Praise for **Stuttering John Melendez**

"John and I harken back to his grade school years, as he and my sisters, Susan and Judi, shared school days. Furthermore, he grew up only a few blocks from my family. We have another slice of life in common, Pappalardo's Pizza Cove. With those credentials, I can, with the utmost of confidence, and no financial bribery, tell you John is a determined, passionate, and talented writer and performer. He looks at the business from both the stage and the balcony, and from those vantage points, his book takes you on a ride that is quite funny. Give it a read, he's our hometown friend and he tells us he's quite famous."

> —**Steve Guttenberg,** actor, comedian, author

"The word 'no' is not in John's vocabulary...unless you ask him to pay for lunch. All kidding aside, he's is a pitbull who will do anything for a friend, a boss, and for a laugh. John is one of the most fearless people I have ever met. It doesn't matter if it's asking O. J. Simpson to autograph a knife or agreeing to fight someone one hundred pounds bigger than him, he will never back down. What I like best about John are the memories that I have of him going out on shoots, the laughs I have shared with him, and when we saw each other after fourteen years the conversation picked up as if we were still working together."

> —**Richie Wilson,** senior broadcast producer for
> *Howard Stern On Demand* and E! producer

"John has beat the odds and earned a front row seat during some of the most iconic shows in entertainment history! This is a book no one else could've written!"

> —**Ross Mathews,** TV personality and comedian

EASY FOR YOU TO SAY

STUTTERING

JOHN MELENDEZ

A VIREO BOOK | RARE BIRD BOOKS
LOS ANGELES, CALIF.

This is a Genuine Vireo Book

A Vireo Book | Rare Bird Books
453 South Spring Street, Suite 302
Los Angeles, CA 90013
rarebirdbooks.com

Set in Dante
Printed in the United States

10 9 8 7 6 5 4 3 2 1

Publisher's Cataloging-in-Publication data
Names: Melendez, John, author.
Title: Easy for You to Say / Stuttering John Melendez.
Description: First Hardcover Edition | A Vireo Book |
New York, NY; Los Angeles, CA: Rare Bird Books, 2018.
Identifiers: ISBN 9781947856196
Subjects: LCSH: Melendez, John. | Stutterers—Biography. | Celebrities—
United States—Anecdotes, facetiae, satire, etc. | BISAC:
BIOGRAPHY & AUTOBIOGRAPHY / Personal Memoirs |
BIOGRAPHY & AUTOBIOGRAPHY / Rich & Famous.
Classification: LCC PN2285 .M45 2018 | DDC 790.2/092/2—dc23

I dedicate this book to my three wonderful kids: Knight, Lily Belle, and Oscar. I have dreamed about having you since I was a little boy, and you have surpassed all of my expectations. There is not a day that goes by that I don't feel proud to be your father. I love you always, Dad.

THIS IS MY AMAZING story. It's the story of an abused, bullied, stuttering, OCD-ridden kid who ends up becoming a staff writer, as well as the announcer, on *The Tonight Show*. Among the many things that happened to me, I became a cast regular on *The Howard Stern Show*, which I had been a fan of since I was a kid. I got the chance to box, something that I always wanted to do—but for me it was in front of a sold-out Taj Mahal! (The one in Atlantic City, not India.) I've had two record deals and an MTV video. I lived the life of a rock star and rubbed elbows with some of the biggest stars in our lifetime. I wrote a song with Joe Walsh. I opened for Mötley Crüe, Ozzy Osbourne, Collective Soul, Ted Nugent, and Cheap Trick all across the country! My album received a good review from *Rolling Stone*, and I got to guest star on *Wings* alongside Steven Weber and Crystal Bernard. I got to be in movies and work alongside Ashton Kutcher, Seann William Scott, and Rodney Dangerfield! As a big fan of *National Lampoon*, I got to write and star alongside *Scandal*'s Bellamy Young in one of

HERE IS A LIST OF MY MOST FAMOUS INTERVIEWS AND QUESTIONS:

their movies! I have been lucky enough to direct stars such as Quentin Tarantino, Jack Black, Hugh Laurie, Charlie Sheen, and Gordon Ramsay. I've hung out with the Kardashians on a regular basis...okay, it all can't be good. I've toured the country with my comedy tour. I had the opportunity to be the head writer of the Kareem Abdul-Jabbar roast. I got to fly in Donald Trump's helicopter, Howard Stern's chartered private jet, and Jay Leno's private casino jet. Heck, I was writing for Jay when he performed at the White House correspondent's dinner, and one of my video jokes even made President Obama laugh!

My prank on his successor didn't exactly get the same reaction.

Still, the most important part was being a father to my three wonderful kids: Knight, Lily Belle, and Oscar. How could this kid from the lower-middle-class Long Island neighborhood of North Massapequa have achieved so much? It is because of the mantra that I have always told myself: Believe in yourself, and never, never accept the word *can't*. Never let anybody tell you that you are not good enough to do something, and most importantly, overcome your fears. Don't allow the naysayers and the doubting voice in your head to take control of your mind. We can all be anything that we want to. It just takes hard work, belief, perseverance, and a little bit of luck.

And one final note before we get rolling here: Much of what I've written in this book about *The Howard Stern Show* is how I experienced things and how I felt at the time I was there. The truth is that I will always love Howard, Robin, Jackie, Fred, Gary, Billy, Ronnie, Scott, KC, and Artie. We had a lot of great times, and unfortunately some bad ones as well.

Anyway, here is my crazy story. Enjoy!

THE HOWARD STERN SHOW: THE EARLY YEARS

AT THE END OF my high school years, I started listening to *The Howard Stern Show* on NBC radio. The dude told it like it was, and I was immediately a fan. I was a seventeen-year-old who still hadn't gotten laid, so I masturbated all the time. I even tried banging a Noxzema jar and nearly burned my penis off. I thought I was crazy. Not for trying to bang a jar of Noxzema, but for masturbating. I would ask my friends if they masturbated and they would say, "No, of course not."

RINGO STARR:
ME: "WHAT DID YOU DO WITH THE MONEY?"
RINGO: "WHAT MONEY?"

I felt like an outcast. Because of my Catholic upbringing, I would mark on my calendar how many days that I would do it each month and try to keep it down to like eight rubs a month, but if I went over, I felt so guilty, like I was sinning so much and giving in to the devil. Anyway, I started listening to Howard Stern and he talked about waxing the carrot all the time. I thought, "Wow, I'm not the only one." Little did I know that my friends were full of shit. Those motherfuckers were beating off so much they lost feeling in their right hands.

I'd listen to Stern while driving for Wholesale Tire—this tire warehouse where I worked off and on since I was thirteen and through college—or when my mom picked me up from the train that I took to NYU. I'd listen to him when I drove to my job selling housewares at Sears or when I was counting electronic parts at Standard Radio. I'd listen to him, Jackie, Gary, Robin, and Fred all the time.

See, I was a huge *MAD Magazine* fan, and this show had the same irreverence. In fact, one of the ways my dad would get me to go to church with him every Sunday was that, after Mass, he'd take me to the candy store, where I'd get one package of candy and one *MAD*. I couldn't wait until the latest edition came out. *The Stern Show* reminded me of just that, *MAD Magazine*.

I had no idea what anybody looked like on the show; in fact, I thought Robin was this thin white chick with long blonde hair. I finally got to see a picture of her in college and I was shocked! She had brown hair! She looked like nothing I had imagined. I used to always listen to "Boy Gary," as they called him, argue with Howard and I was like, "Gary, man, shut the fuck up! Why are you trying to win a fight that is unwinnable?" I felt bad for him. I mean, he seemed somewhat normal.

When I was stuttering my way through NYU, I became friends with this wannabe stand-up comedian named Mitch Fertel. He and I became good friends. He was interning for Howard, and his dad wasn't happy about the lack of pay, so I asked Mitch to hook me up with an interview if he ever decided to leave, and thank God he got into a major car accident and I got the job. (By the way, it's never been proven that I cut the brake line.) Mitch was fine, but he didn't have a way to drive in anymore, and his dad had had enough of him working for free. Mitch didn't really like doing the celebrity interviews anyway because he felt they were hurtful. The show needed a new guy with a total lack of conscience.

ME: "THE MONEY YOUR MOM GAVE YOU FOR SINGING LESSONS?"
RINGO (INSULTED): "I BOUGHT FISH AND CHIPS."

Um…*hello!*

Mitch mentioned me as a potential replacement, and after hearing that I stuttered, Howard wanted to hire me sight unseen. Little did he know that this job of interviewing celebrities was what I had been perfectly groomed for since birth. My fifth-grade teacher wrote in my report card to my parents the following: "John tends to ask outrageous and penetrating questions in class and stutters when excited."

This teacher unknowingly wrote my résumé for my future job.

In sixth grade, they had this assembly for all the boys on human sexuality. They put all of our dads in the seats behind us. All of the other boys had questions but were too afraid to ask, so they would write them down and hand their questions to me, and I would then raise my hand and blurt out:

"How many holes does a girl have?"

"If the fastest sperm gets to the egg, then why are there are so many fat kids in the world?"

"What is a clitoris and where do we find it?"

To this day, I still don't know the answer to that last one.

I'd heard Mitch do the interviews when I used to drive in to Sears, and I'd think to myself, this job would be perfect for me. I had done a good job interning at Polygram in the Video Department, and Gary got a good recommendation from my boss, and Mitch set up the interview for me. The night before, my mom and I went to the Sunrise Mall and bought a black jacket at JC Penny and a pair of grayish denims at the Levi's store. I got a haircut, as per Mitch's advice, and I rode the train in from Long Island for my interview.

I remember meeting Gary in the lobby. I thought to myself, *Oh, come on! His teeth are not green like Howard says on the air, he's such a liar—they're blackish brown!* Gary took me into Scott the Engineer's studio, which reeked of cigarette smoke, and I did the interview. Who knew that the whole time they were taping it? I couldn't have known. I was fixated on Gary's huge teeth, and I thought to myself, *Man, when Gary was a kid, his tooth fairy must've shown up with a wheelbarrow.*

Well, Gary called me a week later, when I was working at my friend Kevin Kalinowski's video store, and told me I got the job. I was ecstatic. I remember my first day. Mitch started showing me around. I remember seeing Robin, who came in limping with a foot cast on, and I was like, "Oh my God, this is the

PAUL MCCARTNEY:

Robin Quivers who I listened to for so many years!" Mitch instructed me that it was up to me to park her car, a gray SAAB with a standard transmission. I met Howard in his office. I was like, "What a thrill. This was the dude that made me feel okay about stroking the sausage," (which also got me a little worried when I shook his hand).

I made him laugh for the first time when we were talking about my parking Robin's car. He asked me if I knew how to drive a clutch, and I said, "Yes of course, of course, that's easy…the gas pedal is on the left, right?" He laughed, Robin laughed, and I felt at ease. I kind of got the feeling that he liked me from that moment. Little did I know that I should have done what Mitch did to avoid the extra work and said I didn't know how to drive a clutch, but I was too eager to please.

I saw Jackie "The Joke Man" Martling from the back, standing down the hallway. I thought to myself, *Hey, he's not as fat as Howard always says on the air. Man, Howard likes to exaggerate.* But then Jackie turned around and I was like, *Oh my God! He looks like he swallowed a beach ball! If he wore a belly button ring, he'd look like a hand grenade!* I met Fred, and I thought to myself, *See, again, Howard was lying—Fred is way weirder than he claims on the air!* I liked Fred—after all, I was a fan of all these guys—but he was just so socially awkward.

I was then schooled on how it worked with Howard's food. This was priority number one. Every Monday morning, I had to go to the nearby bodega and pick up a six-pack of Volvic water, five green apples, and ten potatoes. I'd have to label the four cassettes each morning with the date and tape number and flip or change them every forty-five minutes. At 7:00 a.m., I'd walk into the studio during a break, hand Howard his apple, flip the cassette that I had pre-labeled, and leave.

I loved being in the studio. It was just a bunch of cool dudes hanging around, chewing the shit, and having a great time. It was way more intimate in the old days. I'd leave the studio and call Gene's Diner downstairs and order four ounces of turkey. Throughout all this I was logging the show on the computer and answering the phones. At that time, it was pretty much just me and Gary in the back producing the show. The funny thing about logging the show on the computer was that Mitch had preset months in advance reminding himself—and eventually myself—that at 9:15 a.m. you had to begin preparing Howard's potatoes.

As the weeks went on, I started to realize how Mitch really felt about Fred. He would pre-log in the subject lines at various times on random days.

"June 1st, 7:30 a.m.: Fred Norris sucks massive cock."

"June 18th, 9:00 a.m.: Fred Norris is a giant asshole."

I later asked him about it, and he told me that Fred used to goof on his comic ability and this hurt Mitch. Gary also hurt him once when Mitch, an aspiring comedian, told him one of his jokes and Gary said, "Don't quit your day job." Mitch got them all back when he became one of the best stand-ups around.

Anyway, back to the potatoes. As well as the reminders in the computer, there was also a note hanging from it that read "9:15 potatoes." Howard was serious about his lunch. As I recall, one time I forgot, and that was the first time Howard ever got mad at me—the first of many, as any listener would know.

POTATO PREPERATION

1. WASH POTATOES

2. DRY THEM WITH CLEAN PAPER TOWEL

3. SET POTATOES ON PAPER TOWEL and BEGIN TO SCAR CUT THEM, ONE INCISION DOWN THE MIDDLE and 4 ACROSS

4. PUT POTATOES IN MICROWAVE and SET FOR 20 MINUTES

5. AS POTATOES COOK, GO BACK TO LOGGING THE SHOW and ANSWERING THE PHONES

6. WHEN 20 MINUTES IS UP, GET POTATOES, PLACE THEM ON HOWARD'S DESK

7. GRAB 4 OZ. OF TURKEY and VOLVIC WATER FROM FRIDGE and PLACE THEM NEXT TO THE POTATOES

8. COVER POTATOES WITH PAPER TOWEL, GO BACK TO WORK.

EVEN THOUGH "WASH HANDS" wasn't on the prep list, most of the time I did it anyway. Howard liked to use the potatoes as bread and put the turkey in the middle. That was his diet in those days, and I have to say, it smelled damn

ZZ TOP:

"DO YOU GUYS EVER THROW UP AND GET BIG CHUNKS IN YOUR BEARDS?"

good. He made it look awfully appetizing, too. Meanwhile, if they had a writers' meeting after, I'd retrieve a very different kind of meal. When I'd get a lunch request from Jackie, he'd say in that high-pitched voice, "Go down to the hot dog/gyro guy downstairs. Get me three hot dogs, everything on it, a gyro with tzatziki and extra hot sauce, and a Diet Coke."

I think Jackie and I shared the same philosophy: if I'm going to get fat, I'd rather it be on the food and not the beverage—unless of course that beverage was beer. Yes, that was one of the places where Jackie and I bonded. We both loved to drink beer. We were the only two real beer drinkers on the show, and man could we put it down. Hence the gut Jackie had. Trust me, it wasn't the food; it was the beer. I have that same gut now—well, almost.

I decided that I had to find a niche on the show, and why not do that by writing a brand-new opening theme song like the Double "O" Zeros had with H.O.W.A.R.D. S.T.E.R.N. I also wanted to show how aggressive I was about being a staff member there. This is where it all started. I realized that in the Double "O" Zeros' theme song, they made fun of Howard being Jewish and having a tiny penis. I thought that I would write a song to go along with what I thought was Howard's style and sense of humor. I recorded it at my friend Mike Sapone's house. I brought it in to the show, and Gary said that it "sounded normal." He told Howard the same thing: "Voff, there's not much to make fun of here."

He couldn't have been more wrong.

As soon as Howard brought me into the studio to hear the song and he played the first two lines of it, jackpot! Radio gold.

Here are the first two lines. Please, people, realize I was a twenty-three-year-old kid from white-trash Long Island making an attempt to appeal to what I thought was Howard's humor. Man was I wrong. The song went:

> *Here's a story about a Jew's success,*
> *Do do do do wah, do do do do wah,*

Howard stopped the tape right there, which pissed me off because I felt the song could only be appreciated in its entirety. I mean, that's like turning off "Hotel California" before they even check in. He said, "Is that how you look at me, John? As a Jew?" I tried to explain that I was just trying to follow the Double "O" Zeros' template, but my argument was futile. He played the next line:

"SINCE YOU LOOK JEWISH, WHY DON'T YOU CALL YOURSELVES ZZ DREIDEL?"
"IN A PINCH, WOULD YOU WIPE WITH YOUR BEARD?"

> *He grew up with blacks, his mind was a mess,*
> *Poor little Jew boy, thought he was a coon*

Yes, people, those were the lyrics. I don't have a racist bone in my body, but I thought this was something that Howard would find funny. He stopped the tape again, and now both he and Robin were on me. "A coon?" Howard said. "What the heck is wrong with you, John?"

Robin was also displeased. I tried to defend myself, but to no avail. He started calling me "Stuttering John" instead of "John the Intern." Not liking the nickname, I pleaded with him to stop. "Howard," I said, "I'll tell you what. Play the whole song through, and then if you still hate it, I'll let you call me Stuttering John."

He was like, "I'm going to call you that anyway."

Now, in retrospect, I realize that my defending myself, and this whole argument, became funnier than the song. Howard picked me apart for over an hour, analyzing the song. Then he had a guest, and he said, "We'll play the rest of this tomorrow."

But then something miraculous happened.

When we got to break, Howard said, "That was great, John. You're great on the air." When I was helping Jackie move some stuff into his sixth-floor walkup apartment on Sixty-Fifth Street, he said to me, "John, we thought Mitch was great and couldn't be replaced, but now it's like, Mitch who?" My friend Kevin at the video store called me and said, "John, you have to ease up, after that song, you might get fired." I knew that it meant something, because after the second day of playing the song, I was riding the Long Island Railroad home, and I said something to the ticket taker, and the guy behind me said, "Hey, are you Stuttering John?" I was like, "Yeah, how do you know?" He said, "I recognize the voice."

Wow, I couldn't believe it! All my life I wanted to be famous—could this really be happening?

Here's the whole song:

> *Here's a story about a Jew's success*
> *Do Doo Da Do Wop, Do Doo Da Do Wop*
> *He grew up with blacks, his mind was a mess*
> *Poor little Jew boy, thought he was a coon*

JAMES BROWN:

"WHEN YOU DO A SPLIT, DO YOU BANG YOUR TESTICLES ON THE FLOOR?"

After dancing the Hora, he had nowhere to go
Do Doo Da Do Wop, Do Doo Da Do Wop
Who would have thought he'd be king of radio
Hail to king Howard, Howard is the king
Howard, Howard, Howard Stern
Tie Scott Muni to a pole, light a match
and watch him burn
I mean let's face it, Scott Muni's throat is a mess
Soupy Sales needs an enema, and Scott Shannon
Wears a dress

Well Howard said we see ya to NBC
Do Doo Da Do Wop, Do Doo Da do wop
It seemed they got jealous of his popularity
Do Doo Da Do Wop, Do Doo Da Do wop

Now Howard makes more money than ever before
Do Doo Da Do Wop, Do Doo Da do wop
He's a king-great, top-rate, ratings whore
Howard is a slut, he's a rich, ruling slut

Howard, Howard, Howard Stern
Tie Scott Muni to a pole, light a match
and watch him burn
I mean let's face it, Scott Muni's throat is a mess
Soupy Sales needs an enema, and Scott Shannon
Wears a dress

That was the song. Recorded in my friend Mike Sapone's basement. That was the song that made them forget about Mitch and realize they had this ambitious, stuttering gold mine at their fingertips.

Getting to work each morning was tough. I had to get up at 3:00 a.m. and catch the 3:57 train leaving Massapequa. Many times I would just miss the train and end up racing it down Sunrise Highway, trying to get far enough ahead so I could park at a station and run up the stairs to the platform to get on the train.

One night they held a Halloween costume party at Spit in Levittown. First prize was five hundred bucks and I owed my friend Jiggs three-fifty for a rental car we took to Florida. So I got some chicken wire, a lampshade, and papier-mâché, and I made myself a giant penis costume. I applied shaving cream from an aerosol can to the hole on top of the of the costume and proceeded to hand out condoms. I won first prize and drove home with the costume proudly displayed on top of my car. It fell off due to the wind and some guy pulled up and asked me for it, and I told him no way. I brought it home, slept for a half hour, and took the train to work. After the show, Meg Griffin, who was the DJ on the air following Howard, heard that I won a costume contest. Not knowing what I was dressed as, she asked me on the air and I said that I went as a penis. She went directly to commercial, and this became another sound bite for Fred.

At that time, I also used to answer the phones. Coincidentally, I had also become quite good at doing impressions of Howard. One day his wife called on the hotline phone, which was a special phone for special people like Don and Alison. I answered the phone as Howard and Alison started telling me some private shit. I immediately said, "Alison, this is John!" and then handed the phone to Howard.

That was the first time Howard scolded me, but I can't say I blame him.

The moment that would change my life forever finally came when Howard called me into the studio off the air and asked if I wanted to do a few celebrity interviews. This was the moment I was waiting for. I mean, next to masturbating, this is the thing I was most qualified for. I knew I could do this. I said yes, I would love to.

My first assignments were Danny Glover and fellow stutterer Carly Simon. You'd think that because Carly was a fellow stutterer it would have made it easier for me, but it didn't. I stuttered throughout the whole interview. I forget now what the questions were, but Carly was so nice. Danny Glover, on the other hand, wasn't as easy. He kept getting irritated, saying that he was there at D'Agostino's picketing that they stop putting pesticides on grapes. He said that he only wanted to talk about grapes, so then, thinking on my feet, I started putting grapes in every question.

"Danny, uh-uh-uh, do you g-g-grapely feel that Mike Tyson should be caged?"

He kept getting irritated, but it was funny. With all of my stuttering, I thought I had failed. Little did I know how wrong I was. Howard played it on the air and loved it; they all laughed their asses off in the studio. It turns out that for the first time in my life, the stutter became a plus. It appeared to be a sign

MARLO THOMAS:

of innocence, which won sympathy from my victims and made my offensive questions somewhat less offensive. I started to get very popular—apparently, the blend of being fearless and humble while stuttering was a perfect mixture.

I never felt that bad doing the interviews because I was doing a comedy bit. I would always say, "Big fan, big fan," most of the time because, well, I was. I would always ask for a handshake or a hug after an interview to let them know that I was just messing around and it was all good. Years later, when I was asking my general manager Tom Chiusano and program director Stephen Kingston for a raise, Steve said, "Well, Howard created you," and I said, "No, no, no—years and years of bad parenting created me."

I started doing more and more interviews. One of my next assignments was to interview Ringo Starr at a press conference. You have to understand, the Beatles were and are my favorite band of all time. They're the reason I ever picked up a guitar in the first place. I was very apprehensive about doing this interview and asked Gary if he thought it would kill my chances of ever getting a record deal. He said no. It might have been the first time he had ever been right in the whole time I was at *The Stern Show*.

Just kidding. Well, maybe not.

I nervously attended the press conference. I stepped up to the microphone sweating like crazy. I said, "Ringo, now since Murray 'The K' is gone, who is the fifth? Beatle?"

Ringo responded, "You are."

I didn't even know who the fuck Murray "The K" was. This also helped me in some interviews, as I was too young to know this shit. Heck, I spent the last ten years of my life just trying to get laid.

Then I asked the embarrassing question. The atomic bomb was about to drop directly on Ringo's head. I asked, "Ringo, w-w-what did you do with the money?"

He said, "What money?"

I said, "The money your mom gave you for singing lessons."

Boom! Wham! Pow!

I could almost see the Batman cards filling my mind.

Ringo paused, the crowd gasped, and then Ringo responded, "I bought fish and chips."

I left convinced that I'd just killed my chances of ever getting a record deal, but I hoped that Howard would be happy. He was. They played it on the air and laughed their asses off. Jackie, a big Beatles fan as well, gasped in disbelief. I loved making all of them laugh. Look, I'm not saying that it was easy for me to be insulting, but I knew what would be good for the show and would please Howard. A few weeks later, I got my first unofficial mention in *Rolling Stone* regarding the Ringo press conference. They referred to me as "some Howard Stern reporter," but, hey, I'll take it.

More and more interviews followed, and the press started mentioning my name in their articles. I would show up everywhere and wait for hours, all night, just to get a few. Why? More interviews meant more airtime, more airtime meant more popularity, and more popularity meant more of me as a fixture on the show that I had been a fan of for years. My mantra? Work hard, harder than the rest, and the rewards will follow. Stay focused on the prize, which for me at the time was more airtime.

I once waited thirteen hours for an interview with Chevy Chase. Thirteen hours! That's how hungry I was. I would then bring the tapes back to the station and sleep on the floor next to Mel Karmazins's office because there was a nicer rug in there and he had air-conditioning. I was getting more and more airtime, but I was dead broke; I had worked for free for two whole years and I was ten grand in debt from borrowing from my parents. Twice, even, Howard gave me a check for a thousand bucks because he knew I was hurting.

I remember interviewing Fred Gwynne from *The Munsters*. He was showing his artwork at an exhibit. I brought my friend/bass player, Abe Hopper, with me. We got there in Manhattan and the hottest publicist/blonde chick I had ever seen greeted me. In a brief conversation, she informed me that I was not to ask questions about *The Munsters* or *Car 54, Where Are You?* I promised her that I wouldn't.

I lied.

She then escorted me over to Fred Gwynne and I nervously began my interview. You have to remember, the publicist stood right next to me, and I had to ask some pretty fucked-up questions—funny, but fucked up. I asked a long string of *Munsters* questions, much to the publicist's chagrin.

"How long did it take you to get off that green makeup?"

"How's Lily?"

"Do you sign your paintings Fred Gwynne or Herman Munster?"

Finally, Fred got a little annoyed when I asked him, "Did Vincent Van Gogh ever dress up like Frankenstein?"

TED WILLIAMS:

"DID YOU EVER ACCIDENTALLY FART IN THE CATCHER'S FACE?"

He responded, "John, I'm going to make believe I didn't hear that question." Then he gave that famous Herman Munster laugh.

He wasn't thrilled, the publicist wasn't thrilled...but Howard sure was.

It became mine and Howard's favorite interview. Just the discomfort factor alone was hilarious. Fred was a good sport. I liked him a lot, especially for having the patience to deal with me.

I interviewed Walter Cronkite. I used the word "friggin'" in a sentence and he scolded me for like two minutes on what has happened to American journalists when they use an asinine word like "friggin'."

I was just happy he called me a journalist.

Tommy Lasorda was promoting SlimFast and I asked him, "How much do you want to bet that Pete Rose is gambling again?"

He got pissed, scolded me, and left.

Kevin McMahon, my producer and friend, would always hide during my interviews because he didn't want to kill his chances of ever working in the entertainment business again. I didn't care at the time. Heck, I was working with my radio idol.

I interviewed Tommy Lasorda again on a different occasion while in disguise. He was on a dais while eating a turkey leg and I pissed him off again by asking him, "Are you pissed that those stupid friggin' Canadians keep on winning the World Series?" He started saying something like, "Who you calling stupid? They're not stupid." Meanwhile, the whole time he was spitting turkey leg bits all over me.

I even got Tommy a third time, in Times Square at a book signing. There were no other reporters around. I was in disguise—suit, hair slicked back, fake glasses—and the publicist was happy that someone had actually come to cover the event. After all, this was New York; there weren't that many Dodger fans here. So she gladly escorted the crew and me backstage, where I had a one-on-one interview with Tommy as he was signing pictures.

I started out with softball questions. "Tommy, what would you want on your tombstone?" Tommy replied with some long-winded answer that he must've given before. Then came the atomic bombs. "Tommy, now that you're fat again, are you going to give the money back to SlimFast?"

Tommy turned and looked at me angrily. "I'm not fat. What kind of question is that? I'm not fat, next question."

TED: "COME AGAIN?"

NOW, I WAS SHITTING IN MY PANTS BECAUSE I'D HEARD WHAT AN ASSHOLE HE WAS, AND I STARTED STUTTERING.

I responded, "Tommy, since you sit on the bench a lot, do your 'roids bleed?"

Tommy angrily replied, "What are you, a wise guy or something?"

The publicist said, "That's it!"

Tommy said, "Yeah, get out of here!"

The crew and I were escorted out, although this time not so gracefully as when we were brought in. Three times I got this guy! How can he analyze baseball players when he can't even recognize the same jackass that keeps asking him these dopey questions?

As nervous as I was doing these interviews, I was starting to enjoy them, in an odd way. I mean, after all, these celebrities had had their asses kissed for so long, it was about time someone cut them down to size, and that someone was me—"Hero of The Stupid," as I was named by an envious Robin Quivers as we were walking past 600 Madison Avenue, the then-home of K-Rock, and a few construction workers started yelling my name, recognizing me but not her. She said, "You see, John, you're the hero of the stupid."

The name didn't bother me. Hey, at least I was the hero of something, and I came from a lower-income, working-class family. To this day, people who want to trash me will call me "Hero of the Stupid," but they don't seem to realize that I wear it as a badge of honor. If Robin believed that the working-class man represented stupidity, then so be it. I was a working-class man, and damn proud of it.

> I started to get more and more popular on the show. So much so that a guy beat me out in registering stutteringjohn.com. When I called him and asked for the domain, he said he would only give it up if I gave him a bunch of money. Of course, I told him I was broke, and he said, "Well, do you have any porn?" Typical Stern fan. Knowing that the show had a ton of free porn, I said sure, and he came to the studio and I gave him a boxful in exchange for the website.
>
> Later on, another guy stole my Twitter handle, except he wanted ten grand. Man, people are messed up.

The interviews continued.

Lou Reed strangled me for asking him if he still masturbated. Judging by his grip...yes.

ME: "DID YOU EVER ACCIDENTALLY F-F-FART IN THE CATCHER'S FACE?"
TED (PISSED OFF): "WHO ARE YOU WITH THAT KIND OF QUESTION?"

Raquel Welch punched me in the nose for asking her, "Are they drooping yet?"

After that interview, I thought that maybe I should sue her. I mean, after all, she almost broke my nose. I went to the doctor to have it checked out and thought that she should absorb the doctor bills—I knew K-Rock wouldn't. But I changed my mind when I fielded a call from Andrew "Dice" Clay the next day. He was waiting to get on the show. As we were chatting, I told him I was thinking about suing Raquel, and Dice was like, "What are you going to tell the whole world, that you got your ass kicked by a chick?"

Hence, I didn't sue. It was getting bad, though.

Steven Grillo and I attended a Spike Lee book signing, where I asked him some questions. He got pissed. We got into my Mustang 5.0 and were about to drive off when a few of his henchman opened my car door and demanded the tape. I gave the tape to Grillo and said, "Run!" He ran but they caught him, wrangled him, and punched him in the stomach. He held onto the tape and I managed to get the tape from him and we played it on the air. It was pretty much harmless, but there were bullies out there and it was getting ugly.

I went to an Eric Bogosian book signing and asked him if there would be a Talk Radio 2. He got so pissed; the security guards dragged me down the stairs by my neck! At the MTV awards, I asked Sharon Stone at the press conference, "Sharon, w-w-will there be any upcoming crotch scenes?" Her bodyguard, a stocky ex-horse cop, stuck four fingers in my mouth—two from each hand— and lifted me out of the room by my mouth! To make things worse, his fingers tasted like mayonnaise, and I hate mayonnaise.

I was like, what the fuck, and pushed him twice, then he laid me out with a right cross. I fell to the ground. This guy was built like a brick shithouse. Then a bunch of people jumped on top of me. I'd decided that was it. I wasn't going to keep on getting my ass kicked when I was protected by the First Amendment. CNN and other news outlets came to my defense, saying that it was wrong, and I ended up suing Sharon after much on-air deliberation. I settled out of court for like fifteen grand.

I started to get more and more famous as a cult hero, although some people got annoyed. One time I was eating a slice of pizza at Penn Station while I was waiting for my train and this guy in a suit got up and said, "This is for what you did to Tommy Lasorda," and threw his orange soda all over me and ran out of the place. I was drenched in Sunkist. He was gone before

ME: "UM...JOHN."
TED: "GET THE HELL OUT OF HERE."

I could see where he went. Heck, I was used to this kind of shit—after all, I got bullied by the neighborhood kids ever since they found out I was a stutterer. They would throw rocks at me, ridicule me. I was called Stutterface, Skip, M.C. Stammer, and Stuttering Prick, which are pretty harsh words to hear from your parents.

I was broke, and it was time for me to leave *The Stern Show*. I nervously walked into Howard's office; I asked him if I could talk to him for a second. He said sure. I told him that I was ten grand in debt with my parents and I couldn't work for free anymore and that I would have to leave. He said not to worry, a TV show was right around the corner and that'd make me some money. He was right, to an extent.

The Howard Stern Summer Show was just a four-week stint as a test. Howard hooked me up with his agent Don Buchwald, a guy I would eventually loathe— the quintessential bully, condescending, egotistical, and repulsive, and I'm trying to be nice. I thanked Howard, not knowing what a piece of shit this guy really was. Don got me $750 a week for the Channel 9 show minus his commission. I started doing the interviews, but this time for television. It was me, my field producer Kevin McMahon, and Bob and Roy, who ran camera and audio. I called us "Team Dude."

We would sneak in everywhere and we became the thorn in the side of the other paparazzi—a word that, back then, I was unfamiliar with. Some reporters loved us, but some hated us because as soon as I pissed a celebrity off, they would leave, and the other reporters would not get their interviews or photographs. Being the consummate wiseass, I used to intentionally piss them off. For instance, I interviewed Matthew Broderick at the premiere of *Jacob's Ladder*. I asked questions like, "I loved your father on *Car 54, Where Are You?*" Then my follow-up was, "Did you drive here?"

Heck, I didn't know that he'd killed someone while driving.

Ignorance, for me, was bliss.

That same night there was some downtime and all of the paparazzi were waiting at the entrance, so I decided that it would be funny to walk to the corner and pretend that I saw Madonna exiting her limo to get into the side entrance. I was like, "Hey, guys, there's Madonna, let's interview her!" I had my crew shooting around the corner as all of these hungry paparazzi came running, only to find me laughing my ass off as my crew shot them rounding the corner, showing their dismay and disproval.

NATHAN LANE:

I interviewed the late, great Joan Rivers. She had the best response, God bless her soul. I said, "Joan, do you think ugly people should be allowed to have children?" and without missing a beat, she said, "No, and I told your parents that."

That was the same Leona Helmsley event where I cornered Imelda Marcos and kept stuttering while asking her, "Imelda, when you fart in front of company, do you blame the family dog?" She looked frightened. She looked like a scared cat trying to become invisible in the corner while warding off a stuttering Siberian husky.

I asked the Dalai Lama, "Do people go up to you and say hello Dalai?" He laughed, but Richard Gere, who worshipped the guy and was hosting the event, was not happy. He kept trying to thwart my questions, saying, "These are very odd questions." Later on, I tried interviewing Gere, and he just said, "You're crazy, man."

I had to hand it to Jackie and Fred for writing the bulk of these amazing questions.

I snuck into the Gennifer Flowers press conference after she was in the *National Inquirer* or *Star Magazine* for saying that she had an affair with then–Democratic nominee Bill Clinton. I screamed, "Gennifer, did Governor Clinton wear a condom?"

The crowd laughed. Gennifer's lawyer was not amused.

"It's a social issue," I improvised, and the crowd laughed again. So I screamed, "Gennifer, was there ever a threesome?"

Gennifer's lawyer said he would put a stop to the press conference if there were any more questions of that nature.

I followed with, "Gennifer, w-w-will you be sleeping with any other presidential candidates?"

The crowd roared, and even Gennifer smiled and laughed. The press conference ended, and a reporter came up to me and asked me, "Who are you?"

I said, "Stuttering John, at least that's what they call me." That interview put me on the map. Heck, even the McLaughlin Report was defending my questions, referring to me as Mr. Melendez.

Wow, that's impressive, I thought.

The New York Post said that I single-handedly saved the nomination for Bill by making a mockery of the press conference. They even came out with an article saying that Bill Clinton feared me more than his opponents.

I asked ZZ Top at a press conference: "Does Sinead O'Connor give you a boner?" They were like, "Who's Sinead O'Connor?" and later, "Yeah, and what's a boner?" I laughed my ass off.

One morning, we were in the studio and I was going over the questions for columnist Liz Smith with Howard and the gang. Andrew Dice Clay happened to be a guest, so he was in the studio. He asked me to ask Liz Smith, "Why are you such a fat cow?" I looked at Howard, and he said sure. I did the interview and asked her the question. That was an interview that I felt so bad about that the next time she was appearing somewhere, I asked Howard if I could just go there and apologize. He agreed. So I went there and apologized and she accepted. We taped the whole thing and played it on the air.

We went to a celebrity softball game in Central Park and we struck Channel 9 show gold. The first up was Roy Scheider. You have to understand, *Jaws* is my favorite movie, and I love Roy Scheider. As we were trying to go interview him, the event's publicists came over and tried to stop me. I tried to reason with them, and the camera crew shot the whole thing. They did brilliant work, because while we were arguing with the publicists, they would pan over to Roy and he just stood there calmly, patiently waiting while watching this debacle! I kept explaining to them that I knew more about Roy's career than they did. Finally, they allowed me to interview him, and I asked him boring "What's he up to" kind of questions, and he was like, "Come on, get to the real stuff." So I began with these questions:

Me: "Are you a Jew, Roy?"

Roy: "That won't do."

Me: "Do you smoke pot?"

Roy: "That won't do either."

Me: "Do you worship Satan?"

Roy: "That won't do either."

He finally was like "time's up" and walked away from me.

Then I asked Phil Donahue if he thought that Oprah would eat until she explodes. He said, "That's not funny."

Finally I got to John Amos from *Good Times*, and I knew the questions so I immediately started stuttering—it may have something to do with the fact that he was holding a humongous softball bat.

IMELDA MARCOS:
"IF YOU PASS GAS AT HOME IN FRONT OF OTHERS, DO YOU BLAME THE FAMILY DOG?"

So I began, "Um…d-d-do you think 2 Live Crew are talented or just another bunch of troublesome blacks?"

He cut me off and said, "How the fuck did you get this job with a speech impediment? That's what I want to know." And then he started making fun of my stuttering while I just laughed.

I asked former presidential candidate Walter Mondale about his running mate. "Walter, were you afraid how it would've been when Geraldine Ferrara got cramps in the office?"

I think he laughed.

I accidentally stuttered and spit on famous disc jockey Alison Steele's face while asking her if she still used tampons. And I felt bad. Not for the question, but for the loogie I hocked on her face.

I got punched by Morton Downey Jr. for asking him when he got his warts removed if he saved them in a pickle jar.

Ray Romano's manager, Rory Rosegarten, later described me when I was on the phone with him seeking management as being a "professional asshole." Howard read a review of the Channel 9 show that pretty much trashed everything but said that they liked me.

A stuttering s-s-star was born, but that would soon become bittersweet.

MY CHANNEL 9 LOVE AFFAIR

AT THIS TIME, I started hitting on the talent booker for the Channel 9 show, Karen. She was a cute Jersey girl with a pretty face, killer body, and a good sense of humor. I was in love. I confided my sentiments to Robin Quivers, and she would help me through the game. I asked Karen out so many times that Channel 9 producer Dan Forman pulled me aside at the end of the first season and told me that I had to stop.

But I was persistent.

Moderately handsome and a fun personality is all I had, and I wanted this girl like no other. She turned me down more times than a ringtone in a library. But again, my mantra is always, "There is no such thing as can't." I finally got her to come to my band's gig in Jersey, and after the gig she invited me over to

SHE JUST TRIED TO AVOID ME, BUT I KEPT STALKING HER. SHE LOOKED LIKE A SCARED CAT IN A CORNER.

her friend's house, where I slept in the same pull-out bed with her! No sex or anything, but I felt her beginning to break.

I finally got her to agree to go to a Broadway show with me. I don't know why, but I chose *Phantom of the Opera*. I thought it was a scary show, not a bunch of people singing opera. Damn, I hated opera! They should given me some kind of clue—maybe in the title. But nonetheless, Karen agreed. Robin took me to her favorite store and helped me find a nice outfit for the show: a suede jacket, nice shirt, pants, and boots. It cost me like $500—but, shit, this girl was worth it!

We made out on the front lawn of her condo that night, and I had my foot in the door.

•••

OUR SECRET ROMANCE CONTINUED, although Karen insisted on dating other guys since she'd just gotten out of a long-term relationship—her first sex dude, by the way, so for me, after the slut I dated prior to Karen, this girl was essentially a virgin. I mean, my ex banged half the high school, and that's just the teachers.

I tried everything to make Karen my girlfriend. When we would drive home from an appearance that she came to, I'd drive up next to her and stick my hand through my pant leg, put my shoe on my hand, and wave to her with my "leg." She laughed her ass off. I would write songs for her that were about us, I'd tell her stories with us in the plot line, I'd make tapes for her with her favorite songs mixed in with my comedy routines.

Eventually, she agreed to go to Atlantic City with me. This meant what we all know it means. Getting laid. Not so fast, though. My Mustang broke down about five miles outside of Atlantic City, but we finally had it towed and checked in. We started fooling around and she demanded I put on a condom, which I didn't have, so I had to get dressed, walk downstairs, find a store that sold condoms, and finally return to the bedroom.

I put the condom on, and immediate shrinkage to flaccidity occurred. I was so embarrassed. I went down on her for like half an hour praying that my dick would rise. It did just enough, but the sex was lackluster to say the least. Shit, I had performance anxiety. Oh, great—now my penis was stuttering. What a freaking loser I thought I was. When I got home, I beat my dick for an hour.

Finally, I got a second chance. She was off working for the afternoon, and I fantasized about her wearing a skirt and that I would bang her while she wore

WARREN BEATTY:

the skirt with no underwear. *Voila!* It worked. We never had a problem with sex again and, man, was it fun.

We finally became boyfriend and girlfriend, but she swore me to secrecy. The only person I trusted enough to tell was Robin, who felt she was betraying Howard by not telling him. But she kept her secret. When Karen and I would leave the Channel 9 studio, I had to duck down in the car because she didn't want anyone to know that we were an item. Karen was Jewish, and her parents weren't thrilled that she was in love with a longhaired Catholic Puerto Rican with a stutter, and her dad forced me to wear my hair in a ponytail whenever I was in the house.

Karen agreed that, at the beginning of our second season at the Channel 9 show, she would come on *The Stern Show* and announce our relationship. At the time, I had told Baba Booey I was dating a girl named Barbara, so he had no idea. I finally introduced "Barbara" to Howard and the gang on the air, and it made a great segment. Gary's jaw dropped, and he was like, "Wait, John, this is not Barbara—this is Karen," and I was like, "Yeah, Gary, they are the same." Howard didn't believe it and made us make out to prove it, which we did. Gary was like, "John, I have a newfound respect for you." Robin admitted to Howard that she felt bad keeping the secret from him, but she had promised. I think he understood.

Karen and I continued our love affair for about a year. Then, about the time I got signed to Atlantic Records and began working on my album, the spark I had for her slowly faded. We broke up, but when I found out she had begun dating again, I grabbed her back immediately. Heck, I didn't want to let her go. She was a good girl, and considering that my last girlfriend had more pipe laid in her than an industrial kitchen, I knew I had to try and make this work.

Karen and I continued our love affair for about a year. During that time, we appeared on the last Channel 9 show, which was The Sternlywed Game. It was me and Karen, Dan Forman and his wife Robin, Fred and Allison, and Howard and Alison. We were asked what the kinkiest thing we had ever done sexually was. I said she masturbated for me in a sauna, and Karen freaked out! Howard, Fred, and the whole place laughed their asses off! She held up her answer card, which read, "I gave him a blowjob at a club."

After the show, she was crying outside of the studio building, and I knew I had to console her. It turns out, she was worried about what her family would think. I was like, "Well, why is it better for them to hear that you gave a blowjob at a club? What was so evil about masturbation?"

She finally got over it.

There was a second segment, which they never even aired, featuring me and Steve Guttenberg. I said that I was friends with him and that I wanted to do something with him for the show, and Howard said fine and to take the crew and shoot whatever we wanted. I interviewed Steve about how he lost his virginity and then I took him to play "knock, knock, runaway." Steve knocked on a door and ran and the homeowner darted out of the house and chased Steve down the block while the camera panned to me as I laughed my ass off. The guy caught Steve, who had to explain what was going on while absolutely scared out of his mind. They played it on the show and Howard and everyone laughed but The Sternlywed Game was too good, and they had to cut something. Howard said that they would air it next season, but due to a contract dispute, that season never came to pass. It was too bad, though, because we would beat *Saturday Night Live* in the markets that we were on.

Anyway, Karen and I went to Puerto Rico together, Aruba, the Bahamas, Jumby Bay. We went skiing in Vermont. We would have sex in the public hot tub at a hotel in Hunter Mountain while people were walking by, but nobody knew, or cared for that matter. We really had a blast, but then she started working with Matt Lauer at NBC. Luckily, Lauer was married at that time, so I knew I didn't have anything to worry about there. That was around the time our relationship finally fizzled out, but we remained friends and still are today.

THE GOOD, THE BAD, AND THE BOOEY: CHAPTER NOINE

There are myriad reasons Gary is off my Christmas card list. I think he's rude and I think he's inconsiderate. He also has a tendency to make up conversations that never happened and conveniently forget conversations that actually did.

— Luis Castillo, K-Rock Board-Op

One time we were doing a bit on the show about who hates who. Gary had made a big show of how, if someone had a problem with him or didn't like him, it wouldn't matter at all. And then, of course, when Gary heard that there was someone who had a problem with him—Luis, the K-Rock board op—he got

CHEVY CHASE:
"DO YOU READ THE SCRIPTS OF THE MOVIES YOU CHOOSE TO MAKE, OR DO YOU GO, *'EENIE MENNIE MINIE MOE'?*"

bummed out and defensive. He started attacking Luis, calling him a really wacky dude and a very strange man, and then told him to shut up. Typical Gary.

Even Howard agreed that Gary made up conversations in his head and negated ones that actually happened. Heck, the interns witnessed him doing this to me. He's a bumbling, forgetful, dude with no conscience. Gary is Andy Capp without the booze. (All right, maybe that's a little harsh. He means well, and he has a good heart, but he also knows where his bread is buttered and has no problem throwing anyone under the bus if it means remaining in Howard's good graces.)

I was starting to get national attention, and my endeavors were constantly being written about in *The Daily News* and *The New York Post*, as well as newspapers everywhere, especially after the Gennifer Flowers interview.

I started to write bits for the show. I had this computer in front of me where I would put the calls up directly so Howard could see them. But on top, I always wrote jokes. After every show, I'd print my jokes and save them. The weird thing was, I'd walk into the studio after Howard delivered one of my jokes that killed and he would never say, "Good job." It was something I had to get used to, because after all, it would undermine his argument that I wasn't funny. When it was time to ask for a raise, I showed up to Tom Chiusano's office with the crate full of my jokes that I wrote and asked for a pay increase. Jason Kaplan and Will Murray, now senior producers, saw me bring the crate to his office; they knew how many jokes I got in. Not to mention the people I discovered on the phones. Here's a list:

i.   "Gary the Retard"

j.   "Wendy the Retard"

k.   "Jeff the Drunk," who I begged Howard to pick up for nine months, telling him that this guy was a gold mine, before he finally did.

l.   "Joe Cancer," whom I named

m.   "Sal The Stockbroker," who I would help write jokes to bust Gary's balls

n.   "Dr. Remulac"

o.   "High-Pitched Eric," who I met in the atrium outside the studio

And many more.

So after I asked Tom for a raise, I told Howard, "Hey, I just asked Tom for a raise, please back me up."

I still got the minimum $2,000 annual bump.

But, hey, I took it. I guess Howard really begged for it.

I continued to write bits, jokes, and even my own interview questions. I'll never forget how my writing career started with the show. I was on the Channel 9 Show. I used to do post interviews with the guests. Well, I did one with "The Underdog Lady," and that Monday morning, when I was letting Howard into the building, he said, "Great job with The Underdog Lady, John." I was so happy, because they were my own questions! The next week, I did the same thing with Daniel Carver, "The KKK Guy," and that Monday morning, Howard said the same thing.

I was ecstatic.

One of the ideas that I pitched for the Channel 9 show was a *Hollywood Squares* parody, although when I mentioned that it was my idea and they agreed to do it, Howard told me that it wasn't. Who knows? Maybe he, Jackie, and Fred had the same idea. But the good thing was that, when they knew "The Underdog Lady" was going to be one of the "squares," Howard asked me to come to a writers' meeting with him, Jackie, and Fred to write jokes and questions for the segment. I was psyched. I wrote questions like, "When you go to the bathroom, do you have to lift your leg?" and stuff like that, many of which Howard used.

> One of my favorite Channel 9 moments was when Howard wanted to do a Dorf golf interview in a jester outfit. Kevin McMahon was instructed to build the set Dorf-style. When we got to the day of shooting, Howard walked out in his big goofy, medieval-time boots that curled up at the toes, and he had to walk up this small staircase to get onto a platform that had a hole in it. He then slipped through the hole so his feet would touch the floor. Problem: he couldn't bend. He was so pissed, he wanted it to be like Dorf, which is really just putting your knees on a pair of shoes. Howard was wearing his jester outfit and tore Kevin a new asshole! I was laughing my ass off watching Howard in the jester outfit, unable to move and yelling at the top of his lungs. It was like watching this angry little person scold his underling from this facacta platform. It was so funny!

CONNIE CHUNG:

Getting back to Gary. He was the guy that, when I first started there, he'd be tired after a night of partying and say to me, as he grabbed the "mystery guest" blindfolds, "John, I'm going to go take a nap in the jock lounge, so please hold down the fort." Willing to please, I was like, "Sure."

This happened a few times, but Gary, being the consummate revisionist history buff, said that it only happened once, after I brought it up on the air years later. Gary was that boss that would forget to tell you to do something and then get mad at you for not doing it. He thought of me as a delinquent and was totally shocked when I revealed on the air that I had been dating Karen—a hottie, a real *tomata*, and one of the producers from the Channel 9 show.

Look, I like Gary, but he was Howard's off-the-air eyes and ears, and also someone who would bend the truth whichever way suited him. He would stop at nothing to betray you. For instance, Gary and I needed to supplement our low salaries by doing gigs and appearances. We each were given a plug at the end of the show, but Howard had gotten sick of doing them, so he would leave after the show, and then a couple dozen commercials later Fred would play a sound bite of Howard saying, "And now here's Fred with the plugs." Then Fred would read them. The problem was that most of the markets tuned out after Howard left. They knew Howard was gone and had no need to air the sound bite of him and then Fred. This was hurting me and Gary, since our appearances were in a lot of these markets that had tuned out. One day Gary approached me and said we should send Howard an email asking if he could read the plugs a couple of times a week before he left. I said I didn't want to do it because I knew that Gary had burned me before. I told Gary that if this ever came up, the email was from the both of us. He agreed and said he would even send it to Howard from his email address and from his computer.

I agreed, but with apprehension.

Gary wrote the email from his computer and I pressed the send button per his request. Well, a week went by, I heard nothing, and then one day KC Armstrong walks out of the studio and says that Gary and Howard were talking in there about the email that I sent to Howard.

I was like, "Wait, KC, the one that *I* sent him?!"

He said, "Yeah, and Howard was pissed."

I asked KC if Gary had told Howard that it was from the both of us, and KC said Gary acted as if it were just from me. He never admitted any involvement.

When Gary exited the studio, I confronted him and said, "How could you, Gary, after you promised me you wouldn't?"

He started getting mad at me for making such a big deal out of it.

I said, "Gary, we had a deal and you promised!"

He got mad at me, but then called me around four o'clock in the afternoon to tell me that he was on the phone with Howard and he admitted that the email was from both of us. But it was too late; the damage was done. Who even knows if he did tell him? At that point, it wouldn't have mattered.

> I remember when Gary and I used to do appearances together when he was single. One time, he was making out with this chick, and with those huge lips, it looked like he was going to suck in her entire head. His lips were like the face-grabbers from *Alien*.

Anything said to Gary was like talking to Howard. The only problem was that his perspective on things was not always accurate. I know this, many of my former coworkers know this, and there are many people that still work there who know this.

Gary's memory of things was usually wrong, and other employees would suffer because of it. Hey, look, don't believe me? This is a guy who couldn't even remember the name of his favorite animated character! He screwed up the name of an animation cell that he wanted. It was of Baba Louie, but Gary said "Baba Booey," and thus his nickname was born.

So I started to mess with him. I would pull pranks on him, goof on him in the studio. Write bits about him with fellow intern and friend Mike Novara. See, Mike knew the ins and outs of "the Booey" as well. The bit was a self-help audio tape called "Gary Dell'Abate's: I don't work for a living," and it was all about how Gary would sleep in the jock lounge, bumble things up, delegate any job that Howard wanted *him* to do, and how every other week he was on a new diet. Gary started to get jealous that Howard liked me.

Look, Gary is a nice guy; he just knows where his bread is buttered. I liked him but disliked him too. I even played "Shower the People" with a whole choir that I put together for his wedding. I loved his wife and visited her in the hospital when their son Jackson was born. But, hey, he threw me under the bus way too many times and it pissed me off, so I looked for funny ways to get my revenge.

CINDY CRAWFORD:
"DOES YOUR GYNECOLOGIST SEND YOU LOVE LETTERS?"

Once we were in the studio, and Gary was planning to take the Gary puppet to an appearance he had in New Jersey. Jackie said, when Gary left the studio, "Hey, Howard, we should rig it so the Gary puppet will break."

I chimed in, "Guys, how about I just steal it?"

Howard said, "John, do you think you can pull that off?"

I said, "Absolutely."

He said, "Do it."

So that Saturday, at the appearance, I had my girlfriend's girlfriend and guy friend drive me to the appearance. I had the owner show Gary around the place while the puppet sat near Gary's picture signing table. I had the dude I was with run into the store, grab the puppet, and then get back to the car. He did, and we drove away laughing our asses off.

Poor Baba Booey.

I called Howard. He and I never laughed so hard. We were picturing just how Gary's head must've been exploding and how many times per second he was licking his lips and grinding his teeth—God knew there was plenty of fake enamel to grind. Gary always tied his shoelaces really tight, and we could almost picture the circulation getting cut off from his feet and the blood rushing right up to his lips.

Gary called me and was like, "John, don't lie to me, but did you steal the puppet, or do you know if Howard knows who did?"

I was like, "Gary, no, man. I'm at my girlfriend's mom's house," then went into a story about a problem I was having with Tom or something just to make believe I was so disinterested in his plight.

Sure, it was mean, but I knew it was radio gold.

He was like, "John, what am I going to do?"

"Gary, are you sure it's not still at the store?"

"No, I checked everywhere!"

"Gary, man, just take a deep breath. I'm sure we can get the guy to build us another one and everything will be fine."

He was like, "Howard's going to kill me!"

Howard and I laughed like crazy. This went on all weekend, and that Monday morning Gary got the wrath. Howard played it brilliantly, and Gary bought it hook, line, and sinker. People started calling up. One guy called in saying that he had the puppet and he was holding it hostage, and then he put the puppet on and it was like, "Voff, Ah need your help, A'hm scared."

I GOT THROWN OUT AFTER THAT ONE.

Finally we gave in and told him after an hour. Ah, revenge was sweet. This was my payback to Gary for all of the times he treated me like shit. Man, was Gary pissed at me, but I had scored many points with Howard, and this bond would eventually lead to me hanging out with Howard away from the show—which annoyed the crap out of Gary.

Here's a short list of the pranks I pulled on Gary and the rest of the staff:

a.   **The Scott Salem Phone Scam**

Scott the Engineer's wife used to call him incessantly in his smoke-filled studio and yell at him. So one day, I taped the two buttons down that the phone rests on and asked an intern to call him in his studio in five minutes. I told Jackie what I was up to and to join me in Scott's studio. We went down there, and Scott was stressed as usual. The phone rang, he picked it up, and started saying hello, and the phone kept on ringing. He kept saying, "Hello, hello…" and eventually, "What the fuck is going on?" Meanwhile, Jackie and I were laughing our asses off. He got so pissed he picked up the entire phone and threw it at me.

b.   **The Gary Stock Scam**

I had a few brokers during the "boiler room" days. I didn't think they were doing anything illegal, but I was making some good dough buying and selling stocks. I hooked Gary, Jackie, and Robin up with them, and we all made money. One day I had Benny, my stockbroker, call Gary after Gary gave him like twenty grand for a "sure thing" stock. I taped the call from behind Gary. Benny told him that his stock tanked and that he lost all of his money. I stood behind Gary laughing my ass off. I told Howard, and we were crying. I was Gary's arch nemesis, and I didn't really care. He had betrayed me too many times.

c.   **The Kaleidoscope Scott Scam**

One day, I decided to buy one of these kaleidoscopes that you twist and it changes colors and designs. I dipped the eyepiece in an inkpad and then walked down to Scott's studio with the intention of telling Scott that he had to check out how cool this particular kaleidoscope was. Unfortunately, Scott's intern grabbed it first, put it up to his eye, pulled it down, and had a round ring around his eye like the dog from *The Little Rascals*. I laughed like crazy. Scott was pissed because he knew that I intended it for him.

GEENA DAVIS:

d. **Scott "The DJ, Music the way you want it" Phone Prank**

I had my mom call Scott to hire him as a DJ while I taped the phone call. I had her say that she wanted to hire him, but the one condition was that he wears his wig because she didn't want a "baldy" standing behind the DJ table uglying up the place.

e. **The Steve Grillo Acting Prank**

Steve wanted to be an actor. I had my *Tony n' Tina's Wedding* friend and *The Sopranos* actor, Sharon Angela, call him with a fake part. Steve went to the audition and I had him do crazy shit. I had him barking like a dog and stuff, I executed it well but Howard lambasted me for not thinking of better bits during the audition. He was probably right. Hey, they can't all be winners, but I didn't think it was so bad.

f. **The Classic Scott the Engineer Twenty-Dollar-Bill Gag**

The standard joke, but for E! I hid in a doorway with a fishing line attached to a twenty-dollar bill. Doug Goodstein shot with a hidden camera from down the hall. Scott walked out of the studio and saw the twenty, bent over to get it, and I yanked it out from under him. He fell for it immediately. Man, he looked at me with hatred in his eyes.

g. **Beetlejuice, I'm Right Behind You**

Beetlejuice was hanging in the back office. I sat in a chair right behind him and called him. Then I started saying how I was going to kick his ass. He started going crazy, not even realizing that I was right behind him.

h. **The Artie Lange Practical Joke**

One night, Artie and I went with a couple of guys from the show to a Yankees game. Artie was doing the "Bally's Weight Loss Challenge" and had to lose twenty-five pounds to get twenty-five grand. So he was staying away from carbs—he ordered two hot dogs at the game but didn't eat the buns. After the game, I decided to pull into the McDonald's near the stadium. I got to the drive-through speaker and started ordering a couple of burgers, and then the other guys started ordering. I looked in the rearview at Artie's face in the backseat, and sweat was pouring from his forehead as he appeared to be contemplating the hardest decision in his life. Finally, he broke down and said in a loud voice, "Order me the McFlurry and two cheeseburgers and a side of fries!" I ordered it for him, then, instead of going to the window to get the food, I just pulled out of the parking lot. We all laughed—except, of course, for Artie. That night, we went to a pizza place; Artie had three slices there and another one as we walked to Scores. On Monday, Artie weighed in and had gained weight.

i.   **The Homeless Game Prank**

I worked it out with Robin that I would edit one of the Homeless Games segments, and I handed her, Jackie, and Fred the answers. This way they would win every bet against Howard. When we played the game, Howard got almost every one wrong. He was freaking out, couldn't understand it. Later on, at the end of the game, we let him in on the fact that he had been had. He took it well, which put me at ease, because it could have gone either way.

The entire E! crew knew that I was the consummate ball-breaker and truth-seeker. After a long hiatus, they pulled me into their booth and showed me a picture of Howard's nose from before, and then one from after. It was obvious that he had gotten a nose job, and they told me, knowing that I'd ask him about it on the air. Howard denied it then, but I heard that he admitted it years later, after I left.

One time Howard was giving us all shit about the Christmas gift that we gave him. I couldn't resist. I had been waiting for this moment for a while. So I went on the air and said, "Howard, you once you gave me a colorful canister of popcorn with my name on it. It had three flavors: regular, caramel, and cheddar. I thought it had to be a joke, and I reached my arm in the canister and searched the bottom, looking for a check!" I treated it like a Cracker Jack box as I searched for the prize! After I left the studio, Mike Gange came up to me in the hallway and said he did the same thing!

Howard blamed that gift on Alison. But it's not like any of his gifts were much better. Look, don't get me wrong. I'm appreciative of any gift, and hey, the guy already gave me a job. But every year, it was another dumbass gift, as per Ralph's design. One year we got a leather writing tablet with Howard's tattoo carved into the leather on the cover. Another year we got a Howard Stern watch. After I left, I heard he gave the staff a Sirius radio with a year's subscription.

PHIL DONAHUE:
"DID YOU EVER USE YOUR GLASSES TO BURN ANTS BY POINTING THEM AT THE SUN?"

Hey, if he's going to goof on everyone else's gifts, he should be able to take having his gifts goofed on, no?

I started to get famous in my own right and went on other shows, like Conan O'Brien, Jon Stewart, and Ricki Lake. Of course, I knew it was because of my success on *The Stern Show*, but I liked to do other things. I would always ask Howard for permission. You have to understand something: I loved Howard and didn't want to do anything to piss him off. I also feared him. There were times, after I did an interview with a magazine or television show, that I would stay up all night sweating in bed, going over the interview, making sure that I didn't say anything that would piss Howard off.

I was asked to be in movies like *Meet Wally Sparks* with Rodney Dangerfield and *Dude, Where's My Car?* I was a guest on a Brandon Tartikoff show called *Last Call*, and afterward Tartikoff pulled me aside. He looked me in the eye and said, "You've got *it*." From a guy of his stature, that meant the world to me. In fact, they liked me so much they asked me to be the cohost. It was five grand a week! It's weird, before I was on that show, "last call" was my least favorite phrase—those were the last words I ever wanted to hear.

It irritated Howard, though. Mel Karmazin would put me down by saying that video killed the radio star. Fuck him. If he thought I was such a "star," then why not pay me like one? Howard would always use the Letterman analogy of how Larry Bud Melman was overused by doing commercials and it oversaturated the brand for Letterman.

Coincidentally, when my friends and I went to Atlantic City, my friends had tickets for us to see Jay Leno and meet him after the show. Jay said to me then, "Hey, John, good job on *Last Call*." Who knew he was watching, and how ironic that he would say that? I wish Howard had the same opinion, but instead the whole thing just irritated him.

My fall from grace with Howard happened over a series of instances, the first being the alleged book deal. I told Howard on the air that I'd been approached about doing a book, and he didn't say much about it. Afterward, he asked to see me in his office—like I was in trouble with the principal. He told me that I couldn't write a book mentioning anything about the show because he might have a book deal of his own soon. I could write a book about my band gigs or anything else, just not the show. Later that day, I called my guy at the publishing house and told him the deal was off. After all, who cares about my fucking band gigs? In those days, me writing a book without mentioning Howard was like telling Captain Ahab not to mention the whale.

Here is what happened:

a. I got interest from a literary agent to do a book about my trials and tribulations while interviewing celebrities.

b. I met the guy who was going to cowrite the book with me.

c. I mentioned it on the air, and Howard told me to come to his office after the show, where he then explained that I couldn't do a book about my interviews or the show because he might be writing a book someday and my book would interfere with his.

d. I called the cowriter and told him I was not allowed to do a book about the interviews or anything about the show.

e. I received a book proposal that the cowriter had written and gave to the literary agent anyway. It was exactly what I told him I couldn't do, as per Howard's request. I was shocked. I feared that this had gone to Judith Regan and other publishers, and that Howard would find out and think it was my doing.

f. I called the cowriter and got his voicemail and said, "What the fuck are you doing? I already told you that I couldn't do this."

g. In a state of panic, I called Robin to tell her what this asshole did—but instead of being understanding, she scolded me. She was very angry with me. In retrospect, I'm guessing she already knew and had talked to Howard about it.

h. That Monday morning, Howard ripped me a new asshole about how I tried to write the book behind his back. Which is so silly. Like, really? I would do that after he told me I couldn't? Did he think I was purposely trying to lose my job?

i. That Monday after the show, the cowriter called me to apologize. He totally admitted that I told him I couldn't do the book but that he went against my wishes, and he felt bad. Too late, jackass.

Howard went ballistic on the air. This was such bullshit. Like I would really try to write a book behind his back. I swear on my life that this whole sequence is true. It didn't matter, though. I started getting labeled as sneaky, and this was

FRANK GIFFORD:

but one of the things that started my on-air downfall with Howard. I fell from grace. More of this type of bullshit ensued. Did it have anything to do with my increasing popularity? Who knows? But I became a target.

A friend of mine, James Karridis, pointed out a story to me that he said made him never want to listen to Howard again. Howard and I were arguing on the air, and he said that if I didn't agree with him and say that he was right, I'd be fired. I had to finally say that I was wrong and he was right just to keep my job. The irony is that Howard, who was verbally abused by his dad—called a moron, and stupid—had become that very same person to us.

He made a choice, unfortunately for us—although it was a type of behavior I was already used to.

Here's what I mean...

"OH NO, NOT AGAIN"

THOSE WERE THE WORDS I uttered with my back against my bedroom door, looking down at the foyer a floor below, as my dad continued to beat the living shit out of my sister Susan. I was five or six, and this was not the first time I had witnessed something like this.

My mom ran down in only her panties and jumped on my father's back, pulling him off my sister. *What happened this time?* I wondered. It turns out she showed up a half hour late. A suitable punishment, I guess. That night, my mom slept in bed with her young, scared-shitless son, her hand gripped around the handle of a carving knife to protect me from my dad.

"Goodnight, Mommy," I said, knowing this was not the last time the slap fest was going to happen. I fell asleep with my sisters crying in the next room.

The stuttering started around that time, and the OCD soon followed.

We all received these open-hand slap beatings, but my sister Joyce got it the worst, my brother Roy the least. He was the oldest and apparently the smartest at avoiding Dad's torrential tirades. He could spot the eyebrows rising, and as soon as they went up, you were given about ten seconds to either shut the fuck up or get your face smacked in. See, my dad wasn't so bad. I mean, at least he didn't hit us with a closed fist. Otherwise, I would find this extremely abusive.

I think my first beating was premeditated. I was alone with my dad; Mom was babysitting another bunch of kids. Yeah, I know what you're thinking: Why the fuck would she leave a young boy home with a dad she knows can snap at any minute?

In hindsight, my mom was an innocent woman off the boat from Denmark at the age of eighteen who soon after met my dad. It's easy to judge now, but this was back in the old days—what did she know?

Anyway, here I am asking my dad to help me with my homework, but he was busy on his bed, engineering papers strewn out across the duvet. He was busy, how dare I interrupt?

I asked him for help; he said he was busy.

I asked again; angrier, he said he was busy.

I knew that if I asked again, I was getting beat, and that if I didn't ask, I would survive unscathed. Unfortunately, I chose the former. Why? I mean, I knew it was going to lead to my ass getting kicked. Well, because I felt guilty that only my sisters got the beatings. I mean, who was I to avoid them? My sisters already abused me enough, calling me "Mama's Boy," and this was my way of proving that I was one of them.

"Dad, can you please beat the shit out of me…I mean, help me with my homework?"

Bam. Slap. Game over. My trust in Dad, gone.

From there on out, it was a confused love I felt for him. On the one hand, he was a hot-tempered maniac capable of hitting his young children at will, and on the other hand, he was this great, smart, funny dad who took us on wonderful vacations, made us laugh, provided for us, fed us.

How could I control which dad I was going to get? I couldn't.

I did try to control it; it's called OCD, aka obsessive-compulsive disorder.

Trust me—much like my stuttering, I truly believe most of it is physiological, a chemical imbalance in the brain. But this abuse was not fucking helping.

My other two beatings were not premeditated, however. The one was because I accidentally shit my pants when he was watching me alone. I still remember the log lying in my underwear like a cigar in an ashtray and my dad upset I couldn't hold it in. Yeah, *boom boom*, what a dick I was. The last was when I was building a go-cart with my friend John Holter. We were eight, and I cut one of my dad's many precious two-by-fours that had been lying in

ARSENIO HALL:

the garage for years, gathering dust. He walked into the garage, saw I used a piece of his wood without asking, and slapped the crap out of me in front of my terrified friend.

Why would he do this, you ask?

Well, my dad is a hoarder with shades of OCD himself. I remember he had this army boot in a vise downstairs for most of my childhood. He'd save everything.

Meanwhile, my face was constantly red from the pain of my incessant crying. My home wasn't safe. I was scared and alone.

I think in some way my stuttering became a tool of defense; I'd rather show weakness, so that the predator would feel bad enough to let me live another day.

No safety at home, and soon you'll see: no safety anywhere else, either.

In kindergarten, I used to walk a mile to school alone. Yes, a four-year-old on his own. I got independence before I knew how to spell it. I think it's because my mom always wanted me to be famous, and she let me walk to school alone in hopes that my portrait would end up on the side of a milk carton. Nowadays, my wife drives my kids two blocks to the bus stop. Things have changed.

My mom, however, is a truly great person. She grew up in Denmark during World War II, and as a five-year-old child she could hear the war planes overhead and the sirens going off, warning people to their bomb shelters. She was one of nine children in a poor family, and she would tell us stories about how she would deliver milk in six-foot snowdrifts. She was also constantly being made fun of for being overweight. She was never heavy, really, but just big-boned, I guess. So she would tell us about getting teased by teenaged boys...and then beating the living shit out of them.

> My favorite story, albeit a sad one, is that when my mother was a little girl, she had a pet rabbit named Peter. They were a poor family, mind you, with barely enough money to feed themselves, let alone a pet. One day she came home from school and sat down for dinner, and as they were eating a stew, Mom asked what the meat was. A silence fell over the table—and you can guess the rest. Poor Mom.

All right. I'm sorry for bringing you down.

Back to my wacky childhood.

"ARE YOU MAD AT YOUR DENTIST?"

AND NOW FOR A LESS DEPRESSING CHAPTER

I had the biggest crush on my teacher, Ms. Wyland. She was hot and I dug her. Where were all of these teachers that bang their students when I was young? Hey, I was at least an inch and a half. I could've pleased. At least with the stutter I'd be great at oral. (Ms. Wyland, you reading this? Wink wink.)

MY NEXT NIGHTMARE ENSUED shortly after and went by the name of the Godfreys. And believe me, they were God-free. A family headed by a maniacal ex-Marine dad who beat his kids with a shillelagh that sat proudly above the three baby pictures on the wall. Parents are fucked up, but let me get back to the story.

My best friend Mitchell England and I were transferred from Eastplain Elementary School to Picken Elementary School because of overcrowding. They sold us a line of bullshit about how it was only the smarter kids they transferred.

Yeah, well, why did they take us to school in the short yellow bus, then?

Anyway, Mitchell and I were on the swing set at Margaret Park, close to my house. Innocent kids, not a harmful bone in either of our bodies. From the far entrance of the park walked the bad kids, Patrick and Daniel Godfrey, Gary Cossentino, and a few other truant eight-year-olds. They walked up to us and asked what school we went to. We said, "Picken," and they said, "Well, we go to Eastplain now, in the sump, so we can kick your asses."

The Godfreys lived around the block. Patrick was the ugliest son of a bitch I had ever seen, big-ass birthmark on his face and hate in his eyes.

I wonder where all that hatred came from? (Maybe they were Jets fans?)

Cut to the shillelagh hanging above the baby pictures.

Why do some parents want kids?

For the next three years, the Godfreys hunted me down like Chris Christie looking for a doughnut, chasing me and my friends all over the fucking place. I was scared shitless of them. Heck, I wasn't a fighter. I was an innocent kid thrown into a whole bunch of bad shit. I was also a performer and starred in

RUSH LIMBAUGH:
"ARE YOU CALLED RUSH BECAUSE YOU'RE IN A RUSH TO EAT?"

the first-grade play, *The Little Carrot Seed*. I sang, acted, and helped the other kids with their lines while on stage. The play was so good that the cable TV station put it on their network, and a local star was born.

Well, this irritated the fuck out of my siblings. Not only was I Mama's favorite, but I was talented and not scared to be the center of attention, something my siblings abhorred, and so they put me down ad nauseam. Although when Susan was around her friends, she would have me sing *The Little Carrot Seed* song. She hated me one moment, was proud of me the next.

In their eyes, I was an asshole. How dare I get all of the attention? How dare Mom protect me from Dad, and not them? I mean, who the fuck was I?

I guess I needed an outlet, so I wrote stories. I got an 8mm camera and shot movies. Performing was my passion. It was also my curse.

For three years, my friends and I were in what we called "The War" with the Godfrey gang. Once, Patrick chased me for over a mile down William Road to the main thoroughfare, Hicksville Road, about a mile away. I outsmarted the stupid son of a bitch, though. He saw me running toward Hicksville and decided to cut through the house's backyard to head me off. I saw him do that and just turned around, ran back down William, made a left on Daniel Road, and found refuge at an old friend's house. I called my mom for a ride home, crying the whole time. Shit, man, this kid was nuts! I was so afraid that they'd kill me. The Godfreys also found out about the stuttering. Patrick, Daniel, and their sister Christine would mimic me as they chased me. "Hey, M-M-Melendez, you retard."

Ah, the joys of childhood.

I turned to plenty of different things to escape. I would read as many books as I could, and I wrote incessantly. I sang in the school chorus, made all-district, and was always given a solo. I was a pretty good trumpet player, able to read music, and I made all-district band. I was a good baseball player as well, three-time all-star and tournament team player. But with all of the abuse going on around me, failure, doubt, and guilt soon followed. Put it this way: I went from a kid who loved attention and loved to excel to a scared-shitless confused boy who started to hide from the spotlight.

My next infatuation was in fourth grade: Paula, a Greek goddess of such beauty she made my heart stop. I didn't know how to let her know I dug her, so I used the "going through a friend" trick. I had my neighbor, Alison, give

HE WAS ACTUALLY A GOOD SPORT.

her something from me. I asked Alison what should I give her—a necklace would be too strong—and we decided on a pack of gum. Well, it started out as a pack, but I was a candy freak, so I took two pieces out of it first. After receiving the almost-full pack of gum, Paula gave Alison a note that she wrote and Alison handed it to me. It was on yellow cardboard and read, "Johnny, thanks for the gum but I'm not interested in being anything but your friend, I'm sorry, Paula."

My heart was broken. Devastated, I talked to Mitchell about it, cried, and spent the rest of the fourth grade wondering if it would have been different if I hadn't taken out those damn two pieces of gum. "How selfish could I be?" I thought, but what fourth grader thinks like that?

How about one who had been told that by my sisters many, many, times? My "selfishness" actually caused my sister Joyce to pull a knife on my dad after church one day. (Oh yeah, my dad is a staunch Catholic— go figure.) As I said, he would reward/bribe us into going to church by taking us to the candy store after Mass. I got my pack of grape Now and Laters and a *MAD Magazine*, and they got their candy. By the time we got home, they finished their candy, but I, being the saver, still had mine. I was down to like five pieces, and they each asked me for one in our kitchen. "Fuck no," I thought. (Well, I was nine, so it might have been, "Heck no.")

Eventually, I decided to cut one in half. Hey, man, I was saving them. It wasn't my fault my sisters didn't know how to candy manage. This was sugar capital to me. Look, even the title says "Now and Later." Have some now, save some for later. It's on the fucking wrapper!

Anyway, my sisters started calling me "selfish" and a "brat," and my dad overheard them needling me and came to my defense, only his eyebrows were raised and Susan knew to run out of the fucking room. Joyce, however, was sick of getting beaten. So she picked up one of the carving knives and pulled it on my dad, warding him off.

"Yeah, you want to stab me," he screamed. "Go ahead, stab me!"

She finally dropped it and he beat the shit out of her. I cried watching this, knowing that it was all my fault, that I should have just given her the damn Now and Later.

Why was I so fucking selfish?

Feelings of guilt ensued.

LUCIANO PAVAROTTI:

By the time I was in fifth grade, Joyce was on drugs. She would run away over and over again, getting beat up every time she came home. Susan couldn't wait to leave for college, and they both resented my mother for not leaving my father. They also resented me because I received the most protection, something they would throw in my face on numerous occasions.

At this time, I was excelling in baseball. By my second year, I was on the all-star team. I would have made it the first year if not for four strikeouts in one game after I witnessed Joyce getting her ass kicked by my father in front of my Aunt Delia, who barely reacted and did nothing. She was my father's sister, and this must've been the norm in the old Melendez household when they were kids.

My first baseball manager was Mr. Kay. He showed up at my house and asked me to show my talents. I was seven; I fielded a few balls and told him that I wanted to play shortstop, he asked why, and I told him because that's the position that gets the most action. I knew this from watching the Yankees and Mets play as a kid. (My dad was a Mets fan, my mom a Yankees fan. I was a Yankees fan. I wonder why?)

I was a great fielder, an incredible hitter, yet I missed the fourth spot for the all-star team by a fraction in batting average. Mr. Kay pulled me aside to tell me how great of a fielder and hitter I was, but that my friend Peter Diaco had a slightly better batting average. Why? Those fucking four strikeouts! That's why! The beatings must have had an emotional impact on me that I wasn't even aware of. I cried like crazy the rest of that game. I remember fielding a ground ball and flipping the ball to second for the force with tears in my eyes. I couldn't handle the rejection. I felt slighted. I went home with my teammate John Cosgrove, and as his mom drove, I cried. He said, "Don't worry about it," thinking he was going to make the all-star team. The whole time I'm thinking to myself, "No, you idiot, you ain't making it either. It's Larry, the Carey brothers, and Peter." I didn't have the heart to tell him, though—let him dream another day.

In retrospect, he probably would've been better off if I had told him then instead of waiting to write it in a book.

Anyway, the following two years I made the all-star teams even when it was only the top three players. I was good, but the shit was about to hit the fan.

"EVER FART WHILE BELTING OUT A HIGH NOTE?"

I was in the school all-district band as a trumpet player in second, third, and fourth grade, I finally quit after the Godfreys told me that trumpet playing would screw up my lips. My private instructor at the time was this guy named Frank Fico, and he had these weird thin lips that curved up then down. I decided to get to the bottom of this, so I went to a lesson and said, "Frank, is it true that trumpet playing screws up your lips?" He said, "Of course not, look at mine." I quit the next day.

My fifth-grade teacher was Mrs. Downes, who my sisters would tell me was named for one of the drugs she took. I needed drugs that first day of school, because in the lunchroom I ran into my arch nemesis, Patrick "The Mole" Godfrey. He walked up to me and said, "The war's over, let's be friends."

Man, was I relieved, but little did I know this would eventually lead to a life of crime. This kid was bad, but I loved him. My mom always used to tell me, "That kid's going to end up in jail one of these days," and I was like, "No, he isn't."

He ended up doing ten years, out in seven for good behavior. Then died of a drug overdose.

We became the best of friends. He taught me how to cut through backyards to get to school quicker; he taught me his secret backyard passageways, which is how he managed to sneak up and away on us all of those years during "The War." He introduced me to his brother Danny, who ended up becoming one of my best friends and still is to this day. We went pool-hopping, which is where we would jump into a neighbor's pool at night. We played knock-knock runaway, where you knock on someone's door and then run away. Only Pat was a rebel and loved danger, so he would have us knock and then we would jump over the bushes of the house across the street and heckle the guy who answered the door. Once we all took a shit in a paper bag and lit it on fire on the front porch of a kid we knew. His dad answered the door, knew what it was, and tried to find us. The kid's uncle came to the door but wasn't as clever and started stomping on the bag vigorously, but his foot slowed as he realized that he was stepping in a pile of human shit.

We laughed our asses off because we were across the street watching the whole thing from behind the bushes. The uncle knocked on the door to get paper towels as we watched our sides splitting open. We started to chant, "Weep Waw," the sound effect from the moving cake from *The Little Rascals*, our favorite show. We were juvenile delinquents and received our first JD cards when we were ten.

REGIS PHILBIN:

At the beach, I would tap a girl on the shoulder and Patrick or Danny would untie their top. Pat and I were fast enough to not get caught by the police, but Danny would always get caught. At field day, I finished in first place in the four-hundred-yard dash, winning the blue ribbon, and Patrick came in second. We had to be fast. People chased us all the time.

Life became a mischievous adventure. Patrick would come over my house with Danny and say, "You want to get chased?" and I'd say, "Sure." We would walk two and a half miles to the mall. When we saw older kids playing with their skateboards, we would yell, "Hey, assholes," and they would chase us. And then Danny would get caught and punched, that slow, fat bastard. We would call and order pizza when Pat's parents weren't home and hide on the roof, egging the pizza delivery boy when he showed up.

We would call people whose paperboy was a kid we knew, disguise our voices to sound adult, and tell them we were from *Newsday* and that their paperboy was complaining that his tip wasn't big enough. They would be like, "That damn kid, from now on he'll get no tip." We were assholes. We would collect on my friend's paper route; we'd say, "Yeah, sorry, ma'am. John Holter's sick and asked us to collect for him." Then we'd go to the Pizza Cove and blow the money on pizza, pinball, and video games.

After a night of truancy, I would feel so guilty. I'd jog home from Pat's house, stopping in front of the statue of the Mother Mary, and I would pray and beg God for his forgiveness. I was never a bad kid before. What had the Godfreys done to me? I knew all of this was wrong, but it was exciting.

We also did good things, though. We participated in the March of Dimes twenty-mile walk twice—although the second time, Pat had the idea that we could cut through Grumman and cut off a few miles, but we ended up getting chased and Danny tore the bottom off of his pants because the fat fuck had trouble climbing a fence. We would Christmas Carol for the poor. Some of our greatest scams were calling people, telling them we were from the phone company and that they should not pick up the phone if they received a call within the next ten minutes because we were having technical issues and someone working on the phone would receive a severe electric shock. We would then call back with a recording of us screaming with electric sound effects in the background. Some people believed us and actually did not pick up.

In the winter, we would skitch, which is where you grab the bumper of someone's car at a stop sign and then get a free ride all through the snowy streets of the neighborhood. But in usual fashion, my mom caught me. See, I had this corn on my toe—it was the beginning of an endless list of foot problems, most of them being trying to remove them from my mouth. My mom used to drag me to a specialist to zap the corn with some Dr. Frankenstein-like electric current. It hurt like hell and he would bandage it up with gauze. I got home one afternoon and decided to go skitching with the Godfreys. So I'm chasing down a car I'd never seen before and my mom is in the back seat. She turns around, realizes it's me trying to skitch on her friend's car, and yells in her Danish accent, "Johnny, get home. You'll wet your corn!"

However, high school was great. My stutter had almost entirely disappeared thanks to how comfortable I had become with my surroundings—except when it came to picking up chicks. My band at the time played a sweet-sixteen party and later, when I was waiting for the bathroom, over walked Kim Dejanero, the hottest girl in school, and she asked me my name. I told her "John." Piece of cake—"J"s were easy. But then she asked my last name, and I started sweating more than Donald Trump at the Mexican Day Parade. I gathered all my strength and screamed at the top of my lungs, "MELENDEZ!" I continued to never get laid in high school.

Nassau Community College, otherwise known as "Thirteenth Grade" or "Turnpike Tech," came next. It was two-year school and I wanted to use the time to figure out what I might want to do while not ditching my band or my friends. Most importantly, it saved my father a bunch of money. My most humiliating moment at Nassau came in an English class after we'd read a Hemingway story. I'd done the assignment but the professor didn't believe me, eventually asking, "If you read it, then what color was the girl's dress?" I tried my darndest to say "yellow," but I couldn't spit it out. The whole class was starring at me, and eventually I blurted out "Green!" The teacher triumphantly muttered "nope," and I was forced to let him win if I didn't want the class to know I stuttered.

In my last semester I took a film and literature course. I started to figure, "hey if I can't act because of the stutter, then maybe I can direct." The next year I transferred to NYU as a film major. I'll never forget the first day of my "sight and sound" course. The professor asked each of us to stand up and then say our names and what we wanted to be. I just about shit my pants. When it was my turn, I stood up and screamed (an old stuttering trick), "My name is John Melendez, and I want to be a director!"

He responded, "Well, there's a guy who knows what he wants to be."

In my head I was like, "No, there's a guy who can't even spit out his last name."

MY OCD MANIFESTO

IT'S AMAZING I'VE GOTTEN this far, having been dealt the awful hand of obsessive-compulsive disorder. I'm pretty sure I inherited it from my dad, because not only was he a hoarder, but one time I heard him on the phone with the hospital where my mom was recovering from something saying to himself, "What's wrong with me?"

It started at an early age. I remember being at the beach and lifting my hands so that they wouldn't touch the sand. When I was in my third season of Little League, I had socks that lost the strength in their elastic and kept falling down. So when I was at bat, I kept trying to pull them up, with each foot rubbing the back of each calf, grabbing hold of the sock and pulling up. I got a bunch of hits and this soon became a ritual.

One time two of my friends and I took mescaline, a form of acid, and went to Action Park, a water park in New Jersey. We had a great time, laughed our asses off, but coming down was a bitch. When I got home, I poured myself a glass of orange juice and started to put the glass in the fridge and keep the carton. Suddenly, it struck! As I went to put the carton in and take the glass out, I had a random thought in my head that I hoped my mother died. Totally scared of the thought, I had to take the orange juice carton out of the fridge and put it back in, only this time saying in my head that I wished my mother wouldn't die. I was unaware of what this was, but it slowly started to manifest into a thing that occupied my mind 100 percent of the time.

That was the start of it, but it hit in full force after I graduated high school and had sex for the first time with my girlfriend, who we'll call Ginger. She cheated on me nonstop but would never admit it. This left me devastated, crying all of the time, and realizing that she lied to me about it left me crawling in my head for comfort. Around this time, in college, I took a math course

"DO YOU THINK THAT HEADBAND ON YOUR MOTHER'S HEAD WAS PLACED THERE BY SPACE ALIENS?"

called Logic, Sets, and Numbers. It taught me how X added to $-X$ equaled zero. This taught my fucked-up OCD brain that if I had a bad thought, I immediately had to undo it with a good one.

~~By the time I started~~ *The Stern Show*, I was at full-blown OCD levels. I finally sought a free therapist after taking a psychology course in college and realizing exactly what I was suffering from. He prescribed Anafranil for me, but it only left me feeling nauseated. I was on my own, a short, stuttering, OCD-ridden Puerto Rican with long hair and smelly feet—which, by the way, is my new Match.com bio. At *The Stern Show*, I would obsess over everything I did there. Whether it was labeling the tapes or fixing Howard's potatoes, I was a mess. I would always scar cut his potatoes four times each. Whenever Robin would do a news story about AIDS, I would have to type it and un-type it in the computer several times just to ensure that I didn't contract it.

I was thoroughly OCD about AIDS ever since I'd contracted genital warts and crabs. The crabs were from when I was dating Ginger. Since she cheated so much, I would cheat to get her back. Plus, I was nineteen and horny as shit.

I also received genital warts from this girl I schtupped in Seaside Heights, New Jersey; there's a reason the nickname for Seaside Heights is Sleaside Heights. This girl even let me talk her into blowing my sexually deprived friend Jiggs. She even blew me while Jiggs went down on her, but then our friends opened the motel door and a paint chip fell from the ceiling and went in my mouth and I swallowed it, and I spent the next half hour choking. And let me tell you, choking and stuttering at the same time ain't as much fun as it sounds. The next morning, I woke up and she was gone, along with my silver ring that my friend Axl made.

The worst thing about genital warts is that the doctor douses your balls and penis in vinegar to find them. I felt like a Cobb salad. Then he sticks a needle in your dick and testicles to numb the warts and then cuts them off. It was more painful than my Billy Crystal interview.

I also thought I had AIDS, because my band had played a gig in Philly and I had met this hot blonde. The following weekend, I took her to Atlantic City and we had sex like four times. The last time, though, she bled all over me. I was sure I had AIDS.

I was also very obsessive about becoming a star in my own right. So when Howard would tell me I was untalented, it struck an OCD nerve in my head. If I walked into the office and had a thought that I wouldn't be successful,

BRUCE WILLIS:

"WHAT IS DISAPPEARING QUICKER, THE OZONE OR YOUR HAIR?"

"WILL YOU DUMP DEMI WHEN SHE GETS DUMPY?"

I would have to walk out and then back in thinking I would be. I was in my own prison, and still am to this day. Alcohol eased the obsessions, as well as curtailed the stuttering, so it became a wonder drug to me.

College was the worst. Writing essays, I would constantly have to type something, then erase it, and then type it again if I'd had a bad thought. If, God forbid, I had a bad thought while I touched a doorknob, I immediately had to touch the doorknob again and undo the thought. I was—and still am—trapped in a living hell.

Once, I was having sex with Suzanna and thought about one of her ex-boyfriends while pulling out and found myself traumatized, especially because two months later we found out that she was pregnant. Thankfully, we concluded that she got pregnant when we were having sex in Atlantic City.

Who knew that Howard was going through the same thing? To this day, however, I don't believe he is cured. After he wrote his book *Miss America*, which had chapters on his OCD, he claimed he was cured one day after having an epiphany. Most therapists, if not all, say that is just impossible; in fact, after the book came out, we were all talking in the studio and he was constantly touching and obsessing on one part of the *Son of the Beach* poster hanging on his bathroom door.

Look, OCD people can spot each other dead on. It's easy if you're also suffering from the disorder. I remember being backstage at a David Lee Roth concert and him saying to me, "So you're a 'C' too?" He spotted it right away.

Here's a typical day for me:

I wake up, get out of bed, and allow myself four footsteps to the toilet. I pee and pull my underpants up, although if I have a bad thought, I will have to pull them down again until it equals three times. Three is my favorite number. Then I count the footsteps back to my bed, and when I have a good thought in my head, I jump back into bed. I then grab my computer with four fingers and place it on my lap. I go down once to the menu bar and then one more time and then click on Safari. I check my AOL mail—yes, I still have AOL, it matches my Crocs. And if you make fun of me for it, I'll delete you from my MySpace account. Then I'll go to Huffington Post, CNN, then Twitter. I'll then go to my three Facebook accounts. If I play a game of Backgammon, I'll have to play three more. Before I'm done with Facebook, I'll have to visit all of the accounts four times, breaking up each cycle with Twitter.

After I do that, I can get on with the various other sites I visit, like MLB, NFL, Yahoo, and Dawgshed. If I have a bad thought while exiting Facebook, I have to go back six more times to each account, totaling ten times. The reason being, it has to be an even number—six is no good because it's the devil's number, eight won't work because anything after would be nine and nine begins with an "n," which negates everything.

The whole time, 99.9 percent of my brain knows this is all bullshit, but there is that very small percentage of doubt, and so why not do it if it eases the mind? Then I go to my notes and begin writing my affirmations. Again, going down to the menu bar and then up and then down once again and clicking on Notes. I write my affirmations, close out, looking at the one that says that I'm grateful for my kids twice. I then do the menu bar thing again and click on Microsoft Word to begin writing more.

After I'm done with that, I get up, get dressed, maybe having to put on my clothes multiple times depending on what thoughts I have, brush my teeth, and then shower, which is another ritual:

a.   Wash hands

b.   Wash arms and armpits three times

c.   Wash legs

d.   Wash left shoulder, right shoulder, then two strokes on left shoulder

e.   Wash face

f.   Wash crotch

g.   Wash ass three times

h.   Shampoo

i.   Condition

j.   Take four steps, grab knobs

k.   Shut off shower while keeping face under the showerhead

I get out of shower and must have a good thought or else I have to go back in and come out again. Brush teeth, brush tongue three times. Apply deodorant, only two swipes under right armpit. Leaving the house is a nightmare, because I have to have a good thought while stepping outside with my right foot. Why right? Because when I was an impressionable kid I heard that the devil is left-handed, and because I am a God-loving Catholic, the left would be bad.

LIZ TAYLOR:

Lines and squares are a problem. I sometimes have to put two footsteps in each square and avoid the lines. I was leaving a liquor store with a twelve-pack of beer and cigarettes once and I was doing the stepping ritual. I was also walking backward because I'd had a bad thought. Some lady came out of her car and told me I shouldn't be driving if I was that drunk. I hadn't even had a beer yet!

And it's all based on fear and doubt. I read in a book called *Brain Lock* by Jeffrey M. Schwartz how a normal brain shifts gears automatically. If a normal brain has a ridiculous thought, that person just moves on and switches gears. An OCD brain will get stuck and won't be able to change gears.

The whole time at *The Howard Stern Show*, I was suffering from this disorder. Doing Howard's mail was a nightmare. I had to photocopy every letter, but I had to have a good thought while I put the letter down on the copy machine. Then I made a copy that went home with Howard, but I had to sort the mail and put it in separate folders. This was by far the most OCD job for me. I would have the interns help me. In fact, Steve Grillo used to compare me to Tom Sawyer, because I would get other people to do my job for me—not because I was lazy, but because I was so OCD it was almost impossible for me to do simple tasks. I had so many rituals, it was awful. I am a prisoner of my own brain.

I can only jerk off in the morning. I can't drink until after noon because, when I lived in Long Island, on Sunday the stores wouldn't sell beers until after noon. This became an obsession for me. The only way I can drink in the morning is if I had a drink after 11:25 the night before, thirty-five minutes before midnight. Thirty-five minutes of something, or doing something thirty-five times—it doesn't matter. Thirty-five is the safe zone in my head.

When I met Suzanna, I used to tell her to meet me in front of my doctor's office. I told her it was my back doctor, but it was really my therapist's office. I used to lie about it all the time. One time when Grillo and Gange moved into my apartment, they found a bottle of Prozac in there that I left behind. They showed it to Howard, and he confronted me on the air about it, and I told him that I took it because I thought it helped me become a better guitar player! I was so insecure about anyone knowing what I was going through.

After I told Suzanna, she used a cigar to burn a button-like ash in my bedroom wall and said to press that button when I felt OCD. We tried everything—hypnotists, spiritual gurus, therapists—but nothing seemed to work. It wasn't until I got to *The Tonight Show* that I found a therapist who hooked me up with a combination of Luvox and Klonopin, which made it somewhat better. It was like, instead of touching every doorknob, I would touch every other one. Whatever, it was still there, but it got a little better. I started to enjoy painting, but with every brush swipe, I had to have a good thought. It was far from relaxing.

I enjoyed painting conceptual paintings. For instance, I collected shrapnel from all of the wars from the Civil War to Desert Storm. I bought it on eBay and painted a canvas light blue and then made a peace sign out of the shrapnel. I made this other one where I spelled "Happiness" out of money and pasted it on a light blue canvas. It had a twenty-dollar bill and a ten-dollar bill, along with a couple of fives and singles and some change. It hung over my *Tonight Show* desk in my office. Well, when a fellow writer named John Kennedy was in there writing a cold open with me, he looked up at the painting and asked why I pulled the money off of it. I looked up to see that someone stole the money!

I assumed it was a janitor or something (or maybe an NBC executive), but I guess money was his happiness.

STUTTERING JOHN AND CONROY ARNOLD

ONE OF THE BEST things that happened to me from being on the show was that I became a voice for stutterers everywhere. They now had a young stuttering person to look up to. I received tons of fan mail from stutterers and their parents telling me what an inspiration I was. One day I received a call from a Manhattan schoolteacher. She told me about a student of hers with a real bad stutter named Conroy Arnold. She wanted me to meet with him and talk to him. I said sure, and a few days later, Conroy showed up to K-Rock and I took him into the office I was using. I sat across from Conroy, and he stuttered so badly I had tears in my eyes. After a while of trying to help him, giving him my methods, I asked him what he was doing that Friday night, and he told me that he was bringing a girl he loved to the movies. I sat there and thought and then just pulled this solution out of my ass. I told Conroy to bring a notebook and pen to the movies. I explained to him that this way, if he couldn't speak to her, he could just write it down, allowing him at the very least a chance to communicate. I also explained that having this crutch at hand might alleviate some of the pressure to speak, thus allowing him to speak more fluently. I gave Conroy a hug, and he thanked me.

Doug Goodstein and I flew out to the Million Man March in Washington, DC as we covered it live for the show. We got our press credentials, but when we started doing phone-ins—let's just say that the people attending were not big fans of Howard. They started yelling things at Doug and me, and they were starting to form a circle of angry marchers around us like a wagon train. That's when Doug and I looked at each other and said, "Let's get the fuck out of here!" We took our equipment and hauled ass and flew back to New York.

Thirteen years later—the Friday that I told Howard over the phone that I was leaving him for Leno—we were all going to Atlantic City. So Suzanna, Howard, Beth, and a few of our friends and I all had dinner that Friday night at a high-class restaurant at the Borgata Hotel. After a great dinner, the waitress came up to me and asked if I would mind speaking to their head chef. I said, "Sure, what's his name?" and she said, "Conroy Arnold."

So I'm sitting there, and over walks this tall, good-looking guy in his kitchen attire. Conroy did not stutter at all anymore! I couldn't believe it. I asked him how he did it. He said, "John, I never put down the notebook and pen, and to this day I still carry it around—not as much for stuttering anymore, now just to write my recipes."

Holy shit! I had chills down my spine, and I do now, even as I write this. I was so proud of him and was also so happy that I could make a positive change to his life. We all have angels, and I guess I was one of his. After talking for a while, I asked him if he got laid the night of the date. He said yes, and I said, "Shit, I should start carrying around a notebook and pen!" To this day I continue to mentor stuttering children. I was even the keynote speaker at the National Stuttering Associate in Chicago. I gave an hour-long speech, but the Q&A afterward was brutal—it took five hours, and we got through three questions.

If you or anybody you know has a problem with stuttering and is looking for help, do feel free to reach out to me through my website.

POOR GUY WAS LIKE, "WOULD YOU?" HE SAID IT IN THAT MR. ROGERS VOICE. THIS BECAME A SOUND BITE FOR FRED.

There was this story about an image of the Virgin Mary appearing in a window in New Jersey. People were lining up to touch it, so Howard sent me there to see what was going on. As I was waiting in line, I called Howard live on the show. I touched the window, and he told me to start crying. The thing was, there were tons of people waiting in line behind me. I didn't want to piss them off, and plus I'm kind of into religion. Finally I said fuck it, so I started fake crying, and Howard and the rest of the show started laughing their asses off. I continued to bawl as all of the people in line watched. The whole studio was laughing. I've always loved to make people laugh. I wasn't even going to put this story in the book, but so many people continue to come up to me and tell me that it was their favorite Stuttering John bit. Hopefully I won't go to Hell for it!

GOODBYE TO BILLY WEST, AND ME...TEMPORARILY

I GOT A CALL from Don Buchwald, who was no longer representing me. He explained that we were about to be doing a show for E! and that my salary would be two hundred dollars a week, about ten grand a year. I said okay, because what else was I going to say?

I called my lawyer, Larry Shire, and he said fine, "but please just ask them to send or fax me a copy of the contract so I can review it before you sign it." A few days later, one of Don's henchmen, Richard Bosch, came into the building, and I met with him in the jock lounge next to Gary's office. He handed me the contract and I assured him that I would sign it, but asked, if it's okay, that he just fax it to my lawyer. He said yes and took the contract back and I was off the E! show! After three weeks, I walked down to Howard's office and asked if I could talk to him. Almost crying, I apologized for asking Richard to send the contract to my lawyer. Howard said, "Yeah, John, just do what we tell you to do, and stop listening to Jackie; he's nothing but a troublemaker."

IVANA TRUMP:

I guess this started when Baba Backstabber and I talked with Jackie in the jock lounge. The truth was that we were all upset with our E! salaries. Jackie was making around twenty-five grand a year and I think Gary around fifteen grand. We were all just expressing our disappointment, and Jackie might have made a joke, saying, "Let's all just say no, there's strength in numbers," but I didn't take him seriously. He was just lamenting like we all were. But somehow Gary went back to Howard with this and blamed it on Jackie. He told him something like Jackie was trying to get us to go against Howard, but this was all bullshit.

> Billy left at this time because the E! show was non-union and Billy was in like three unions—AFTRA, SAG, and I think another one. His agent told him that he could get thrown out of the unions for working below the union rate, which is what the show was paying him. Billy told me that Howard called him at home, and when Billy answered the phone, Howard said, "Hey, big shot." Then Howard said he couldn't understand why Billy wouldn't do the show. Billy said that it went against his unions and that he could get thrown out. Then believe it or not, Howard said something like, "Well, why don't you just do it until you get caught?" Billy said no. It's hard to believe that a multimillionaire superstar would tell a lower-paid member of the show to break his union agreement.

Well, Billy stayed for a little while longer but then got into a negotiation over money with Tom and decided to get the heck out of there. After Billy left, Howard was talking to Robin in the studio off the air and in between commercial breaks, saying something like, "Can you believe Billy left? What does he think he's going to do? Doesn't he realize that the only reason he gets voiceover work is because people hear him on this show?" I remember that conversation like it was yesterday. I thought to myself, *Wow, is Howard that big of a megalomaniac? Is anybody worth anything to him outside of the show?* Shit, Billy went on to voice Bugs Bunny, and that's just the tip of the iceberg.

I loved Billy, he was a riot to hang out with in Scott's studio, and I knew that the show and I would miss him.

This would soon become a trend.

THE INSIDE SCOOP ON DON "THE DOUCHEBAG" BUCHWALD

YEAH, THE REAL ASSWIPE that got into Howard's brain before there was Marci Turk. He was a bigger bully than Howard—well, almost. If you are a *Star Wars* fan, think of Howard and Don as the Sith. Buchwald was the evil emperor.

This is how our tumultuous relationship began. Jackie knew all about Buchwald, which is why he never sought representation from him. It was incestuous. Here you had Howard, Robin, and Fred all represented by Buchwald.

At the time of the Channel 9 show, Howard suggested that Don should represent me and deal with my Channel 9 contracts. So Don was able to get me $750 a week from the Channel 9 show, my only salary at the time. But when the Howard Stern Channel 9 show first aired, I became an overnight television success—so much so that when Channel 9 put together their advertising packet, they featured Howard, Robin, and myself on the cover. It was awesome. It meant that, although I wasn't making very much money there, I was able to do appearances, sometimes four in a week at $750 a clip. Eventually, when the second season of the Channel 9 show came around, Don offered to represent me. I was ecstatic at first. I mean, maybe he could do for me what he did for Howard…I was wrong.

It started out okay. He got Channel 9 to double my salary, and the interviews continued and my fame kept rising. *Rolling Stone* and *Entertainment Weekly* both did big pieces on me, as well as *The New York Times*. Don's rule was that I had to tell him about any offer, except for stuff to do with my band's gigs and appearances. Little did I know that this was his way of controlling me, making sure I didn't get anything too big where I would leave *The Howard Stern Show*.

It was a perfect system of giving the underlings a taste of things, but nothing too big. I got offered a T-shirt deal through Don that I wasn't that into but begrudgingly took. I asked Don, "Well, why wouldn't you offer Howard or Robin a T-shirt deal?" He said something like, "Because they're too big for that." It was upsetting, but I reluctantly said I'd do it but then told him that I wasn't comfortable with it. I didn't want my picture on a T-shirt at the time—I was after something bigger.

Man, did he rip me a new asshole.

"I worked weeks on this," he said to me in his office. Then he did what he usually did and turned to the phone behind him and said, "I'm going to call Howard. I am just representing you as a favor to him."

I said, "I'll do it, Don! I'll do it! Please don't call Howard!"

He put the phone down and I took the money and went and took pictures for the shirts. This is what Don did. He would do this on numerous occasions. He used my love and fear of pissing off Howard against me. Heck, I was a kid. I didn't realize just how badly he was manipulating me. One day, at the height of my "Stuttering John" fame, after interviewing Gennifer Flowers and when all the shows were talking about it, I again set up a meeting with Don and asked if he thought he could get me on the talk show circuit. I said, "You know, like Letterman or Joan Rivers."

He said bluntly, "What are you going to do?"

I was deflated. I said, "I don't know, Don—be funny, tell stories about my escapades and such."

He pulled the same shit again. "I'm going to call Howard. I'm only representing you as a favor to him." I again panicked and pleaded with him not to call Howard, which he agreed to, but who knows—in retrospect, while I'm writing this, he probably told Howard anyway. Something like "John's feeling his fame" or something like that. In the meantime, Don did nothing to get me a bigger salary at K-Rock. He said that he tried, but my salary remained at ten grand a year, and then Mel doubled it to twenty after my third year. So in the three or four years I was there, I made thirty thousand gross. But again, I wasn't complaining; I could always leave, but I wasn't ready to do that just yet. I had to wait for a bigger offer to come around.

So now I knew two things: Don didn't really want to represent me, and he saw no value in me. I was convinced that if I did get any offers, he would turn them down. Who knows how many came through?

Now, as I mentioned, Don wanted no part of the band or my appearances. So at one of Howard's birthday shows, I met a guy named Michael Kaplan who was in the record industry and knew a vice president at Atlantic Records, Craig Kallman. Craig asked me to bring a demo of my band and bring my guitar and

"DON'T YOU THINK THAT IVAN LENDL LOOKS LIKE IGOR FROM THE OTHER SIDE OF THE NET?"
"WHEN YOU GET OLDER, WILL YOU HAVE SOMEONE HELP YOU OVER THE NET?"

play a few songs for him. So there I was, just me, my guitar, and Craig. I started playing a few of my songs and he was into them. He said he really liked them and asked for my demo, which I gave to him.

After five days, I called him while driving to a gig. He picked up the phone and I asked him what he thought of it.

He said, "John, the tape you gave me was blank."

What an idiot I was!

I dropped off a new tape and he called me back and said he liked it. The next thing was for my band to perform for him, so we drove to my gig at Septembers in Jersey with Craig, his girlfriend Isabelle, and my girlfriend Karen. We had become very friendly at this point. The place was packed! They were turning people away. This couldn't have been better. My band rocked—we did originals, covers, and comedy songs, with me telling jokes in between every few songs. After the show, we got in Craig's car and he told me that I could consider myself signed.

All my life I had wanted a record deal, and now it was mine!

At first it was an EP deal, which is about five songs. But I partnered with this producer, Randy Cantor, and we churned out some pretty cool songs, and Craig upped the deal to a full-length LP. I hired entertainment lawyers from Grubman, Indursky, and Schindler, and they negotiated the deal.

I never even thought about telling Don. First, he wanted nothing to do with my band, and second, I didn't want him to fuck it up. Remember, this is the same guy who basically told me that I was nothing. Why would anyone in his or her right mind trust this bully to negotiate a deal for their band? The day I was about to sign the contract, I got cold feet, and I thought I might as well tell Don as a courtesy before I signed it.

He screamed at the top of his lungs and circled around my chair like a hawk scoping out its prey. I pleaded with him, saying, "Don, you wanted nothing to do with my band and I haven't signed anything yet." He screamed at me some more, I said I was sorry, and I left. I tried calling him a couple of times, but he wouldn't return any of my phone calls. I talked to Gary about it and he wondered how this could possibly be a big deal to Don. I finally said fuck it and signed the deal the next day.

Don and I rarely spoke after that. I sent him a letter apologizing, but I really didn't feel that bad.

MARTINA NAVRATILOVA:

When Benjy Bronk and I started contributing to the show's writing on a daily basis and our E! contracts came around for renewal, we both asked Scott Einziger for writing credits on the show. Scott approached Don and asked him about it, and Don's response was, well, we don't want to give them full-fledged writing credits because then they're going to want more money, so let's phrase it like this: Some written materials were contributed by John Melendez and Benjy Bronk.

Scott couldn't believe how low Don would go, but he had to comply. This was just the world of "The Firm," and you took what they gave you and asked for no more, or else you faced the wrath of Buchwald and Howard. Jackie used to say that Howard and Don would split the pie, give Robin and Fred a slice, and then let the rest of us fight over the crumbs. Jackie was right, we all knew he was, but if we rebelled, we'd be abused. Don listed himself as a "consultant," yet the guy didn't have a funny bone in his body. He would come to the creative meetings and blurt out some unfunny bit that was so bad it made us all uncomfortable. I'd even feel Howard cringing. The guy was a dolt that latched onto Howard and ran with it.

The last scumbag move by Don and Howard was when we were about to shoot the video for my single, "I'll Talk My Way Out of It," and I asked Howard if he would make a cameo in it. He said flat out that he had to think about it, and the next day explained to me that he couldn't be in it because one day, well, one day he might want to do some business with MTV, and this would dilute it.

Are you fucking kidding me?!

This guy acted like such a douche to me. I'm sure he asked Don and Don wanted nothing more than for me to fail. So here I had Sting, Gene Simmons, Gilbert Gottfried, Jackie, Gary, and Nuno Bettencourt, but no Howard! Fuck, even Sting did it, but no fucking Howard! It was like when everyone on the show came to my wedding except for Howard (and Fred, of course), even though it was in the Hamptons—where he coincidentally commutes from now.

I used to get a call every morning from this guy on a pay phone in God knows where, saying that he couldn't believe that Howard wasn't coming to my wedding. I tried putting him through, but Howard never picked up the call.

It turned out to be Benjy. So when he started with us, I was happy that he knew what a dick Howard could be even before working there. I'm sure Don made that decision about the video. I swear, I used to fantasize about getting a voodoo doll of Don made up on the off chance that the stupid thing might actually work. Now, of course I know they don't actually work, but it sure helped me sleep better at night. This guy was and is the ultimate bully, and the only way to silence a bully is to out-bully him, which I was in no position to do. I just had to grin and take it, all the while knowing that I had to get out of this place.

Well, that's my chapter on Don. I regret ever meeting him.

JOE WALSH AND ME: I DON'T LIKE YOU EITHER

CRAIG ASKED ME WHO I wanted to write with, so I said one of my idols, Joe Walsh. Atlantic flew me out to California and I went to Joe Walsh's house in the hills to write a song. I was ecstatic. This was like a dream come true! I arrived at Joe's house and he invited me up to his living room. He had a mike set up on a stand and he had some music tracks of his new songs on his audio equipment. Joe stood in his living room and sang a couple of songs, just him. It was the first show I'd ever been to where the main act offered me a beer between songs. I couldn't believe it. I had my own personal concert performed by Joe Walsh. Later that night, Rick the bass player, a few other guys, and Joe's girlfriend came over, and Joe and I started working on the song while drinking beers, snorting coke, and smoking pot.

Joe came up with the title "I Don't Like You Either." We started writing lyrics like, "I don't like my ex-wife's lawyer," and "I don't like paying for my pot." We wrote all night while playing pool. I went to my hotel that night and drove back to Joe's house the next morning to record the song. When I pulled up, Joe came out looking pretty disheveled. I said, "Joe, do you have the lyrics?"

He said, "Oh, yeah, be right back."

He went back in his house and then walked out five minutes later and said that he couldn't find them! Thank God I had a pretty good memory. I remembered most of them, and I wrote the lyrics down in the studio. We recorded the song with Joe and me on guitar. Fuck, I was jamming with

OLIVER NORTH:

Joe Walsh! After the recording session, we started mixing it. Joe left for like three hours with his girlfriend, and when they came back, they were both wearing train engineer caps. Joe told us that he'd just bought a train car! We mixed the song, and I flew back home. It turns out Atlantic didn't think the song fit my album, but it is available on iTunes.

> One time I wrote a song for my album with Mark Hudson, of Hudson Brothers fame. He was Kate Hudson's uncle. He was staying at the Trump Plaza and we got stoned and wrote this song called "If I Had A Say," which made the album. He would tell me stories, and he told me one about how he was doing a show with the cast of **The Brady Bunch**. He had heard some things about Florence Henderson. After a rehearsal Florence came into Mark's dressing room and asked him if he had heard about her. He said yes and she asked what he'd heard and he told her he'd heard that she gave great helmet washing, which is what he called blowjobs. She said that was true and proceeded to blow him right then and there. Mr. Brady didn't know what he was missing!

MY CRAZY TIMES WITH SAM KINISON

Sam was probably the nicest celebrity I've ever encountered. He treated me like a friend I hung out with Sam once at the China Club in LA. He introduced me to Katey Sagal, Chris Squire (from Yes), and Julian Lennon as if I were the funniest guy since Lenny Bruce.

Sam pulled me aside and took me into a bathroom stall and opened up a full magazine page of coke. I hadn't seen that much pot before, let alone coke! He did a couple of lines with me, then reached into his pocket and pulled out a white pill with green and red dots on it. He said, "If you get a little freaky, take one of these."

Later on, there was a big commotion on the stairwell. Sam was in the process of strangling Arsenio Hall because of some joke Arsenio made about Sam's dead brother. They pulled Sam off Arsenio. Afterward, Sam, drunk and coked out of his mind, drove me in his Camaro up to his house in the hills. His stomach was literally pressed against the steering wheel. That night Sam and I smoked a doob on his balcony. Truth is, I wouldn't put the doob near my lips because I was convinced that, with all of the whores Sam banged, he must've contracted AIDS. I was just so OCD about getting AIDS. One of Sam's friends drove me back to my hotel that night.

Whenever Sam came on the show, he was always drunk as fuck, and he came with a big entourage and tons of champagne. The funniest time was when he saw Fred in our office and pushed him against the back of the door and said, "I love you, Stuttering John." Sam thought Fred was me, and that must've irritated the crap out of Fred. I was nervously laughing my ass off inside.

I think that was the same day that Sam flaked on doing Joan Rivers's show and claimed it was because of "bad Chinese food." I loved that excuse so much, I thought about making it the name of my band.

One time, I went to see Sam when he was at the Westbury Music Fair on Long Island. Unfortunately, I came to the second show. He was fine for the first, and was even nice enough to have Jackie open up for him. When I first got there, I went backstage to say hi and he was pretty messed up. He was drunk and on God knows what drugs. Well, Sam went back out and was bombing horribly. He couldn't get a joke out and was just mumbling. People started booing and running down the aisles, yelling at Sam and demanding their money back. Sam looked at me and said, "John, help me out." I froze; I didn't know what I could do. I loved Sam and I felt so bad for him. Finally his people escorted him off the stage. Poor Sam.

The last time I saw Sam, my friend Lenny and I were in LA trying to get our band on some big convention show. We ran into Alan Stephen, one of Sam's Outlaws of Comedy, and he invited us to see Sam at the Trancas in Malibu. We went, and Sam was killing it. He was doing new material about the Iraq War and it was so fucking hysterical. He would goof on how the missiles had cameras on them, and how General Schwarzkopf and his cronies would probably watch the tapes over and over again as if it were a football game while some poor Iraqi soldier was about to get hit in the face mid-scream.

After the show, he invited Lenny and me to his house in Malibu. It was me, Lenny, members of Ozzy's band, and various other celebrities. We were hanging, drinking, doing coke. Sam would turn down bigger celebrities than

LIZ SMITH:
"WHY ARE YOU SUCH A FAT COW?"

me from getting in his gate. That's how Sam was to me. He was such a good friend. Later on, Lenny and I went to sleep on Sam's landing. The next day, we woke up to two familiar voices. I looked down and saw Sam and his neighbor, Buddy Hackett, holding out their revolvers and exchanging gun stories. It was fucking surreal!

We said our goodbyes and left, but who knew that would be the last time I would see my friend Sam? A few months later, I was driving from my girlfriend's house in Jersey and heard the news of Sam's death. How sad and ironic that a then-sober Sam was killed by a drunk driver. I dedicated my Atlantic Record to him and my friend Abe, who had died around that time—two great people who died way too soon.

LIFE ON THE ROAD

"There were two chicks, one was really hot. I banged the other one."
—John Melendez to *Tonight Show* writer Rob Young

WELL, ONE THING IS certain: being on *The Howard Stern Show* definitely increased my sex life. It started out when I would do appearances at strip clubs. I would do a dance contest and then get oral by one of the strippers in the closet. Then came my record deal, where I toured all over the country. After I signed the deal with Atlantic, I partnered up with producer/musician extraordinaire Randy Cantor. We started writing songs at his home in Bensalem and recording in his home studio. Craig liked what he heard and decided that the EP would be an LP. Along the way, Randy and I penned a song for a movie soundtrack called *Airheads*. It starred Brendan Fraser, Adam Sandler, and Steve Buscemi. We wrote "I'll Talk My Way Out of It" in about ten minutes, recorded it, and turned it in. Well, it turned out that not only did Atlantic want it for their single, the *Airheads* people wanted it as *their* single!

My days on the road were epic. One night, we were in Dallas at a sold-out show at a club called Dallas City Limits. Right before we went on, this chick named Heather begged me to let her go down on me. Later on, I had my first threesome in a hot tub on top of the Omni Hotel in Dallas. I always invited people back to my hotel after the gig. Well, these two hot strippers took a liking to me and we had sex everywhere from the hot tub to my room. They were telling me how big my penis was…well, let's face it, strippers get paid to lie. I was thinking, shit, my album only sold fifty thousand copies and I'm getting this? I wondered what Pearl Jam must have been getting.

We opened for everybody: Collective Soul, *Mötley Crüe*, White Zombie, Cheap Trick, and David Lee Roth. After the gig opening for Cheap Trick and David Lee Roth, Cheap Trick complimented my album, saying that it sounded like a good Cheap Trick! David Lee Roth invited me back to his trailer to smoke some weed. This motherfucker rolled a doobie the size of a cigar. I saved the roach and laminated it! We got so wasted that my friend puked on the side of his trailer.

Those were the days. We even opened for Ozzy Osbourne at Jones Beach.

On the air, Howard had Ozzy call in and tell me that he wanted my band to open for him. I was so excited. Ozzy said that he loved my album and started listing the songs he liked. He said that he liked "Plush" and "Interstate Love Song." I slowly realized that he wasn't talking about my band—he was talking about Stone Temple Pilots. I was devastated, and I didn't know what to say. I was hoping that he would say a few of my tunes but instead he continued with "Sex Type Thing" and "Vasoline."

Finally I was like, "Ozzy, that's Stone Temple Pilots, that's not my band."

He was like, "Oh, really."

Howard started laughing. They'd all pulled a fast one on me. It was a brilliant prank.

We hung out backstage with Ozzy and I had someone videotape it. We were partying and laughing, and then the next week I gathered my friends around the TV to watch the video and up comes my kid on a swing. My wife had taped over it! After we opened for Ozzy, while he was on stage, I decided to climb up to the side seats above the stage. There I saw this black curtain, so I decided to push it open, and there I saw this guy with a microphone singing Ozzy's songs, doubling his voice so he would sound good. It was like the Wizard of Oz! He was like, "Shut that curtain!" (Sorry to ruin it for you, Ozzy fans.)

The days on the road continued. We opened for Ted Nugent across the country. The road was awesome. I think I had sex in every town. While opening for Collective Soul in Florida, I noticed this hot blonde with gargantuan breasts

BEA ARTHUR:

"WHAT HOLLYWOOD STAR WOULD YOU LIKE TO NAIL MOST?"

in front of the stage. After our set, I walked out in the crowd, found her, and brought her back to my trailer. Then, as I was walking out of the trailer, the Atlantic rep was walking into my trailer. She was cute, so that same night I brought her back to my room and we fooled around.

In New Orleans, after the gig, we walked down Bourbon Street, and there was this hot blonde with the most perfect body I had ever seen, in an American flag bikini. The band and I went inside and she came in and I smooth-stutter-talked her and took her back to her place and we had sex. The next day, she introduced me to her parents. The life of a B-list rock star!

I was dating the black female singer in my band that played on the Channel 9 house party show. It's true when they say once you go black, you never go back, because, well, she never came back.

It was just a potpourri of sex. I started dating one of my Stern coworkers. She was this cute Nicole Eggert lookalike, and I flew her with me to an appearance. We messed around there, but at the appearance I met an ex-*Playboy* centerfold. I set up a date with her the following week as I was coming back to do the Cleveland funeral. That Thursday afternoon, in New York, I shot a comedy sketch with Gilbert Gottfried on Conan O'Brien's show, then flew back to Cleveland. The Playmate picked me up, and on the way she told me that her boyfriend said it was okay if she had sex with me. We went to the bar and ate spicy Buffalo wings. That night, we went back to the hotel and she went down on me while sticking the tip of her finger in my butt which hurt but hey, I wasn't going to refuse because that led to intercourse—shit, I was having sex with a former centerfold!

After sex, we went to sleep, but I overslept! I got dressed without shower-ing and rushed to the funeral. Heck, my band was going to perform there in front of ten thousand people—my single, "I'll Talk My Way Out Of It." Then it hit me...thanks to the Playmate's finger coinciding with the Buffalo wings, my hemorrhoids were ablaze. My ass was fucking killing me! Now I had to go on stage and perform! When it was time for me to sing, my rectum was hurting more than Beetlejuice's brain trying to solve a math question. My ass was on fire, as Artie Lange would say. I painfully sang through the song, although Johnny Cash's "Ring of Fire" would have been a more appropriate choice! I was like, "I'll tell you some lies, ouch, and I'll, ouch, talk my way out of it, ouch!"

BEA GOT PISSED AND COMPARED HOWARD TO HITLER.

One of my favorite stories is when I called DirecTV and asked them to postpone my subscription since I would be traveling for a while, headlining at the Punchline in Atlanta. The girl on the line sounded cute, which usually means that she's a pig, but she asked me why I was canceling and I told her about the Punchline. She said she was in Alabama and that Atlanta wasn't too far from there. I told her to follow me on Facebook, which she did, and she truly was cute. She came to my gig, I did well, and after the show, I brought her back to my hotel room and we had sex. After the sex, she said she was going to give me free DirecTV for life! Then I sucked her boobs for a free NBA package and went down on her ass for free Telemundo.

Okay, that last part was a joke.

WHEN I FIRST MET MY WIFE SUZANNER

AROUND THIS TIME, I got an offer to be a member of the cast in *Tony n' Tina's Wedding*, an off-Broadway show that had become quite popular in its ten-year run. I was cast as the best man for like three grand a week for a six-week run. Hey, it was good money and I loved to act, so I figured, why not? I might even meet a hot chick.

The show is about an Italian wedding gone awry, and I, like most of the cast, played a gumba Mafioso wannabe from Long Island. To make that work, I needed to do something about my hair, and so I got this gay dude Benjamin (pronounced Ben-ha-meen) to cut it off. He braided it because I wanted to save the hair, because I feared going bald, so I figured if I started losing my hair, they could make a wig out of my own hair. It didn't help that I kept calling Ben-ha-meen, Benjamin. Like, after the fifth time I could see he was getting angry. Who the fuck changes the pronunciation anyway? Well, he cut it off and shaved a little around the edges, and gone were my gorgeous locks. I started going to rehearsal at *Tony n' Tina's*. At first I didn't see any girls that were my type and I was a little bummed. A girl finally came up to me on opening night, while I was rehearsing the song I had to play during the ceremony, and I looked up. She said, "Hi, my name's Suzanna," and I reluctantly said hi back. She said that she heard I had gone to NYU and that she did too. I nonchalantly

MIKE WALLACE:
"HOW CAN YOU BE SO OLD AND STILL HAVE PIMPLES?"

said, "Cool," and I went back to practicing the song. I knew she thought I was a complete asshole, but I made a note in the back of my mind that she was kind of cute.

Keep in mind, however, that Howard had sent the E! crew there to tape me, so I was a little more nervous than usual. Well, when we did the show, I looked for the girl but I couldn't find her. It turned out that for the show she'd put her hair up Guidette-style, wore way too much makeup, and completely transformed into another person. Heck, she was a great actress, and I didn't recognize her. Before the next show, her grandfather died and she left the show for a week. Her understudy played her. I was like, man, whatever happened to that hot chick? Well, after the week went by, there she was again, sitting outside of Gus's, where the show was run. I said hi and asked her if she was the understudy. She got irritated again and was like, "No, it's my part. Last week you worked with my understudy."

D'oh! I messed up again; this girl must've hated me! So now I had to win her over.

That night, there was a large group in the audience who all worked at *Playboy*. They turned out to be big fans of mine, so they invited me and whomever I wanted to bring to the after-party at a downtown Manhattan club called Tattoo. I invited a bunch of the cast, including Suzanna, and we all went to the club. She asked one of her best friends, Alice, to come. She had just started and was also pretty hot. In fact, at this point, I didn't know who I should hit on first. I was really concerned with who I had a better chance of bedding down.

Yeah, I'm a horn dog. Sue me.

Well, they had a dance floor, and this guy was dancing with Suzanna, trying to drunkenly make a move on her. I could tell she wasn't interested. I saw the opportunity and took it. I grabbed her, pulling her away from him, and started dancing with her. Then we talked and we laughed and I laid her down on the couch next to the dance floor and we had our first kiss.

Soon after that, I asked her out on a date and she said yes. We met at a movie theater to watch *Interview with the Vampire*. I was completely grossed out by the blood and the veins in that movie, and more importantly, I was faced with the holding hands dilemma. I knew this would be the moment of truth. If I went to hold her hand and she seemed not into it, then I knew she was not into me. On the other hand, if she willingly held it, it meant things were

WHOA! MIKE GOT CAUGHT OFF GUARD. HE WAS STUNNED FOR A MOMENT, AND THEN RESPONDED: "HOW COULD A MAN LOOK THE WAY YOU DO?"

looking good. I reached out, and she didn't pull away. Yay! Then, the final test: if I rubbed my thumb along her hand and she rubbed back, she was definitely into me. She did!

After the movie, we walked out and she hailed a cab. I begged her to come home with me, but she refused. I thought that was a good thing—after all, I wanted a girl who would not be that easy. We continued to do the show, and one day she agreed to come with me to get my new headshots done. We went to the photographer's downtown apartment, and he started taking pictures of me in all different poses.

We took a picture together for kicks, but who knew this would be the beginning of a very long love affair? That eventually we'd get married?

As we walked from the photographer's office, we started talking about past things we'd done. I told her that I had a song in *Airheads* starring Steve Buscemi, Adam Sandler, and Brendan Fraser. She told me that she went to NYU with Adam Sander. I asked her if they dated, and she said yes, but it was to get back at her former boyfriend, who'd cheated on her. Heck, it could have been worse, I guess. She could have said that she'd dated Rob Schneider.

I asked her who was funnier, Adam or me, and she said I was.

She must've really wanted to date me.

See, I thought this could be a deal breaker. I always said that I didn't want to date someone who had been with a celebrity that was bigger than me. Which probably rules out three-quarters of the population, but whatever. I knew this would become an obsession if I didn't end this, but at the same time, I really liked this girl.

We were friends, and soon enough we were finished with the show, and I asked her to come home with me. We had sex and she started coming over regularly. We dated for a little bit, but then as my stint ended, we went back to our previous relationships.

Around this time, we had a few days off from the show. Karen and I were on the outs and I still thought about Suzanna. I had seen her once before, when I was doing interviews at a celebrity Academy Awards party. She walked by me with her boyfriend and she waved. Anyway, we had a little time off and I was going to go to the Hamptons for some R&R, and I had a choice: Did I want to ask Karen, or did I want to ask Suzanna?

LEONARD NIMOY:

I chose to call Suzanna. She was more fun, and I missed her. I knew that I had some making up to do with her. You see, a) I was the one who left her the first time, and b) when I was covering the gay parade for the show, I was supposed to meet Suzanna to talk but I got busy and accidentally blew her off. She wasn't very happy about that, to say the least. I rode my bike down to the *Tony n' Tina* space on top of Gus's and waited for Suzanna to walk from the church. I sat on my bike across the street, and when she came out, she saw me, I waved, and she waved back and smiled.

I came back that night and apologized and convinced her to come home with me. She agreed, and I explained to Suzanna in the cab that I had always envisioned being with a girl that had a Drew Barrymore look.

Which I thought was Karen. Ironically, Suzanna did in fact look like Drew Barrymore, but I couldn't see it. In fact, I was not entirely attracted to Suzanna at first. I remember telling my therapist that I thought she was just okay-looking. He came to the show and told me, "John, she is gorgeous"—and my therapist was gay! When we got up to my apartment, we decided to play strip backgammon, and she was so cute and innocent playing the game that I felt myself starting to fall in love. We made love that night, and I knew that I was falling deeply in love with her. Even though the Adam Sandler thing would pose an OCD nightmare for me, it didn't seem to matter. See, I didn't care that much about Adam—it was just that I knew I would have to undo the OCD thought any time his name came into my mind. For instance, if I walked through a door and thought *Adam Sandler has Suzanna*, then I had to walk out of the doorway and say in my mind, *John Melendez has Suzanna*. I knew that if it weren't Adam going through my head, it would be someone else. Which turned out to be true, when I found out about the other few past ex-boyfriends.

Look, Suzanna was no slut—she had had very few boyfriends for a twenty-eight-year-old. At least she was with Adam before he became famous, so it wasn't like she was a fame whore or anything. God, I knew that for sure if she was with me.

I told Suzanna I really had to get out of *The Howard Stern Show* because I just couldn't take Howard putting me down all the time. I called her that night and asked her to come to the Hamptons with me, and she said yes! We went to the Hamptons and stayed at some hotel. We had great sex in the Jacuzzi and really had a fantastic time. We played backgammon on the beach until the tide swooped in and ruined the game.

"IS YOUR PENIS POINTED LIKE YOUR EARS?"

This is how brainwashed I had become from Howard. I knew I was in love with Suzanna, but the Adam Sandler thing was a problem for my OCD mind, and also Suzanna had a birthmark on her face like Alison, Howard's wife, and I thought Howard would say I was trying to be like him. To give you an idea, when I used to walk in with Howard in the morning, he once said to me, "John, I wish I had it as easy as you." In my mind I was like, *Yeah, right, I have extreme OCD.* It never dawned on me what he was referring to until he was coming out with his second book, which was all about his battle with OCD. Then I got it. I was afraid to tell him that I had it too, because then again, he would say I was trying to be him. This shit really bothered me. But that was his usual lament. When I did bits on my radio show, he would say I was trying too hard to be him. It bothered the fuck out of me.

Around this time, Suzanna told me that she was pregnant. Her Jewish parents wanted me to marry her before she started showing. I loved Suzanna and planned on marrying her anyway, but I didn't want it to look like a shotgun wedding. Besides, having a kid first is how us Puerto Ricans do it. Coincidentally, I had already told my therapist that I was going to propose on Christmas Eve. Well, I told Howard that I was having a kid, and he said to me on the air that I should abort the kid because I wasn't fit to be a father. It took every ounce of my being to not kick the shit out of him then and there. Later on, when my now very pregnant wife showed up at his birthday show, Howard repeated that same line and told Suzanna to abort the kid.

What the fuck was wrong with this guy?

•••

HOWARD HAD HIS FIFTIETH birthday party at some bar in Manhattan. My present was to tape everyone at the party and make him a CD of all of the birthday wishes. I hung out with Dave Chappelle at the party.

Two other Stern staffers and I started smoking a joint at the party. We took a few hits each and then I invited Dave over to partake. As soon as Dave put the doobie in his mouth, two security guards came up to him and told him to put it out. Dave said something like this, "What the fuck, man, these white boys have been puffing on this stogie and you boys do nothing, but then a black guy takes a hit and you're all over me like flies to shit!"

•••

ART GARFUNKEL:
"HOW DID IT FEEL TO BE PAUL SIMON'S BACKUP SINGER?"

I WAS STILL DOING the interviews, and now they were for E! I pissed off Billy Crystal, who I was a fan of. I asked him if I could ask him a few questions, he said, "Who are you?" and I said, "Paul."

See, at that time, I had to start wearing disguises because more and more people would recognize me. This time I had a suit on and greased my hair back. I then asked him how bad he thought David Letterman did hosting the Academy Awards. Billy said that he thought David did a great job. Then I asked him if there'd be a *Mr. Saturday Night 2*. Noticeably more annoyed, he was like, "Yes, there will be a *Mr. Saturday Night 2*."

Then the bomb was delivered.

"Billy," I said. "How long were you married before you started cheating on your wife?"

He blew up, and eventually said, "And you can take this tape to Howard and shove it right up Howard's stupid fucking ass."

"But, Billy, we're big fans of yours," I replied.

He was like, "Yeah, right, and now you'll all go on the show and laugh, but it's not fun, it's not fun." Whew, that was tough. That response became an impression fans did for years. It was modified in a way and became "It's not fun, and it's not funny."

I would try every disguise in the book. I'd dress up in a fake moustache, fake teeth, greased hair, glasses, suit and tie. I considered putting in "Gary" teeth, but I would have lost thirty IQ points and dislocated my jaw. Ralph Cirella had a friend at *SNL* that did the makeup there, and we had some interviews to do that night at the Essence Awards, so I went to the *SNL* studios at 30 Rock and had this guy give me a prosthetic nose, a prosthetic chin, teeth, moustache, and glasses. I wore a suit and tie; the whole procedure took like three hours. Then we walked up to the red carpet at Madison Square Garden and a cop guarding the red carpet saw me and said, "Hi, John…"

D'oh! All of that for nothing.

I still managed to interview people, but it was getting harder and harder to pull it off. I knew I had to find another niche on the show if I planned on keeping my steady stream of airtime going, so I consciously decided to take my ball busting into the studio. You don't understand—when I was a kid, my friends and I would hang out at the handball courts in high school, each illegally buy a six-pack, and eventually form a circle and one by one rip each other a

ART WAS NOTICEABLY ANNOYED, AND HIS WIFE ANGRILY REPLIED, "HE'S NOT HIS BACKUP SINGER."
I FELT BAD AFTER THAT ONE. I'M A BIG SIMON AND GARFUNKEL FAN.

new asshole. From "yo mama" jokes to things more personal, everyone and everything was fair game. After years of that, I became an expert. I would look somebody up and down like the Terminator. I'd make mental notes of their clothes, their shoes, their haircut, and then hold onto that information, and as soon as they threw a zinger my way, I would pounce.

After five years, Howard started to beat me up on a regular basis on the air. It hurt and I had to get out of there. I didn't want to relive all of this abuse that I ingested from my dad, siblings, and the neighborhood bullies. I was experiencing the same feeling that I did with my father—one day, he's great, the next day, he's beating the shit out of you. People would ask me if Howard was a nice guy off the air and I'd say, "Yes, he's a great guy off the air."

They'd say, "Oh, so on the air is all an act?"

And I would tell them, "No, off the air is all an act."

See, you have to understand: I really looked up to Howard, I loved him, he was my radio idol, and I am very sensitive, so when he would beat me up on the air, it truly, truly hurt. I always wanted to please him. Part of the reason I busted Gary, Fred, and Jackie's balls on the air was to make Howard laugh. We would go out to dinner all the time. I honestly thought of him as a friend—only on the air, he was such a prick sometimes that I didn't know which Howard was the real one.

I remember leaving the studio one day feeling so bad, after Howard had laid into me saying things about how I'm not talented, I'm not funny, I'm an ingrate, and the only reason I'm on the show is because I stutter. He said the only time I'm funny is when I'd stutter. I almost cried right there in the studio. I went home and wrote a song called "I Don't Know" about my depression due to his abuse. I actually recorded it in Scott's studio with Scott producing.

These kinds of beatings weren't only thrown my way. Fred told me that one of his songs on his album was a song about Howard—it was called "Don't Talk Down To Me." Gary once told me that, at one point, Fred was so fed up with Howard's abuse that he wanted to leave the show and audition for *Saturday Night Live*.

I didn't only want to do radio. I wanted to do television, movies, and stand-up comedy. One time, on the air, Howard said he liked me the least because I always wanted to do outside things. Later on, a show producer that still works there pulled me aside and said, "Isn't it weird that Howard looks down on ambition?"

BURT REYNOLDS:
"WHAT'S THE CLOSEST YOU'VE BEEN TO DOM DELUISE WHEN HE CUT THE CHEESE?"

•••

AROUND THIS TIME, I took a pregnant Suzanna to see *The Cable Guy* starring Jim Carrey. She started complaining about being in pain and I was like, "Come on, honey—the movie isn't that bad," and she was like, "No, John, I think I'm going to have the baby."

We left the theater and lay down in my bed as I timed her contractions. I was exhausted, but she wanted me to stay awake. I tried to order *The Bridges of Madison County* but instead accidentally ordered *The Three Tenors*. I'm not sure which I anticipated would be more boring, but I then had to order *The Bridge of Madison County* while timing her contractions, and I started dozing—man, was that movie a fucking sleeping pill. The contractions started getting closer as I started getting closer to putting a gun to my head from this stupid fucking movie, so we got up and took a cab to NYU hospital to give birth to our first child. Months before, I had made a tape of all of Suzanna's friends telling her to push and wishing her well. I played the tape over "Jeff Beck's Guitar Shop."

Hey, I was in love...with Jeff Beck.

Nah, I loved Suzanna, and I wanted the birth to be extra special. Her friend Alice started grabbing her leg and telling her to push, and I was like, "Hey, Alice, no offense, but this is between my wife and I, so scram." She apologized and left, and we prepared for the birth.

I called into my afternoon radio show during the labor, which of course Howard told me he had done first. I told him on the air that if it weren't for him, I wouldn't know how to breathe—a line Gary once repeated, because, let's face it, Gary couldn't write his own material even if Rodney Dangerfield rose from the grave to help him.

Finally, my baby boy was born! He was beautiful. It was a great day. I was finally a father, something I had dreamed of all of my life. We brought him home to my Manhattan apartment and the parenting began.

Then, some idiot, some enemy to all men, invented this breast pump machine, which is a machine that sucks the milk out of our wife's breasts so *we* can do feedings at three o'clock in the morning! Who is this asshole? I remember walking by her when she was in the bathroom, with her gut hanging out because she just gave birth and the things sucking milk out of her

THEN I STARTED SCREAMING DOWN FROM THE SECOND FLOOR OF A MALL, "BURT, WHY DID YOU HIT LONI?" THE MALL SECURITY ESCORTED ME AND MY CREW OUT.

tits, making this sound like *whoosh-ka-ka-ka whoosh ka-ka-ka*, I walked by and said, "Hey, honey, you look like a cow!"

Never tell your wife she looks like a cow. I'm telling you. I didn't get a blowjob for a month, and that was from the breast pump machine!

It's weird having sex with your wife when she's producing milk too. We were having sex, and I was on the bottom and she was on top, and milk squirted out of her breasts, right into my face! And that's not good, because I'm lactose intolerant! My wife's breasts were huge, but every time I squeezed them I felt like I was juicing an orange.

I was exhausted. No, not from the sex, but for doing these late-night feedings. Suzanna and I would take turns, and one night I was on our couch, which thank God was low to the ground and was on the carpet, and I was so tired from the early *Stern* hours that I fell asleep lying down on the couch next to my kid, and when I woke up two hours later, my kid had fallen off the couch and was sleeping on the floor! Maybe Howard was right about me not being fit to be a father. My son was fine, though.

Hey, parenting is a work in progress.

•••

I KNEW I HAD to get away from the show, and I told Suzanna that. Howard is a good guy sometimes, but like most of us, he has his faults. Once, he sent down an edict allowing only the on-air staff to drink the free water that was provided by Poland Spring, a show sponsor. No interns or off-air personnel were any longer allowed to drink the free water. Ann Marie McCann, the office administrator, had to enforce this rule. How fucking ridiculous? Howard's logic was that he didn't want to take advantage of his sponsors. Okay, Howard, I can understand that, but then why not reach into your wallet and buy a case of water, you cheap fuck?

I had auditioned for the show *Wings*. The producers told me that my audition was the only one they laughed at, and so I got the part as a guest star on the show. I was so happy, and Howard begrudgingly let me do it—but not before mentioning that they wanted him first and were using me. Before the show aired, Howard refused to read the on-air commercials that NBC was paying for. He would go to the live read, see what it was for, and then refuse to read it and tell Fred to play the prerecorded commercials. How fucking petty?

CONAN O'BRIEN:

When Robin got *The Fresh Prince of Bel-Air*, he was all over that, but me? How dare I? Six months later, we were in the studio, off the air, and Howard said, "John, I saw your episode of *Wings*—you were really good."

In my head, I was like: six months too late, don't ya think?

> When I guest starred on **Wings**, at the end of rehearsal Crystal Bernard asked me to come into her dressing room. I did, and she sat across from me, looked me deep in my eyes, and said, in a soft, sexy, Southern voice, "Now what's a cute guy like you doing married?" She was hitting on me, and it took every ounce of my being to turn her down, because I wanted to be faithful. Now that I'm divorced, I regret not hitting that. Just kidding.

DOWN GOES CHIUSANO!!!

Tom was an avid golfer. He and his father were like the top golfers at his country club in Pelham, New York. One day on the air, I challenged Tom to a hole of golf. I sucked at golf, but my plan was to get into his head. Robin bet Tom a grand that I would beat him, and the bet was on. Look, I'm not saying that I get lucky but I do. Plus, I'm an avid competitor. I beat Jackie and Gary at racquetball. I destroyed Gange and his brother in tennis while playing them at the same time. I made mincemeat of Robin on the tennis court, so why not take down Tom?

The date was set, and the E! camera guys drove out with me to Pelham Country Club. It was a nice sunny day. I started drinking beer. There were plaques all over the walls of the club of Tom and his father winning all kinds of golfing accolades. There were trophies that Tom and his dad received. All of the people at the club knew Tom and of his golfing prowess. I looked into the E! camera and said that I would beat Tom by getting into his head.

We hit a practice hole and Tom annihilated me, but now came the real thing. We started the hole. It was a par three. I hit a decent shot, but on the next shot I hit the fucking E! guy's camera. I demanded a reshoot, and Tom accepted. The next shot, I made it right on to the green. I couldn't believe it...neither could Tom. Meanwhile, every time Tom took a shot, I kept saying, "Beep da biddley bo." It was an old *Little Rascals* reference when they were golfing. They had a chimpanzee that broke all the clubs and kept saying, "Beep da biddley bo." Richie Wilson, our E! cameraman and friend, was laughing his ass off.

We were on the green. I hit one near the hole, setting myself up to make a ten-foot putt to win. Tom choked and hit it over the green. All I needed was to make this putt and the victory was mine. I concentrated and made the putt, much to Tom's chagrin. I ran around the hole like a lunatic, celebrating my victory while Tom looked on in despair! While we drove back in his golf cart, I kept yelling to all of his golf buddies saying how I beat him. Tom looked straight ahead and said, "This is the worst day of my life." I'm glad I could help, Tom.

BACK TO SUZANNER

I FLEW SUZANNA AND Knight out to LA for pilot season in hopes that Suzanna could fulfill her dream of getting a TV show. She auditioned for a pilot called *New Jersey* and quickly became the first choice for the lead, in the eyes of Danny Zucker (the writer) and Robbie Benson (the director). I was ecstatic. She had an agent and would get thirty grand just for the pilot! I was already thinking of how I would spend that money on a BMW. Danny was a friend of mine, but he had no idea Suzanna was my wife. He finally found out before Suzanna's last audition and called me to tell me how great she was. The part was between two girls, but she was still their number-one choice. All she had to do was audition for Warren Littlefield and a few other NBC execs. I was so happy for her and couldn't wait for my car.

She called me after the audition, and she wasn't very happy. She didn't think that it went well. I was worried, and sure enough, later on, it turned out that Warren wanted a Drew Barrymore type. Geez, man, Suzanna looked like Drew Barrymore! What the fuck was wrong with him? Suzanna was devastated. She felt she was getting older and that she had to score something soon. I wanted to cheer her up and profusely pounded away at the computer, writing our love story. I flew out to stay with her and Knight for the weekend and handed Suzanna the script that I wrote for her to star in. She was so appreciative, and it cheered her up. It was a role she was perfect for—unless Drew Barrymore wanted it.

JEWEL:
"ARE THEY REAL OR IMPLANTS?"

SHE HATED ME SO MUCH. ROBIN AND I WENT WITH HOWARD WHEN HE WAS A GUEST ON *THE TONIGHT SHOW,*

When Suzanna got back from Los Angeles, we decided it was time to have another kid. We rented a small studio apartment in a rent-controlled building that I got through a friend I had met at an appearance. We needed to spend time there, since I was close to financing my film and we would have to shoot in Manhattan if I got it. Suzanna was about to start ovulating, so as I drove over the Bayville Bridge toward Manhattan, I knew I had to try and impregnate her that night. I purposely hadn't masturbated so I was ready, looking for another child, which I had always wanted. We got into the apartment on Fourteenth Street and made love that night and I unleashed my poison, and a month later we found out that Suzanna was pregnant. My Puerto Rican and Danish sperm was pretty potent, and Lily Belle Melendez was born on December 7 of that year.

> Around this time, I gave Knight a yellow Labrador puppy named Gunter as a birthday gift. We were in this tiny Manhattan apartment, and around three in the morning the dog had to take a shit. So I go down to Fourteenth Street in my pajamas, the dog shits, and I pick it up. Then he shits again, and I rummage through the garbage to find something to pick it up with. We lived across the street from this happening Manhattan nightclub that had just opened called Spa. So while I'm picking it up, I look and Derek Jeter and his buddy go walking past me, and Derek says, "I hope there's some hot girls here." Of course—he's picking up women, and I'm picking up dog shit.

Meanwhile, Howard, Beth, Suzanna, and I would go out all the time. Former E! show Executive Producer Scott Einziger used to join us with his wife Maya, but then he left to produce other television shows and did a show called *Are You Hot?* Howard not only sued the network, but he also sued Scott personally. Yet another person who ultimately left the show on bad terms. Even in Scott's last week, Howard beat him up on the air, talking about how this was the only job he could possibly do. Then Scott went on to win an Emmy for producing *The Amazing Race*.

I still had fun with Howard, though. Once, Howard, Suzanna, Beth, Ozzy and Sharon Osbourne, and I were all having dinner at Nobu in Manhattan. Well, at one point, Ozzy went to the bathroom. Keep in mind that the bathrooms at

AND I SAW HER STANDING IN FRONT OF HER DRESSING ROOM AND APOLOGIZED, AND SHE WAS LIKE, "YEAH, WHY WOULD YOU ASK SUCH A QUESTION?" THEN HOWARD WALKED BY AND SHE HUGGED HIM AND SAID SHE WAS A BIG FAN. NOTE TO JEWEL: HOWARD WAS THE ONE WHO SENT ME OUT TO ASK YOU THAT, DUMMY!

Nobu had an ocean waves soundtrack playing on the speakers, I'm guessing to help people relax, or pee faster. Anyway, Ozzy's in the bathroom for a while and then finally returns and says in his barely coherent Ozzy voice, "Where is the fucking ocean? I pulled a chair up to the window in the bathroom and kept looking out, but I couldn't see any ocean. I kept hearing it, but I couldn't see it." We all laughed our asses off.

Those were the good times spent with Howard, but we never discussed business and I always knew it was inevitable that the wheel would spin, as Gary and I would say when we had no guests booked, and it would eventually land on me—meaning the verbal on-air beatings would come soon enough, so I might as well enjoy the nice Howard, just like I had with my father: enjoy the good aspects even though the bad was around the corner.

S-S-STUTTERING JOHN TAKES THE STAGE

SINCE I WAS EIGHTEEN, I had always wanted to do stand-up. I would write jokes and record them on my answering machine from various locations, pay phones, what have you. I was constantly writing my act on my computer. When I was at NYU, I was jealous of Mitch Fertel when he told me that he was going to be a stand-up. I had always wanted to be one, but there was one problem…I stuttered. I was so afraid that I would get up there and stutter on every joke. I remember telling my therapist, the one that I saw for OCD, about this fear. I was just terrified. I was used to being on stage with the band, and I would do comedy songs and tell jokes in between songs, but the thought of getting up there—just me, no guitar, no band—scared the crap out of me. I used to go with my wife to see stand-ups and be so completely jealous that they got over their fears to get up, and they were confident enough, yet I wasn't.

Then one day, at thirty-five, I had an epiphany. I thought to myself, "Hey, if I can ask celebrities about their bowel movements, why can't I get on stage?" I put together my five-minute set and brought my wife to the NY Comedy Club in Manhattan. I was so nervous. It was my turn, and I went on the stage and I stuttered through the whole set! Sweat poured profusely from my head and body. I turned my five-minute set into an hour. At least that's what it felt like.

TOM HANKS:
"DO YOU THINK OF ROSIE O'DONNELL TO PROLONG THE SEXUAL ACT?"

I walked off the stage in utter despair. My wife tried consoling me, though I still felt like a complete failure. But I truly believe that we have angels in our lives, and I was about to meet one of mine. Al Martin, the owner of the club, saw my set and walked up to me and said, "John, I have another room. I want you to get up right now and do the same set."

I didn't have time to think.

So I did, only this time I got plenty of laughs and barely stuttered! I was so happy. I thanked Al, and I'll never forget what he did for me. After that, there was no stopping me. I had faced my fear head-on. This has been my mantra in life: Never let them tell you that you can't do something. Sometimes the person telling you that is yourself. I truly believe that we all have that voice in our head that talks us out of doing things, that tells us we can't do something and puts us down. I think the goal is to not let that voice interrupt your life. Sure, we are all going to have self-doubt, but the key to doing what you want is to believe in yourself. And here's another thing: Do not take it all so seriously. One of the things that I tell stutterers when I mentor them is to learn to laugh at yourself. Stuttering is not who you are, it's just something that you do. I tell them to inform those that they're speaking to that they stutter before saying anything else. That way, all of the pressure to speak clearly is alleviated.

•••

I STARTED THE "STUTTERING John and Friends" tour a few months later, recruiting other comics that I thought were great and who could do the bulk of the time while I hosted. I figured this way I could build up my act and make money doing it. My wife and I would go to all the clubs looking for the right guys. One night we went to the Comic Strip, a famous uptown comedy club, and we saw this guy named Modi, who I thought was as funny as hell. I asked him to be on my tour.

That night, who else walks on stage? Mitch Fertel, who had now changed his last name to Fatel. He was up there to rehearse his set for *Letterman!* Wow, he was great. After the show, we hung out with Mitch at a diner and I congratulated him. He had reached his dream. He didn't let what Gary or Fred said to him bring him down. He was on *Letterman* a few nights later, and Howard loved it. He played his set on the air, and I was so proud of him, and yes, a little bit jealous—but that's just part of being human, isn't it?

TOM WAS COOL. IN FACT, WHEN HE SAW ME AS HE WALKED UP THE STAIRS, HE SAID, "ALL RIGHT, JOHN, LET ME HAVE IT."

I needed one more comic to add to my tour, and I found him at the Boston Comedy Club—a short, bald, energetic guy named Jim Norton. He was awesome, and I immediately asked him if he would join my tour. He said yes. I also added Melrose Larry Green, a *Stern Show* fixture.

I had my tour set, so I started working on my act. I did a set at the Comic Strip, where the owner Lucian gave me a few tips. I did a set at Carolines on Broadway, where I wrote a chunk while in the bathroom and then did it right on the stage and it killed. I kept doing the NY Comedy Club and started getting really comfortable on the stage.

The first two nights of my tour were December 5 and 6 at Rascals Comedy Club. The first night was at the one in West Orange, New Jersey, and the second was at the Rascals on the South Shore. Well, after the show on the sixth, Melrose Larry and I decided to go have pizza at a Manhattan joint after the long ride back from Jersey. My cell phone was dead, so we just ate a few slices of pizza and I let Melrose pay. Shit, I was about to have another kid and had already doubled up on mortgage and rent!

I got home around one or two, and my wife was pissed. She said she was trying to get ahold of me and that she was having contractions! I took her to the NYU hospital and the labor began. I was so freaking tired, and the doctors told me to walk her around the hospital to get the dilation bigger, so that the canal would be big enough to have the baby. I was so tired and drunk that I was like, "Suzanna, I don't want to walk anymore."

She was like, "If you don't walk me, I'll call my mother and have her do it!"

Fuck that. Her mother hated me from day one, and I think it was because I was Catholic and they were Jewish, so she probably felt guilty for killing my Lord and Savior, I don't know. Well, Suzanna had a long labor, but then our beautiful baby girl was born, Lily Belle Melendez! I was so happy.

The comedy tour continued, but I couldn't use Jim Norton anymore. He started working on *The Opie and Anthony Show*, and they would goof on Howard. I feared Howard's wrath, so I asked him if I should still use Jim and he said that he'd rather I not. I talked to Jim and he suggested I use his old roommate, Jim Florentine.

I was like, "Jim Florentine? You mean Jammin' Jim, the guy that used to open for my band and who had like one good joke? That Jim?"

MICHAEL J. FOX:

"ARE YOU A MEMBER OF THE LOLLIPOP GUILD?"

Norton said that he was really good now. So I went to see him, and he was funny, so I added him to the tour. The only thing about Jim was that this crazy dude, Vinnie Mazzeo Jr., that booked us told me that Florentine would bad-mouth me behind my back all of the time. I confronted him about it, but he denied it. Later on, I had my doubts, but that's another story.

I toured all over the country, making sometimes up to fifteen grand a weekend. Modi used to joke with me and say that he couldn't believe that I was learning to do stand-up in front of three thousand people a weekend! My five minutes soon became fifteen, and then thanks to hard work, I finally got it up to an hour. Modi and Jim used to compliment me on how natural I was on stage. They would say that it seemed like I had been doing it for years, which in a sense was true, since I was the class clown since elementary school.

P-P-PRIVATE PARTS

AFTER PUBLISHING HIS BEST-SELLING book, *Private Parts*, Howard signed a movie deal. The writer and producer interviewed all of us, but it turned out that I wasn't going to be in the main frame of the movie. The story was only up until the time Howard left NBC and I was a few years after that, so as dejected as I was, I understood. They told me to come down to the last scene in the movie, at Bryant Park where AC/DC was to play, and hang in the crowd, and maybe I'd get in a shot. When I came to the casting office at the shoot, the producer said, "Oh, hi, here—why don't you sit with the other Wack Packers?" She then escorted me to a room filled with Crackhead Bob, Fred the Elephant Boy, Beetlejuice, and Hank the Angry Drunken Dwarf. I was like, "Miss, I ain't a fucking Wack Packer!" Someone came and explained to her that I was an employee, and she apologized. But, man, talk about adding insult to injury. It was bad enough that I wasn't in the movie—but now *this*!

In retrospect, it was kind of funny, and Baba Booey and I had a good laugh when I told him. Later on, they said they wanted to shoot a scene with me. I was walking around for months complaining about not being in the movie, and Len, the writer, got wind of it and wrote a monologue where I complain. We shot

MICHAEL WAS SUCH A GOOD SPORT AND IS ONE OF THE NICEST CELEBRITIES OUT THERE.

it in Times Square, and I just walked up to the camera and started spewing my anger and distaste for not being in the movie. To tell you the truth, I didn't stick to the script and basically improvised the whole thing, including saying, "Howard says I'll be in the sequel. Well, suppose this movie fucking sucks and there won't even be a fucking sequel!"

I remember spitting and stuttering profusely in the first take. Betty Thomas, the director, said, "Let's try another one, because we can't use that one because you're spitting all over the camera." I said, "Sure, but I bet that's the one you'll use." Sure enough, I did two more takes...but that spitting one made the final cut.

DUDE, WHERE'S MY CAR?

WAYNE RICE, THE PRODUCER, cast me in *Dude, Where's My Car?* So I flew out to LA and went to wardrobe, as we were going to shoot my scene the next day. I asked Danny Leiner, the director, how I should look, and he said the more disheveled the better. So I took his advice and hung out drinking all night. I tried to get a spot doing stand-up but couldn't, so I ended up at the Whiskey Bar and saw Matt Damon there, and we drank and talked for a while about the way his Red Sox blew it to the Mets in 1986. He was so down-to-earth as he told me how upset his father was about that Bill Buckner game, and how they knew the Red Sox would somehow fuck it up. After all, Matt was alive during the Bucky Fucking Dent home run days.

The next day, we shot my scene. My character's name was Gene and he basically lived in the closet. I came out to say hi to Ashton Kutcher and Seann Michael Scott's characters and then peed on the plant behind them.

It was an Academy Award–worthy performance!

While I was on set, however, Ashton Kutcher got into this big twenty-minute argument with the director because Ashton insisted his character would enter the living room in his underwear. The director demanded he wear shorts because, well, Ashton is hung like a horse and you can see his huge schlong through his underwear. I offered my solution to the problem and just said, "Ashton, why not wear two pairs of underwear?" He responded, "I already am!"

RICHARD DREYFUSS:

Damn, that motherfucker was not only good-looking and banging Mila Kunis, but if Bill Buckner had been hung like him, there's no way that ball would have gone through his legs.

THE FLUNKY VS. THE JUNKIE

MY WIFE AND I were watching *Celebrity Boxing* in our tiny Manhattan apartment, and it had like Danny Bonaduce fighting Barry Williams. It said they got paid thirty grand to do it, and I was like, "Why would they agree to do that for such little money?" The next morning I was on the air with Howard and we started talking about the show, and I said that I couldn't believe they would box for such little money.

Howard asked, "Why, John? How much would you want to do it?"

I said I would have to make at least a hundred grand.

A few minutes later, Crazy Cabbie called in to challenge me. You have to understand, Cabbie was always jealous of my relationship with Howard. He would have loved to be going out to dinner with Howard and sleeping over at his house like I did. Howard asked me if I would fight him.

"For a hundred grand? Sure," I said.

Keep in mind, Cabbie was six two, 260 pounds, and an ex-Army lunatic.

Tom Chiusano came in the studio and explained that there would be no way he could raise that kind of money to put on a fight. What a moron he was for saying that. One of the higher-ups at K-Rock complained to me later, asking why Tom would let his advertisers know he was unable to raise that kind of money. Many people started calling in demanding that the fight happen. Tom was cornered, and he finally acquiesced and said he had to talk to the sales staff to see if he could make it happen.

Donald Trump called in, as I recall, and said that we could do the fight at the Taj Mahal, one of his Atlantic City casinos, and just like that the fight started to solidify. It was to be five rounds lasting two minutes each, with another two minutes in between for rest.

I was a little nervous; after all, this guy was a monster. But, heck, that was a lot of money. And truth be told, I always fantasized about being a boxer. It was a dream of mine, so why not live it on someone else's dime? It was like my own little Fantasy Island. I got a trainer from my friend Lisa Ripi, my masseuse and acupuncturist, who I got through Jackie. Lisa got Super Heavyweight Kickboxing Champion Derek Panza to teach me how to box, and Joel Gold and Steve Weinbeger trained me in endurance and weights. I trained eight times a week, six days in a row with one day off. I would jog on Tuesdays and Thursdays and then spar those nights. It was excruciating. Derek told me that after training with him for two months, I'd be able to knock someone out with just a jab. In retrospect, I believed him. He taught me how to box and throw a punch correctly. I didn't know what Cabbie was doing, but we were serious.

I once sat in Derek's office and asked him if I could get killed during this fight.

He said, "Don't worry, John. Not only are you not going to get killed, but you're going to win this fight."

Derek had this plan for my first sequence of punches. After the bell rang, I was going to come up to Cabbie and drop down low and give him a jab to his stomach. Then, when he dropped his hands, I'd deliver an overhand right to his face. I lay in bed every night going over this sequence before I fell asleep.

We were both getting a hundred grand for the fight—win, lose, or draw. I got paid another seventy-five hundred for putting "GoldenPalace.com" on my back, and I made a deal with Trim Spa for fifteen hundred to say after the fight that the next time I wanted to lose weight, I wouldn't work out, I'd just take Trim Spa. I also booked my comedy tour at the Taj for the night of the fight, and that got me another nine grand.

Hey, if I was going to risk my life, I might as well get paid for it.

I had my mouthpiece set up by a dentist. He asked what color I wanted, and I said purple. Who knows why, but it was probably a color that I didn't have an OCD problem with.

Tom Chiusano had me go to some cheap K-Rock doctor for my physical. This guy was older than the mountains. He could have been Larry King's babysitter. This guy had this disheveled examination room. When he went to take my blood, he asked me to hold his tray of medical tools. It took the motherfucker like a year to walk across the room to take my blood and another year to find a vein to shoot. This was almost as terrifying as the fight.

As the morning of the fight approached, I got so incredibly anxious. Shit, this dude Cabbie was a Neanderthal with not much of a brain. I'd actually say that Baba Booey was smarter than him. My wife and I were driven to the fight the day before; I did radio interviews for the affiliates on the way there, with GoldenPalace.com temporarily tattooed to my back. I was told by one of the DJs that I was a three-to-one underdog in Vegas!

We finally got to Atlantic City. I jogged briefly along the boardwalk that night and then we had dinner, where Donald Trump came to greet us at our table. Donald had been a friend of mine ever since I interviewed him and Marla Maples at the Trump Plaza in New York City during an event. I'll never forget that night, because Donald asked me to come inside and asked me what my plans were for that weekend. I told him Suzanna and I were going to Atlantic City. The next day at work, I got a call from his people comping me at the Taj, including massages! Heck, after the fight that weekend, I was flying home with my wife, Howard, and Beth in Trump's helicopter!

I went to bed early the night before the fight, and when I woke up the next morning, I could barely eat. Derek told me that I had to eat something, so I forced down a few bites of oatmeal and made my way downstairs to the dressing rooms. I did a warm-up with Derek, punching his hands, took a piss, and got into my trunks. Howard came backstage and said I didn't have to do this. He was concerned about my well-being. That's kind of nice when I think about it. I said to him, "Howard, not only am I going to go through with this fight, but I am going to win." Donald Trump came backstage to wish me luck, and then it was time to play the waiting game.

The place was packed, completely sold out. There were celebrities there, like Evander Holyfield, Jillian Barberie, Don King, and Bert Sugar. We were given the ten-minute warning, and then Derek came up to me and told me that he wanted to try a new first sequence of punches. I'd been visualizing the fight plan for the last three months and told him no fucking way! He said okay, and then informed me that we were going to walk out Mike Tyson style, with our arms on each other's shoulders. Derek taped my trunks up and we were ready.

We were then told they were about to lead us out, and I suddenly had the urge to piss! Fuck!

This always happened before I performed, and usually I had to shit as well. Derek said we didn't have time to retape my trunks, so I stood above the toilet and took a piss with my shorts still on. Thank God they were made from that waterproof material, or else I would have been drenched.

HARRISON LAUGHED. HE'S PRETTY COOL, AND THE RUMOR IS THAT HE'S ALWAYS STONED.

We began to walk out Mike Tyson style and I heard everyone commenting on me. Vinnie Favale, resident *Letterman* employee and kiss-ass, said that I looked scared. This infuriated me and gave me some food for thought in the way of revenge. Vinnie's one of those jackasses who once told me he didn't invite me to his party but invited Gary because he liked Gary better. I walked into the ring, and they introduced legless and armless Celestine to play the National Anthem on a keyboard with her tongue. After she was done with her performance, Michael Buffer introduced Cabbie and me.

The day of reckoning had arrived.

Derek Panza had kept it from me that Cabbie's headgear had double the thickness of mine. He had sparring headgear and I had amateur boxing headgear, but since this wasn't a sanctioned fight, there was nothing my trainers could do and Derek didn't want to freak me out. He also had planned that I would not sit between rounds. I think this was what Joe Frazier or George Foreman did to intimidate their opponents.

The bell rang, and I came out strong, delivering the first sequence of punches and landing them all. I kept on punching. All the angst, all the buildup had me tearing ass on this dude. But I started to lose my breath, too, because a) I had a tendency to hold my breath when I punched and b) Cabbie kept laying his 260 pounds on top of me. I guess that was his strategy—either that or the fat fuck was just too out of shape.

After a slew of punches, I heard an excited Artie Lange yell, "Holy shit, Stuttering John is kicking his ass." I liked that he said that. Of course, he was also happy because he bet like ten grand on me for the fight. One of my favorite moments was after the third round—they asked Evander Holyfield who he thought was winning the fight, and he said, "I think Stuttering Joe is winning."

I guess that dude got hit in the head one too many times.

People starting chanting "Cabbie sucks," and then all of the naysayers like Tom Chiusano, KC, and Robin started admitting that it was I who was winning.

But in the fourth round, I took a right cross from Cabbie, and for a split second I said to myself, *just let him hit you again and lie down.* The punch hurt and I was dead tired, mostly from holding this fat fuck up for half the fight. I let Cabbie land another one, but then I came to my senses and said fuck this, I'm not letting him win. I ain't quitting, I have never quit a day in my life, and I wasn't about to start now. So I started retaliating with a string of punches. I remembered hearing

MICHAEL CAINE:
I HID BEHIND A PILLAR WHERE MICHAEL WAS SIGNING AND WAITED FOR HIM TO ARRIVE. WHEN I STUCK MY HEAD OUT AND
SAW THAT HE WAS COMING, I JUMPED OUT AND STARTED ASKING HIM QUESTIONS.

Baba Booey after like the fourth round telling Howard that I looked bad, and there was a pile of blood on the floor in front of me. The truth was, it had nothing to do with Cabbie. You see, my last week of sparring, I did eleven rounds, three of which were with Derek—and he beat the fuck out of me, causing my nose to bleed profusely. Cabbie just irritated a preexisting injury.

But who could blame Da Da Dummy? He bet against me.

The bell rang and the last round began. Cabbie had but one shot and that was to knock me out, but he was exhausted. We exchanged a bunch of punches and then the fight was over. The crowd was cheering me like crazy, and when they announced I had won by a unanimous decision, the place went nuts.

I gave a *Rocky*-like speech, thanking my wife and kids. At first Cabbie wouldn't even shake my hand, he thought he had won. Later on, he finally shook my hand. After I sat down to be interviewed, I started feeling really anxious on the air and was having a panic attack, so I left. When my wife and I got into my room, she had a *Rocky* movie poster waiting for me. How sweet. She wanted to have sex with me while I wore my belt, but I was too anxious. The whole time, in the back of my head, I thought to myself, *I did it*. It was just another time that I believed in myself—I overcame my fear and faced it just like that. I proved to the thousands who were there and the millions listening at home and in their cars that anything is possible. Most of all, I proved it to myself.

I did my stand-up show that night, with Howard and Beth in attendance. Howard even said on the air that Monday how good I was. Sunday, we flew back in Donald Trump's helicopter. What a weekend—what an experience that I'll cherish forever. It was the experience of a lifetime. The following week, on the show, I was applauded. Gary even told me he spoke to Fran, one of the higher-ups at E!, and that she said, in reference to me and the fight, "See, that's a real man."

That was nice of Gary to say.

JACKIE MARTLING-922-WHINE

I ALREADY TALKED ABOUT the first time I met Jackie. He gained some fame on Long Island due to his call-ins to Bob Buchman, the morning jock on WBAB. I used to listen while driving to Nassau Community College. He was on the

LATER ON, IN A BOOK, HE COMPARED ME TO A SNIPER IN THE WAR.
"WHEN YOU KISSED CHRISTOPHER REEVE IN DEATHTRAP, DID YOU GET TURNED ON?"
"DID SIR LAURENCE OLIVIER EVER HIT ON YOU?"

air with Buchman, plugging his (516) 922-WINE joke line. Apparently he had like twelve answering machines in his mom's attic in East Norwich, and people could call in and hear a bunch of crappy jokes.

Well, they weren't crappy. Mostly, I would call the line when I was *on the crapper*. We didn't have cell phones then, so what the hell else was I going to do? I already read my latest edition of *MAD Magazine* twenty times.

Anyway, I guess Jackie got the break of a lifetime by becoming a part-time member of *The Howard Stern Show*. I used to listen while counting electronic parts at Standard Radio in Farmingdale. I used to picture him and Fred sitting in chairs next to each other, handing Howard jokes, which ultimately was an accurate assessment.

I was excited to meet Jackie. Heck, he was a likeable guy. After I'd been on the show for a few days, Jackie and I became friends, so much so that I was helping him load furniture into his shit hole roach-infested sixth-floor walk-up on East Sixty-Fifth.

Jackie was borrowing the dump from another comedian, and he eventually handed it over to me. I remember throwing a shoe at a cockroach the size of a baby's arm. Jackie would invite me to Bayville, a North Shore beach town, to hang out. When I started dating Suzanna, we would go there and hang with Jackie and Nancy. The best was when Jackie had us walk up four flights of stairs in his first house to prove to us that he had a water-view house. We literally got to the attic and had to pull up a chair and stand on it to look out the tiny attic window to see a bit of the Long Island Sound through the dirty window, the trees, the bushes, and the tops of three houses.

After the first time we left, Suzanna said this was the only place besides the city that she could live, so the next day I looked in *Newsday*, saw a listing, sold my Infinity stock, and bought my first house. I am an Islander; I like the city, but I love the tranquility of a house, grass, and the beach. I had bought a thousand shares of Infinity stock for seventeen dollars, then another thousand at like thirty, and then sold it, profiting about $300,000! I put a hundred down on the house, and much to Jackie's chagrin, we were essentially neighbors.

I couldn't really afford the mortgage on my meager K-Rock salary, so Jackie and I would commute together. Man, he was grouchy in the morning. And he wasn't keen on the idea, anyway. He had his rituals that he liked to do in the morning. Drive to the same deli, grab a coffee, listen to the news station

PETER JENNINGS:
"DOES DIANE SAWYER GIVE YOU A CHUBBY?"

1010 WINS, and not talk. He would drive over the Fifty-Ninth Street Bridge instead of going through the midtown tunnel to save the $3.50 in tolls, the cheap fuck. His excuse was that it was closer, but I wasn't buying it. After a long spell of silence, I asked, "Hey, man, how are you?"

He snapped, "You see, this is why I don't want to drive you, because I don't want to tell anyone how I'm doing."

I was scared of him in the morning. I would just sit there quietly. I know I really irritated him once when it was pouring rain outside and Jackie was in my driveway. I had overslept, so I ran out in my underwear with a handful of clothes. He was pissed. I can't say I blame him that time.

This wasn't the first time I had driven with Jackie. When we were doing the Channel 9 show, I used to take the train to work in the morning, do the radio show, get a ride with Robin to the Channel 9 show, and then afterward Jackie would drive me home to Long Island. Well, not exactly. Jackie would drop me off fifteen minutes from my house, off of the LIE because he didn't want to inconvenience himself by driving me to Massapequa and back. It's like the time he refused to give Eddie Murphy a ride home when Eddie was a struggling comic, and look how that turned out.

Jackie is a good guy, but Jackie is all about Jackie. Read this quote from *Radar Online*, when Jackie tried to get back on the *Stern Show* after walking off for his third and final time:

> "In fact, fairly soon after 9/11, when everybody in New York was so disheartened and depressed, I wrote Howard another very sincere email, saying I really wanted to return to the show and that I thought the horrible tragedy was a perfect window for me to return, for us to reunite. That New York badly needed anything that would symbolize any kind of 'return to normalcy,' especially anything that would lighten things up at all, and judging from the hundreds and hundreds of emails and the people I ran into everywhere I went (even to this day), so many of the listeners were rooting for my return that it seemed like an ideal time to bury the hatchet, let bygones be bygones, or simply tear down whatever walls that were...
>
> in the way, and make the show whole again."

PETER JUST LAUGHED HIS ASS OFF.

What the fuck was wrong with him? He tried using a tragedy to get his job back? I know his heart was in the right place but come on, Jackie! New York would feel better? I'm sorry, Joke Man. I don't think all of New York is focused on you and *The Howard Stern Show*.

But that's just one of Jackie's flaws. It's Jackie's world and we're just part of it.

Don't get me wrong, but the thing I learned over the numerous conversations I had with Jackie was that he was optimistic and forgiving when it benefited him. For instance, if Nancy had a problem with somebody but the guy was nice to Jackie, he would say in that high-pitched voice, "But he's a good guy..."

All right, I digress. Jackie was one of my best friends on the show. He and I hung out together, smoked weed together, went on trips to Cancun and Puerto Rico together. We were buds. One time before I bought the house near his, Jackie unexpectedly crashed at my place, and the next morning I asked him if he brushed his teeth and he said yes.

I said, "Wait, you had a toothbrush with you?"

And he said, "No, I used your roommate Mike's."

Fucking gross! And that's fucking me saying it!

I could not wait to get on the air and tell Howard, which I did—but Jackie denied it. He said he was just pulling my leg, until my roommate Mikey called in and said, "John, I just checked my toothbrush and it is wet." Jackie definitely used it! We goofed on him for a while on the air.

I was developing a skill at becoming the resident informer and ball-breaker. Breaking balls was something I did all my life, but this was a new way to reinvent myself when I was starting to get recognized too often when I did interviews. You might say, "Wow, you're a snitch," to which I would say, "But did it make great radio? Yes!"

I rest my case.

I might not be good at a lot of things, but one thing I am good at is figuring out a way to survive. Jackie and Booey became my incessant targets for ridicule. Gary because he was a big-toothed backstabber, and Jackie because, well, he was wacky. Put it this way: Jackie once told me that he wanted to construct an underwater pool tunnel connecting two of his neighboring houses. Granted we were both drunk, but that motherfucker was serious. It seemed like a good idea

KATHLEEN TURNER:

"HAVE YOU EVER FARTED IN YOUR HAND AND SMELLED IT?"

to me at the time, thanks to the weed, but I logged it away and couldn't wait to spill this shit out on the air. I ultimately did, and we laughed our asses off.

Here's a list of wacky Jackie ideas:

1. Consult a doctor from the pennysaver and get his toenails chopped off. (I always thought it would be a funny practical joke to send Jackie into an Asian nail salon to get a pedicure and watch their reaction to his nail-less toes.)

2. Become mayor of Bayville.

3. Build a wall separating us from Mexico. (Wait, that's not his.)

4. Create a cooking show with Bobby Flay called *Boy Meets Grill*.

5. Become a stand-up comic.

6. Record a music album.

7. Buy five houses. In response, one brilliant caller called in to the show and said, "Jackie, since you have five houses, shouldn't you own a hotel?"

8. Jackie wanting to start The Jackie Martling Museum at one of his houses.

9. Jackie asking guests and having Grillo ask guests to sign a page of a joke he wrote when they appeared, so he could one day wallpaper a room in one of his houses with all of the celebrity pages.

Look, I love Jackie. I really do. He was my partner in crime in a lot of ways, but I think he made the biggest blunder in show business history: he decided to enter it. Nah, just kidding. But that last one was the worst in my opinion. It was so backhandedly obviously a boost to his ego. I mean let's face it, he wanted to passive-aggressively let the celebrity guests know he was the one writing the jokes. That's like me going up to Tom Cruise after his appearance on *The Tonight Show* and asking him to sign a script of a bit or segment that I wrote. It was just dead wrong, and I don't blame Howard for being pissed about it. We would have to go through a strict path if we ever wanted an autograph from a guest on *The Tonight Show*, and the requests were few and far between. I remember asking Jay if I could get a picture with Barack Obama, and he was like no fucking way. I felt like a dolt. Sadly, Jackie didn't seem to mind. The worst was that he got Grillo to do his bidding sometimes, which put an added pressure on his tiny brain. I'm sorry, I shouldn't have said tiny—I meant extra tiny. Put it this way: Grillo works for a lighting company now where he shows off new light bulbs, and I'm pretty sure this is the first time a light bulb has ever gone off above his head.

Anyway, back to Jackie.

Suzanna and I finally decided to get married. After all, we had a kid already. So we rented a house on the beach for an entire month, but then realized later on that the tide was slowly rising and we'd have no room for the wedding tents by the time the date rolled around. In our desperate search, we found another house down the block that we could rent for the day. It had a nice deck for our wedding band, the famous Nerds, from New Jersey. They were friends since I did many gigs with them. Anyway, we had a beautiful day, June 28, a sunny Saturday. We invited about two hundred people. I invited Robin, Jackie, Gary, Fred, and Howard from the show. Howard didn't attend, and neither did Fred, although they gave me nice gifts.

Unfortunately, Jackie came. I kid because I love, but the truth is, Jackie decided to go up and jam with the Nerds and it was cool for about two minutes, but he would not get off the stage. I went up and asked him once after ten minutes, but he refused. The people were holding their ears after drunk, pot-influenced Martling cranked the guitar up and muddled through bad lead after bad lead as if he were playing with mittens. I finally grabbed Baba Booey and was like, "Gary, this is Godawful! Please help me get him off the stage!" Gary took control and went upstairs to the upper deck and yelled to Jackie. "Get the fuck off the stage, you're ruining the wedding!"

Finally, thank God, Jackie put down the guitar, and the Nerds went into their brilliant rendition of "Bohemian Rhapsody" to help us all forget the white trash noise we had just endured for the last twenty minutes.

The funniest and worst part of the wedding was that we got married by a priest and a rabbi on the beach. I told everyone to come in shorts and bathing suits, because the thing I hated most about weddings was that you had to get dressed up. Therefore, this one was to be totally casual. While the wedding party and my wife were all proceeding down the aisle, the rabbi turned to me and said, "Do you have the check?"

After the ceremony and the pictures, Mike Novara, who was my best man, and I ran down the beach and jumped into the water while the wedding videographer was taping us. Well, the wedding ring expanded due to the cold water and my finger shrunk and the wedding band that I paid two grand for

KAREEM ABDUL-JABBAR:

"WHO'S THE BEST WHITE GUY YOU EVER PLAYED AGAINST?"

"WHY DID YOU CHANGE YOUR NAME FROM LEW ALCINDOR TO SOMETHING AS STUPID AS KAREEM ABDUL-JABBAR?"

slid right off. I started looking around in the water for it panicking. Suddenly, I remembered the videographer was taping the whole thing and shouted at him to turn the camera off!

Suzanna thought that I planned it, but I was devastated. I was so massively OCD about it that it ruined our honeymoon in the Bahamas. A few years later we were hanging out with Jackie and Nancy on the beach and I was about to go swimming. I had since bought a union ring in Denmark that I used as my wedding band, and I gave it to Suzanna to hold so that I wouldn't lose it. As we were walking back to our house, I asked her for the ring back, and it turns out it had fallen out of her pocket.

Maybe we weren't meant to be married.

•••

LATER ON THE NIGHT of the wedding, we all went back to the initial house I had rented to watch the Tyson/Holyfield fight. You know, the one where Tyson bit Holyfield's ear off—which made us all a little bit jealous, having just listened to Jackie's "jamming." Anyway, we all got even drunker and more wasted, and Jackie passed out in front of the basement door. Keep in mind, there were only two bathrooms in the house and I had like fifty people there. So Jackie passes out in front of the door, and my friend Danny was coming up from the basement bathroom. He starts trying to open the door and starts banging it against Jackie's head!

Boom! Boom! Boom! Boom!

Jackie did not wake up. Suddenly, Nancy sees what's going on and runs to Jackie and grabs him by his shoes and drags him away from the door to free my friend Danny from the basement. I told this story, and thanks to Fred's brilliant sound effects, it made a funny bit for the air.

Fucking Jackie. Man, I wish you were drinking again.

MY FAVORITE JACKIE STORY

JACKIE USED TO WRITE jokes for Jackie Mason in Jackie Mason's Midtown apartment. One day, Martling wrote Mason a really good political joke. Mason said, "Did you write this, Jackie?" Martling said that he did, and Mason responded, "You, my friend, are a genius." Martling couldn't have been more thrilled and proud of himself. Later on, they walked into the elevator, and it had an elevator man who had to pull the cage-like door shut before you can go down to the lobby. Mason said to the elevator man, "First floor," and the elevator man pulled the door shut, and Mason said to him, "You, my friend, are a genius."

Poor Jackie. We had some fun times, though. I remember when Howard had a party at the Rainbow Room at Rockefeller Plaza, 30 Rock, like forty-two stories up. The bathrooms were jammed, so Jackie and I smoked a joint near the elevator shaft and then we both took a leak down the grate, our urine probably turning into ice by the time it reached the bottom.

The best was when we were in Philly. We all took a bus there from our studio in New York to do the funeral show of John DeBella. We were at a posh hotel and we all got fucked up—well, at least I did. Howard and Jackie were in a bathtub with Jessica Hahn, who was a *Playboy* centerfold and fresh from the Gene Profeta Televangelist sex scandal. She had these huge gorgeous tits, and they were all in the bath. Howard called me and told me to jump in the bathtub, which I did. I came running in the room and jumped into the tub. Jessica was repulsed, and allegedly the water turned black.

As we were on the bus ride home, Jackie fell asleep, so I took Jessica's lingerie and slipped it into Jackie's suitcase. When Jackie got home, thankfully he realized it was there and immediately buried it in his backyard before Nancy could find it, although it was too late to quell her anger that brought on the infamous Jackie speech: "I want to take this moment to apologize to my wife, Nancy. What I did was stupid, it will never happen again…I love you…and, Howard, please don't make a mockery of this."

Ugh! I think my dick might have curled into my abdomen. Great radio, though—although I'm sure that's not what he intended. Poor Jackie. There he was, apologizing to a woman who banged some dude on the front lawn of a Long Island home.

Then again, man, the things we do for love…

The Lon Chaney of stutterers.
Photo Credit: Doug Goodstein

A young John at Scott Walker's bar mitzvah.
That's Pat Godfrey and Gary Cosentino in the back. Gary kept pulling my clip-on tie off.

My band Stiff Minister at the highschool battle of the bands.
Me and bass player, Bob LaValley (left).

In New Orleans—I'll sweat my way out of it!

My Danish mom, the viking on her eightieth birthday.

My dad and I shortly before he passed. He was a funny bastard. When we were at his chemo session,
I said to him, "Dad, I posted our picture on Facebook and people said I looked like you. I wanted to kill myself."
He said, "They said I looked like you? Now I want to kill myself."

My wonderful three kids: Knight, Lily Belle, and Oscar.

Man, they grow up quick.

Faces for radio. I'll never forget driving back from Albany and hearing my song,
"I'll Talk my Way Out of It," on the radio
Photo Credit: John Halpern

S-S-So, Joe, is Don Henley really that big of an ass?
Photo Credit: Kristen Casey

Me and Suzanna. I'm the one on the left.

Crazy Cabbie and me before the fight.
That's one crazy-looking dude—and he don't look so good either.

Me after winning in a unanimous decision.

The late great Robin Leach took this picture when we were at Rao's in Las Vegas.
Bill offered me a cigar but I refused. God knows where that's been.

Another picture from the Stuttering John and Friends Tour,
this time with Nick Di Paolo, me, Mark Mercer, Modi, and Bob Levy.
Photo Credit: Mark Mercer

The Stuttering John and Friends Tour with Melrose Larry Green,
me, Bob Levy, Jim Florentine, and Artie Lang.

One of my favorite comedic actors ever, Albert Brooks.

Howard actually told his staff to set up fake Twitter accounts.
Where have you gone, Howard, and who has taken your place?

My crew headed by my friend Doug Goodstein.

Turning Vegas into Chin City

The writing staff at The Tonight Show. *A talented bunch of motherfuckers.*

Jay took a picture with everyone from the staff before the show ended.

Doing a bit with Jay during the gas shortage.

"Is this thing on?"

MY FAVORITE JACKIE MOMENTS

1. During one of Jackie's contract disputes with E!, they had to put up a black wall to hide Jackie from the cameras.

2. When we would go to the bathroom during a commercial break, I would pee, and Jackie would sit on the toilet, not close the door, pull down his pants, and just unload while still carrying on a conversation with me. It was like, "yeah, so Nancy, *boom, splash, fart noise*, she wants to have, *boom, splash, fart*, dinner tonight, *boom, splash, fart noise*, and then he'd get up, pull his pants up, and leave!

3. Jackie and I would go the Friars Club—yes, he would pay, but little did you know that if he didn't go there he would be charged anyway, because he had to pay like $250 every quarter, so essentially the meal didn't cost him anything, but I still do appreciate it. I loved it there. We would both order the same thing: half a roasted chicken, well done, a salad, mashed potatoes, and a French onion soup, which was where Jackie had the line that I still use today: burn the cheese on top, and when you think it's burned enough, burn it again. One day, we took Gary there, and Gary ordered the shrimp. Jackie and I watched in amusement as Baba Booey wrapped his inner-tube-like lips around each shrimp and ate it like a reverse shit. He just vacuum-sucked that thing right into his mouth. It was like, "Ah, nows ya see it, ahnd nows ya don't." I couldn't wait to get on the air and tell the story. I did, and Jackie, Howard, Robin, and I goofed on him and laughed our asses off.

4. We were in LA doing an appearance, and Jackie and I watched Gary suck in M&Ms like a kissing gourami does a morsel of food—it was like ffffwwwwoommmm! In the mouth. Gary loved chocolate, so it was like a fast-speed wet vac. Then he would have a sip of his drink and wrap those gargantuan lips around the straw as if it were Jenna Jameson wrapping

I HAD NO IDEA WHO THIS GUY WAS, BUT HE HAD THE BEST ANGRY RESPONSE. HE SAID, "OH, GET AWAY FROM ME WITH THESE STUPID QUESTIONS, YOU BLOODY FOOL!"

her lips around a cock. Again, I couldn't wait to bring it up on the air… which I did.

5. Jackie's "pissing on his mom's face" story is my all-time favorite. See, Jackie and his buddies decided to drive to Michigan for college. Jackie's mom wanted to go, so they got her a bottle of sherry, and Jackie and his mates bought a ton of beer. They had a pail in the car so they wouldn't have to stop to pee. Jackie took a leak in the pail while all of the windows were open. Emptied it out the window, and the piss came flying back into his mom's window and nailed her right smack in the face! Thankfully Jackie's mom had a sense of humor, which leads me to this story.

6. When Jackie was a little boy, his mom would be sitting in her chair in the living room. Jackie would say, "Hey, Mom, where are my socks?" Jackie's mom would look at him and say, "Do you know Helen Hunt?" (This was way before there was a famous Helen Hunt.) And Jackie would say no, and his mom would say, "Well go to hell and hunt for them."

7. When we were at the MTV awards in Manhattan, we decided to do a drinking show. The game was to see who could drink the most. I started to get really buzzed, as we all did. Jacob Dylan was one of the guests, and I decided to interrogate him about his Jewishness. Jackie could not stop laughing, it was the funniest thing. Meanwhile I was so drunk and annoying, I accidentally spilled my beer on Jacob Dylan's beautiful, expensive suede jacket. He was so pissed, and Jackie just continued to laugh uncontrollably.

8. Jackie once told me that he took a shit off the Bayville Bridge.

9. One morning, I got a call from Nancy in the office, and she said to ask Jackie to take off his shoes and socks in the studio. I asked why but she was like, just do it. So I went in to the studio and said it. Jackie took off his footwear to reveal that his toenails were painted in red nail polish. I guess he had passed out drunk, so Nancy decided to fuck with him.

10. We all attended a Jackie book signing of all old jokes that weren't Jackie's. The party was at Carolines in Manhattan, and we went back to Jackie's favorite hotel room in the St. Moritz. We were hanging out in his room drinking and getting stoned, and I asked everyone to tell their favorite Jackie story. Larry "Ratso" Sloman had the best one. He asked, "How funny is it

JAMES EARL JONES:
"DO PEOPLE EVER CONFUSE YOU WITH JAMES EARL RAY?"
"HOW MUCH DO YOU GET PAID TO SAY 'CNN'?"

that Jackie, a guy who wants everyone to know he writes Howard's jokes, put out a book of other people's jokes?" I laughed my ass off.

11. Howard once beat a naked woman's ass with a huge fish and Jackie took it home, cooked it, and ate it.

12. I asked Jackie, when we were walking into a racquetball court at the NY Health and Racquet Club, why he never decided to tell his own jokes in his act. I said, Jackie, you're a storyteller, but he said that Henny Youngman once told him that nobody wants to hear about your life. Well, no disrespect, Henny, but it's been fairly profitable for Leno, Seinfeld, Kinison, and the zillion other comics out there.

13. Jackie's one OCD thing about performing was that he always had to go on stage with red socks.

14. Jackie once was nice enough to let my family sleep at his house on the beach. It turns out his house was flea-infested and we received a combined three hundred fleabites all over our bodies.

15. When Jackie had hemorrhoids, Nancy used to have Jackie get down on all fours and she'd insert the Preparation H tube up Jackie's ass.

16. Jackie, Fred, Gary, Nancy, Billy and Vee, Billy's wife, all recorded the hidden track on my Atlantic album called "One Thing." It was an anti-FCC song, and at the very end, Jackie strums his guitar and does a two-minute rendition of all of the infamous Jackie laughs.

17. When we went to our sexual harassment required class at K-Rock, before the teacher entered, Jackie drew a big cock on a piece of paper and taped it to the television at the front of the room.

18. Jackie would eat Buffalo wings by inserting the whole piece in his mouth and then pulling it out with just the bone left—à la Fred Flintstone.

19. One time Jackie stuck his finger up the ass of a guy that mooned him and went back to eating his Buffalo wings without washing his hands.

20. At every one of his shows, he would tell his last joke and then begin selling merchandize on stage. It was so embarrassing. I'd never seen a comedian in my life end his show and immediately turn into a snake-oil salesman on stage!

"WOULD YOU LET YOUR KIDS SLEEP UNSUPERVISED IN A ROOM WITH MICHAEL JACKSON?"
JAMES WAS ALL RIGHT. AFTER ALL, HE IS A FELLOW STUTTERER.

THE FINAL JACKIE DEPARTURE

I DID NOT WANT this to happen. I kind of feel responsible because I was the one who hooked Jackie up with my entertainment lawyers at Grubman, Indursky, and Schindler. I got them when I needed lawyers to secure my record deal, and I had two good attorneys there: Larry Shire and Don Kaplan. Larry was like the rock star, good-looking attorney, and Don was like the consummate nerd, with the only thing missing from his collared dress shirt being a slide rule.

Anyway, Jackie wanted representation and he asked me if I knew anybody. I suggested Larry, and Jackie fell as in love with Larry as I did. Little did I know that Larry was the catalyst in Jackie's departure. Howard, Fred, and Robin were all still represented by Don Buchwald, and Jackie didn't want any part of that.

He had walked off the show due to a contract dispute twice before, but I knew this would be the last one. Why? Because I knew Howard was fed up with all of Jackie's shenanigans. There was already tension, as Howard was convinced Jackie was the rabble-rouser of the disgruntled. I knew he was at his breaking point. I remember when Jackie was considering making this fatal move, we were standing in front of the elevator doors in the lobby of 600 Madison Avenue, home of K-Rock. We awaited the elevator to go downstairs and I said, "Jackie, look, stick it out for five more years, then you can retire a millionaire and never have to work again."

He said no, that he'd had enough and wanted to be paid what he felt he was worth. Now, mind you, I was making $35,000 a year and Jackie was making like $700,000. I think he wanted like $800,000, but still, to me it was a lot of money either way. Why leave that?

We'd all had enough of Howard's abuse, but, man, you stuck it out this far. Take it in the ass for five more years and then live the rest of your life on the beach like Tim Robbins in *The Shawshank Redemption*. Jackie left the show. What a dumb move from a very bright man. Larry had convinced Jackie he would be able to get him more money, and Jackie was brainwashed.

DON CORNELIUS:
"O.J.—INNOCENT OR GUILTY?"

Tom Chiusano met with Jackie one last time and offered him a little bit more and told Jackie that this was their last offer. There was no more negotiating, take it or leave it.

Unfortunately, Jackie left it.

Larry had him convinced that he could out-negotiate Mel Karmazin, but that wasn't going to happen. Jackie was going to lose, and lose he did. He lost his job, then his wife, then his passion for drinking beer, then his comedy gigs dried up, and his pay went way down. It was very sad. I loved Jackie; I didn't want to see him go. We all missed him.

Jackie had heard that I goofed on him after his departure on the air, and I'm sure I did, but I pretty much just goofed on his decision. I watched his five houses become two after three went to Nancy. I liked Nancy, but at the time I always felt that she had to prove how smart she was. She always felt she was just as responsible for Jackie's success as he was, and that always annoyed me.

In retrospect, at least I didn't support a guy leaving the highest-paying job he could get in exchange for nothing. Everyone knows you don't leave a job until you have another one lined up. That's the first rule of business. Yeah, Nancy was a tough one. They would fight all the time, but hey, most married couples do. Yet I always felt that Nancy was jealous of Jackie's success. The four of us went upstate to a bed-and-breakfast once, and we were at a restaurant having dinner. Nancy asked Jackie for something and Jackie said, "Yes, your Majesty"...and then opened his eyes and looked at Nancy and said, "Oh, did I say that out loud?" I laughed my ass off.

HI, MY NAME IS FRED, MY NAME IS ERIC, MY NAME IS FRED NORRIS. HI, MY NAME IS FRED, MY NAME IS ERIC, MY NAME IS FRED NORRIS.

WHAT CAN I SAY? Fred is a very damaged individual, much like all of us on *The Howard Stern Show*. We're all just people who left one dysfunctional family for another. Howard suffered abuse from his father the same as I did. Although I got my ass kicked, Howard only got put down a few times—but it was

HE FREAKED OUT ON ME.

damaging nevertheless. I think, though, that Howard has always strived for his father's acceptance. It has helped him and hurt him in many ways. Robin was molested by her father. Jackie, believe it or not, didn't have many stories to tell, and Gary, from what I remember, had a crazy mother.

And then there was Fred. Poor Fred.

The scared child stuck in a hard, stiff, tall body. Fred has always been so incredibly socially awkward that the last thing you'd want is to be stuck in a conversation with him for over five minutes. From what I recall, his biological dad named him Fred, but his stepfather's name was Eric, or vice versa—I just know that one of them was a drunk and abusive to poor Fred. So because of that, one time Fred changed his name to Eric but never told us. Finally it was revealed to us and then all jokes ensued, because nobody knew which name to call him. I mean, he already had changed his last name from Nukkis to Norris. Shit, this guy has changed his name more times that P. Diddy. I then pulled the clips of him saying both first names and wrote a song parody to Eminem's "My Name Is" that my engineer buddy Brian Kelsey produced. Howard loved it and played it for a week, but then suddenly it vanished.

I mean, you figure it out. Fred played the bits, he had the files, but somehow he lost the recording?

He's a character.

I've always felt that Fred was envious of me.

Look, there's not one of us main people on the show that didn't want to get out at one point or another, but the difference is that I got out. I got out for a brighter future. I was leaving for a better gig. Fred's head must have been spinning like Linda Blair's. I reminded him of everything that he wasn't. I was young, aggressive, and ambitious. I was not afraid of rejection. I was not afraid to fail. I was not afraid to perform. Even when Howard and I went to see Fred's band, he wouldn't sing to the audience. He literally would turn his back to the audience.

I had dreams beyond *The Howard Stern Show*. I was the rebel.

Fred wanted to get a record deal and tour the country—I did.

Fred wanted to be an actor—I got to be in movies and on sitcoms.

Fred went out on tons of voiceover auditions yet got few or no jobs—I got the most coveted announcing gig in all of television.

DAN RATHER:

"WHAT'S THE FREQUENCY, KENNETH?"

This drove Fred absolutely nuts.

He would call me an opportunist. A wheeler and dealer. You know, like Howard. But I think I know another reason why Fred hated me, and it's all about the off-Broadway play, *Tony n' Tina's Wedding*. You see, I always try and help people, because what else are we here for? So one time Fred's wife Alison asked me if I could get her an acting role on the show, and well, I did. The problem was she got the role of the nun that has to make out with one of the groomsmen, night after night. This couldn't have made Fred happy, plus Alison became very friendly with many of the cast, including myself, and we would all go out drinking after the shows.

One night, I went with Howard and our ladies to watch the play, and Alison was doing a very good job at her role, practically getting molested leaning on a pillar on the stage. We goofed for hours on the air about it. Fred wasn't happy. But then we brought in the actor that kisses her, Patrick Buckley, a very dear friend of mine—but more importantly, this good-looking blue-eyed Italian with a nice svelte physique. We had him do the scene with Alison, and I thought Fred's head was about to explode.

Howard said, "John, why don't you try the scene with her?"

Before I even got close to her, Fred blew his top. He wasn't having any of it. Howard tried to calm him down, but Fred hated me.

•••

DURING MY FIRST MEETINGS with Fred, I had to order the breakfast, and Fred would ask me for French toast and a coffee—though he used to ask Mitch for two packs of smokes wrapped in tinfoil so Howard wouldn't know he was smoking again. He was afraid of Howard. He was just a scared little kid still afraid of his daddy. It makes me feel sorry for Fred. Fred wasn't all that happy there.

Fred can lie all he wants, but I know, his wife Alison knows, and many fans know how angry he would get when Howard abused him. Once, Fred was going to leave. He was in a crazed state, and his wife called in to talk him down. Fred had a very bad temper. This guy could dish it out but he just couldn't take it.

I think he hated me the most because I didn't fear him. I goofed on him, and that tore him up. He must've been like, *Who the fuck is this new guy ripping into me?* But truth be told, not only was I a fan of Howard, but I liked to make him laugh. Hearing him laugh at something I said or did made my day. That's the

HE JUST LOOKED AT ME FOR A BRIEF MOMENT, STUNNED. HOW THE HELL WOULD I KNOW THAT A GUY ASKED HIM THIS BEFORE HE BEAT THE FUCK OUT OF HIM?

kind of contagious personality he had. It's not like I didn't make my family and friends laugh—after all, I was the perennial class clown—but making Howard laugh was even more special because I looked up to him. And I'd do it, even if it meant goofing on the rest of the staff. Keep in mind that they goofed on me, but thanks to my upbringing and friends, I was just particularly good at it—a consummate, stuttering ball-buster who had thick skin, especially when it came to stuttering. Howard, Fred, Jackie, Artie, any of them goofing on my stutter meant nothing to me. I was secure in my own stuttering body, although I was vastly insecure in other aspects of my personality.

As for Fred or Eric or whatever, he admitted on the air that my getting a record deal inspired him to get back into music…and to the fans, I apologize.

Nah, Fred's not a bad guy. I mean, he would give me great gifts for Christmas. Way more generous than Howard's, but then again a cookie puss is a better gift than what Howard dealt out. Fred gave me miniature Peavy and Marshall amps, a wah-wah pedal. Howard gave me a canister of popcorn. Fred was also fun to write with. He really is a very funny man. He's a good musician as well, but I'll never forget the time he choked during the recording of my song "One Thing" at The Hit Factory in Manhattan. Billy West knocked his guitar solo out in one take—and Fred took like twenty-five. I think the whole experience made him nervous, but that can happen to anybody. At the end of the day I have to say that I like Fred. He is a talented motherfucker. It's just unfortunate that he doesn't feel the same way about me.

ARTIE LANGE—DR. JEKYLL AND MR. HYDE THE HEROIN

My history with Artie starts as the most pleasant experience imaginable yet ends dark, twisted, and sad. We met in the green room at *The Howard Stern Show* when he came in with Norm Macdonald to promote their movie *Dirty Work*. I came by the green room to say hi, and Artie welcomed me with a stream of compliments. I complimented them both on the trailer, telling them that the movie looked pretty funny. I'm a big Norm Macdonald fan, and when Gary and I went to *SNL* and went to the bar for the after-party, Norm couldn't have been more gracious. It was one of those things that neither Gary nor I were aware

LESLIE NIELSEN:

of. Many famous people listened to the show and were big fans of ours. It never dawned on me. It was completely humbling.

Anyway, Norm was on the air with Howard, and eventually they brought Artie in. Artie was a smash. He was extremely candid, and Howard immediately fell in love with him. Let's face it: Artie Lange was a lovable guy. I liked him the moment I met him, but things turned for the worst in the years to come.

After Jackie made his final departure from *The Howard Stern Show*, Howard was fed up. He was extremely angry and Robin joined in, and that was the final nail in the coffin. Thus the revolving door of the Jackie chair commenced. Jimmy Kimmel and Adam Carolla, Richard Jeni, Jeffrey Ross, Craig Gass, Doug Stanhope, Greg Fitzsimmons, A.J. Benza, and, of course, Artie Lange all took a turn in the chair, each for about a week.

It was stressful for many of these people. Richard Jeni, one of the funniest stand-up comedians that I have ever seen, talked to me in Scott's smoking closet, asking me how I thought he was doing. I knew what Howard felt but had to pretend it was my own feeling to protect my trust with Howard. I told him, "Richard, you're doing great, but maybe just speak off the cuff. You know, the show is about reality. If I were you, I wouldn't go into my act or anything."

I remember hanging with Jeffrey Ross for the brief time I was a friar at the club. (I had to get out, the dues were killing me; no wonder Jackie had to hock his T-shirts and knickknacks on the stage.) Anyway, Jeff asked the same question as Richard, and I repeated the same answer.

Howard wasn't thrilled with Craig Gass because let's face it, he was no Billy West. Billy knew when to go into an impression; Craig either didn't have the confidence or didn't have the wherewithal to do so. Howard felt he had to lead him to it, and even then Craig was too oblivious to bite.

Jimmy Kimmel and Adam Carolla were all right, but Adam just never shut the fuck up. Besides, they already had careers and I'm sure they wouldn't have made the move even if they were offered the gig. I remember once Adam decided to cut me off in the studio, telling me to shut up, and I wanted to punch him in the fucking face.

I couldn't stand A.J. Benza. That macho, mobster-wannabe shit just didn't do it for me.

I can't remember much about the other guys, but the one who really stood out to me was Artie Lange. I thought he fit in perfectly, but there was a problem: he laughed in that raspy tone at his own jokes incessantly. Soon after, I caught his appearance on *Conan*, and he did the same annoying laugh after every joke. Now my plan came to action. I went in the studio, stood at the podium, and asked Howard if he saw Artie's appearance. Howard said, "No, how was he?" So I did my rendition goofing on Artie's incessant laughing. He had no comeback; he just sat there and shut up. I swear to you, people, this was a conscious effort by me to ensure that Artie got the job. I disliked A.J. with a passion, and I wanted Artie.

Anyway, after my trouncing, Artie did not speak on the show the rest of the morning. When I returned from making copies of Howard's mail, one of the E! producers, Robin Eadzinski, had put a Post-it on my desk. It read, "Fuck you for killing Artie."

What the fuck, dummy? I was *helping* Artie.

Later, Artie confessed that the real reason for his silence had nothing to do with me. Rather, it was that Howard had said on the air that Artie wasn't part of the show. Heck, Artie was a damaged, sensitive guy, as we all were, and hearing Howard say that made him sad. The good news, though, was that he stopped the raspy laughter after every joke. My plan had worked. I don't care what you think, this is the God's honest truth. I would swear on a stack of Bibles, I did it to help Artie, not hurt him.

But how do I get the second man in the running, A.J. Benza, off the show?

This happened completely unintentionally. I'm smart, but not that smart. On his fatal day, I was doing the phones, as I always did. I had a computer screen that went straight into the studio, with an adjoining screen directly in front of Howard's face. I would put phone calls up and write jokes on there as well. Anyway, I was getting about 70 percent of the calls coming in from people who hated A.J., and the rest were supportive of him, and quite frankly, that's being kind. Anyway, I would put them all up. When it came to the calls, I wouldn't try and sabotage the poor guy's employment. Anyway, Howard is as Howard does, and he kept taking the negative ones. That was entirely his decision, not mine. Finally, A.J., in his Mafioso tough-guy voice, was like, "Let me tell you something, Howard. If Stuttering John puts one more negative call through, I'm gonna smack him in the face."

So I called in from Gary's closet—I mean office—went out and answered it on my phone. Put it on hold, put up a fake name and wrote, "This guy hates

GREGORY HINES:

A.J. and has dirt on him." I went back to Gary's office and Howard picked it up immediately. Then I just roasted him.

"Hey, does A.J. stand for arrogant jerk?"

"A.J., your career is disappearing faster than your hair..."

He walked out of the studio and into our offices. I stood up, waiting to see what this goomba was going to do. Well, the bitch slapped me, and I went into hot-tempered Melendez mode. It took Gary and KC to hold me back. One thing was certain: A.J. was gone, and I knew it. I swear to you, it was not intentional, but I single-handedly gave Artie the job.

We talked on the air for the rest of the morning. Howard didn't want A.J. to be canned, but they asked me. They said, "John, are you okay with A.J. still working here?"

I said, "Sure, but it doesn't mean that one day I won't punch him in the jaw."

This became a big problem.

Donald Trump called in and said, "John, I'm smarter than you, and this is your payday. I'm rich, you're not, walk out right now and sue. You'll get millions."

I couldn't do that. I would never sue Howard or the company, although in retrospect it was pretty sound advice.

Anyway, the decision was made. A.J. was out and the Jackie chair was Artie's. Artie should still be giving me 10 percent of his earnings for that. I took a punch for that fat fuck.

•••

So the Artie years commenced. He was legendary. The perfect addition to the show. At first Artie tried writing jokes for Howard like Jackie did, but it didn't take him long to realize that just wasn't his thing. Howard finally told him just say what you want, and boy did he. It was like Jackie who? Artie had leaped to fame so rapidly that he became the most liked on the show, even more than Howard. Look, Jackie was great, but Artie was a juggernaut. He was funny and fit right in. Jackie realized his mistake and sent Howard numerous emails asking for his job back, but it was too late. Artie had replaced him. Howard was free of Jackie and his shenanigans forever.

It wasn't long before Artie and I became good friends. He was my closest friend on the show, like Jackie before him. I had just started doing the Stuttering John and Friends comedy tour at that time. I had a gig booked in Boston at the

Comedy Connection, and Artie walked up to my desk and said, "John, I want to start doing comedy again. Do you think I can do some time at your show?"

I said sure, but I already had most of the money allocated. I had Nick Di Paolo for $2,500, Jim Florentine for $1,000, and Modi for $700. I also had Melrose Larry Green for $100 and had run out of hotel rooms. I told Artie the most I could give him was $500, and he said fine, and I added him to the bill. Little did I or anybody else know, he was the hottest thing on the bill. I had booked Doug Goodstein and the E! crew to shoot the road trip and the tour, but got cold feet at the last minute, as I didn't want to feel Howard's wrath if it rubbed him the wrong way.

I wish, in retrospect, that I had never canceled the shoot. The road trip was legendary. We began the first show in Boston, and the Artie chants had already begun. I had the wherewithal to put Artie on last, and he killed. The people loved him. All five shows had sold out. It was a great time for all of us. Modi, someone who we all thought was bisexual, endured constant abuse from Nick as he jokingly said yah, big-nosed motherfucker spreading the AIDS all over the place. Nick was classic, probably the angriest man on the planet but one of the funniest. Nick couldn't stand the fact that he had been doing stand-up for twenty years and I had just started and I was making the most money. After my set, he would get on stage and say, "Well, that was adequate."

I love him, though.

Our wives came with us on this road trip. Nick was on the stage killing, but then suddenly he snapped. Either someone said something he didn't agree with or it was the time when somebody in the front row was writing our jokes down, but at some point, he just lost it. He started cursing out the crowd. I was sitting next to his wife, Andi, and was like what the fuck just happened? His wife was like, I have no idea. I asked Nick afterward and he said, "Ah, I was just getting bored."

I would put Melrose Larry Green on—not because he was funny doing his wretched act, which consisted of old borscht belt jokes, but because when he started bombing and people started booing and throwing things at him, he would lose it and just start saying, "Fuck you! Fuck the Red Sox, you bean eaters. The Red Sox suck. The Patriots suck! Fuck you! Fuck you!" Then he would run around on stage giving the entire crowd the finger. Howard saw our show after the fight in Atlantic City, and he said, "I don't know if Melrose

MARC CRISTIAN (EX-LOVER OF ROCK HUDSON):
"WHO GOT HIT IN THE FACE WITH MORE BALLS—YOGI BERRA OR ROCK HUDSON?"

is either completely insane or a genius." He was like Andy Kaufman. He was a hell of a novelty act.

One night after the shows, we were all having a few beers in my hotel room. Melrose was there, acting crazy as always. He always claimed his craziness was an act, but we all knew better. Anyway, he got up to leave and after he walked out and shut the door, Nick said, "One day that guy's going to kill somebody." We all agreed and starting talking about how crazy he was.

Suddenly we hear a knock at the door. It's Melrose, completely pissed off. He's like, "I heard that, Nick. I'm going to kill somebody? Fuck you, and fuck you, John and Artie, fuck you all," and then he walked out. The motherfucker had had his ear to the door listening the whole time!

On the ride back from Boston, we pulled over at a gas station convenience store. I put a burrito in the microwave and took a shit in the toilet as it was cooking. We had Modi drive because he was the only one sober since he didn't drink. I got a blowjob from my wife in the back seat while Nick was in a heated argument with his wife over directions and anything else that pissed him off at that moment.

The Monday after we got back, Artie, knowing how big he was, said, "John, I'd like to do more gigs with you, but I'd like to get paid more." So I agreed and started paying $2,500 a weekend. I was getting like $10,000 a gig, so I'd usually net about $4,000 for myself. Eventually, as Artie got bigger, he and I split the money, then we'd split it but the agent fee came out of my share. But why not? Artie had become so huge it was the right thing to do. It's almost as if *The Howard Stern Show* was his calling. Everyone tuned in to hear what he had to say. We continued to tour together, which truly was a highlight of my life.

The road stories continued.

One time we were doing the Improv in Ontario, California. We were in the green room with Sam Simon and his *Playboy* Playmate girlfriend was there. It was about time for me to go on, and as usual I had to take a quick shit. The toilet was right next to where everyone was hanging. Keep in mind, the green room was small. I went to the bathroom and let a quick meat missile out of my ass. *Foom!* I got up, washed my hands, and walked out to see the Playmate completely disgusted. I said hi and she reluctantly shook my hand.

Artie was disgusted that I would constantly lose my checks. We had gotten paid for a Bar 51 gig in San Diego and Artie said, "John, I think you dropped

TO WHICH, AFTER A SEEMINGLY PLEASANT REFLECTION, HE RESPONDED, "ROCK HUDSON."

something." There on the hotel lobby floor was a check for $5,000. Artie banged the hottest groupie that night. Brown-haired hottie with a great body. I was married, but man, I was jealous.

We once did a gig at George Washington University in Washington, and I lost a cashier's check for $10,000 while taking a piss on the side of the highway when we were driving home. I needed it to pay my new condo mortgage. Do you know hard it is to get a new cashier's check from a university? Sheeeet!

We were at The Funny Bone in Columbus, Ohio. Dave Stroup, the owner, wasn't there for Saturday's shows. They had a female manager there. Artie got so tanked on Jack Daniel's on stage that he started to challenge people to fights when they got up to go to the bathroom. People constantly bought him shots. He had already done about an hour and he was fifteen minutes over, and the manager looked at me and said, "Are you going to stop this?"

I said no.

Later on, she wrote the owner, Dave, a note that he passed on to me. It read: *The shows were all sold out, Artie Lange was completely inebriated, and Stuttering John had no control of the show. That being said, we ran out of three brands of beer and have never sold that much alcohol in one night ever.*

That was pretty much it. Our shows were like one big party for us and the fans. People would buy Artie shot after shot while he was on stage. This was after he downed a bottle of Jack Daniel's. After three Saturday shows at the Funny Bone in Columbus, Ohio, we pulled over at the Steak 'n Shake drive-through on the way home. Artie ordered like half of the menu. I wrote everything down to use on the air. That Monday morning was by far one of my favorite moments on *The Howard Stern Show.* You see, the Sunday night before, I drank Tropicana orange juice that had maggots in it. I went into the studio to talk about Artie's Steak 'n Shake order and we all goofed on him, but then I told the orange juice story. I kept gagging every time I talked about it, and Artie started goofing on me, implying that I was trying to get a lawsuit going against Tropicana. This whole segment lasted an hour, everyone in the studio and in the E! control room were laughing their asses off. After the segment, Scott DePace, the E! director, came up to me in the hall and said, "John, that has got to be one of my favorite hours ever on the show. It was one of my top-ten funniest hours ever."

Recently, Artie texted me that he finally listened to it and he laughed his ass off.

AL FRANKEN:

That's how Artie and I had become. We were partners in crime, and we would have a great time on the air. Whenever I would try to wedge in a joke, Artie would put his tongue between his teeth and act as if he were pulling a hubcap off with a crowbar. He'd do the hand motion and it was so funny. I started doing the same thing to him. Once Artie made a Barry Larkin joke, which we knew Howard would never get since he wasn't a big sports fan and I gave him the crowbar. Howard never knew that this was going on—it was just our little funny private thing that we'd do to each other on the air.

We were at the Funny Bone in Pittsburgh. The owner was an annoying little twit that we all couldn't stand. He put us up in his office: Artie, Nick, Florentine, Modi, and me. After each of our sets, the guy always had a little annoying quip. To Artie: "You're a regular whippersnapper up there." To Nick: "You're a thunderbolt up there." The guy was a tool. The place was sold out; in fact, they added a sixth show because of the demand. The bathroom was a walk away, so Nick, Artie, Modi, Florentine, and I started pissing in his office garbage pail. While backstage, a groupie came back and just got completely naked. Another hot blonde came backstage as well, horny for any of us, but since we all had wives and girlfriends, she ended up sleeping with Modi. Oh, the shit Nick gave him the next day. "I see you're spreading the AIDS again, hooknose."

I had my best improv line ever that night, too. I was doing crowd work and I asked a guy in the front row what he did for a living. He told me that he worked for Coke, and without skipping a beat I told him, "So does Artie."

The crowd loved it.

We did the Electric Factory around Christmastime. There was a huge blizzard outside and my SUV was sliding everywhere. It was a twelve-hundred-seat venue and I didn't know if anyone would show due to the inclement weather. I mean, who the fuck is going to come out during this blizzard, right?

The place was jammed, and the Philly faithful didn't disappoint as far as proving that they are the nastiest fans in the world. These are the people that snowballed Santa at an Eagles game, for shit's sake. They had a kangaroo court underneath the spectrum for drunken disorderly conduct offenders. There's a reason these fans are voted the nastiest on the planet year after year by a ton of magazines. The city of brotherly love, my ass!

It was time for the show to start, and Nick decided it was a good time to tell me that I was not a comedian. Not meaning that I sucked— I had just

"WHAT WAS THE BIGGER DISASTER: BILL MORRIS (I MEANT TO SAY DICK MORRIS, THE DISGRACED SENATOR) OR STUART SAVES HIS FAMILY?"

started—but that I didn't make a living at it like he does. What a pep talk from the "cugine of mean." Maybe he was just trying to prepare me for the fans?

Nah! That's just Nick. I called Suzanna from the side of the stage for a boost afterward, though.

I went on stage to thunderous applause, but when I started my act, after every joke a guy in the front cupped his hands around his mouth and screamed, "You suck!" After every single joke for fifteen straight minutes, "You suck!" Later on, the same guy came up to me and said, "Hey, John, big fan, big fan."

When I introduced Modi, before he could even get to the microphone, a guy screamed out at the top of his lungs, "Sit down, you fag!"

Amazing…he thought was gay too.

When Artie was on, a guy in the left bleachers kept yelling after every joke, "You fat fuck!"

You've got to love Philly. What a great time.

The touring continued, but a lot of times without Artie. Why? Because "The Reverend" Bob Levy decided to convince KC to do his own tour after seeing the success I had with mine. This infuriated me—not because I didn't think that they should make money, but because they would use my regular players. Artie, Florentine, Di Paolo, shit, even Melrose Larry Green! Bob saw the value in Artie and jumped right on it. Suddenly I was competing with my own tour! I started to branch out and book new guys—Greg Fitzsimmons, Mike Bocchetti, Doug Stanhope, Yucko the Clown, Craig Gass, Russ Meneve, Otto and George, and Gilbert Gottfried.

JETPEW

ONE TIME Jim, Di Paolo, Modi, and I were flying back from a gig in Cleveland, and Jim and I had the worst case of gas imaginable. So we started farting incessantly. We were laughing our asses off as passengers were getting winded. One fat black lady was like, "That ain't right, that just ain't right." Di Paolo repeated his usual line: "Twenty years in comedy, three HBO specials, and I got to put up with this shit?"

JAMES LOVELL (APOLLO 13 ASTRONAUT):
"WHICH ONE OF THE ASTRONAUTS HAD THE BIGGEST PENIS?"

Modi was asleep with his huge giant nose facing the air. I blasted a long, loud, pungent bit of Puerto Rican noxious gas out of my ass. I watched Modi as his huge vacuum-like nose inhaled the stench. I slowly watched his beak-like nose twitch, then his eyes slowly open in horror, and he screamed, "Oh my God, you people are animals!"

Jim and I couldn't stop laughing. The flight attendant walked over to us and told us to stop, but Jim and I couldn't control ourselves. God knows what we ate. We unloaded another beefy barrage, and finally the flight attendant got on the loud speaker and said, "Look, I know what you guys are up to, but if you don't stop, we are going to land this plane and have you removed from the aircraft."

Oh, the pain…of having to hold in what we had left until we landed.

It was one of my favorite fart stories of all time.

THE ARTIE MELTDOWN

THIS WOULD BE THE start of a gradual descent into no man's land that I experienced firsthand before any of the other *Stern* cast members. We were in Tempe headlining The Tempe Improv, and we just got finished with five sold-out shows. We were hanging in Artie's hotel room—Artie, Modi, Jim, the club owner Dan Mer (RIP, and no, Artie didn't kill him), and me. I liked Dan. After all, he convinced me to do a door deal the second time, and I nearly doubled my gross per weekend.

Anyway, we're chilling in Artie's room. I'm not sure if Modi or Jim were still there, but suddenly Artie snapped. He flew into a tirade. Why should I have a bigger room than him? He was the real star. How dare I get a bigger room? He did more time, he drew more fans. Mind you, I never requested a bigger room, but Dan probably just did that because I had worked there in the past. And fuck, man, I put the shows together, promoted them on the other radio shows in Phoenix, and attended promotional events for the radio station in exchange for plugs. Here I was getting beat up by a guy who only a year prior was begging me to put him on my tour. I was not only embarrassed that he snapped in front of Dan, but I was also fucking pissed as shit. Who the fuck was he?

"HOW DID YOU GO TO THE BATHROOM IN YOUR SPACE SUIT?"

"DID YOU EVER RUN OFF A BATCH IN SPACE?"

Keep in mind, I could give a shit about room size. I'm usually half in the bag and use the room for three things: to eat, shit, and jerk off. All I needed was a bed and a TV with a porn channel. We were supposed to have been booked first-class sitting next to each other on a flight the next morning, but I got up extra early and flew coach on an earlier flight just so I didn't have to see the son of a bitch. That week on *The Howard Stern Show*, I wouldn't even look at him. Finally, that Friday, he came up to me and was like, "John, I'm sorry about all that shit I said in Tempe. I'm really sorry."

I accepted his apology and we moved on.

Another example came after we were leaving Howard's fiftieth birthday party. It was a beautiful white-themed room with Colin Quinn doing a roast of Howard and all of us. I was asked to call Colin and give him the skinny on everyone, which I did for like an hour and a half. I even had the pleasure of helping him craft some jokes, which was an honor for me because I think Colin is brilliant. This is how down to detail I am: the place only had Heineken beer, which I refused to drink, so I paid an intern to go down to the deli and pick me up a twelve-pack of Coors Light.

Anyway, after that party, we were all going to go back to Artie's for the after-party in Hoboken. Artie insisted on driving his Mercedes there, but I refused to let him—heck, he was bombed. He started getting angry and hostile, so I took the keys from Dana, his girlfriend. I literally stood in front of the driver's side door. Artie was pissed, threatening to beat the shit out of me. I refused to let him kill himself, and we got a sober person to drive us all there in Artie's car. This behavior continued at lunches, where he would just snap. I recall after one gig, with Sam Simon, Suzanna, Artie, and Dana in the car, Artie had the limo driver pull over just so he could puke his guts out. He was falling, and falling fast.

Our friendship continued, as did our bookings. The bookings became fewer and farther between because he had his own thing going, plus he would do shows with Levy as well. Around this time I was on *I'm a Celebrity...Get Me Out of Here*, got offered *The Tonight Show*, and negotiated a deal.

One day after the show, Artie and I were sharing a cab and I asked if he would come to my place because I had to talk to him. He agreed, and we took a cab there. I had this OCD thing where I felt I had to tell Artie the news at my place so if I had any negative thought I could undo it in my own place; it was my

OCD safe haven, if you will. It was then and there that I told Artie I was leaving for *The Tonight Show*. He was happy for me but felt I should have told Howard before I signed the deal. I was like, "Look, Artie, there's no freaking way. I'm not going to tell Howard and have him fuck it up on me." If that happened, I would be out two gigs, and I couldn't afford to risk that. Artie disagreed, but he would soon find out just how right I was.

•••

MY LAST DAYS WERE approaching, and I made the most of them with my buddy Artie. I came up with the bet that he couldn't hit a fast-pitch female softball pitcher in Las Vegas. We put a grand on it. It's one of the funniest memories I have with Artie, since we made the bet on the air and the date of the softball bit was after I would be gone. Artie knew this secret information, and so he kept insisting on me putting the money down on Howard's console on the air. Howard couldn't figure it out; he was like, "Artie, why does he have to put the money down now?" Artie just kept responding, "Put the money down now, John!" Howard couldn't figure out why, but I knew. This was the last time I could ever trust Artie—after that, all bets were off. But, man, was it funny to me.

When I finally gave my two weeks' notice, I thought it was only fitting that I do my last week on the air. I felt I owed it to Howard.

Initially Howard said he was happy for me, but by the following Monday all that had changed. He claimed he went out to dinner with multimillionaire fat ass and CEO of Viacom Mel Karmazin and that Mel got into his ear, telling him how dare I leave after all Howard had done for me.

What a fucking hypocrite.

This was a guy that left WNEW after they treated him well, left Viacom for Sirius after they treated him well, and was now saying that I shouldn't have left. This was the same piece of bloated horse manure that once, after a Christmas party one year, tore up a hundred dollars into little tiny pieces right in front of me to show off how rich he was. (I collected the little pieces, thinking I could tape them back together, but that was futile.) Later, we had a Tequila-drinking contest. Boy, Mel could handle his booze. On the other hand, I ended up puking all over Manhattan and almost had the girl driving me home take me to the hospital. Anyway, that Monday morning, Howard

APPARENTLY, IT WOULDN'T HAVE MATTERED, AFTER THE RECENT ALLEGATIONS

started the rant. "How dare John not give me the opportunity to match *The Tonight Show* offer?"

Tom came down into the studio, exclaiming that maybe he could have matched it.

Puuuhhhhllllllllleeeeeeeaaaaassssssseeeeee! This cheap fuck would rather get cancer than give me a raise!

After an hour of this bullshit, I asked him, "Tom, would you have matched the $500,000-a-year salary from *The Tonight Show?*"

He said no. Case fucking closed.

But, whatever, I endured the week of abuse. I owed that to Howard and the show. Fred couldn't stand that I was leaving. Artie said, "Howard, I told John he should have told you first," which was fine by me, since that was accurate.

A few years later, Artie confessed to me that at one time he was up to try out for the host of the CBS show that followed Letterman after Kilbourne left. They were doing two-week tryouts for various hosts, and the show's producer thought Artie would be a good fit for it, and called Howard to get his blessing. Howard was furious.

He was like, "Rob, you can't steal my guy."

And just like that, Artie was out a gig.

This is a fact, and Artie told me the story.

Now think about it, folks—all that time that Howard bashed me for leaving for Jay, saying Jay or I should have told him first, all of that abuse I took—well, my fear of him fucking up the deal had been well founded. The motherfucker did it to Artie. Heck, there had been rumors that Howard had Buchwald stop sending Fred out on acting auditions because he feared he might lose him.

KURT RUSSELL (AT A POST-GRAMMY BASH):
"DON'T YOU THINK IT'S TIME THEY STOP GIVING BONNIE RAITT SO MANY FRIGGIN' AWARDS?"

ARTIE LANGE 2. NO!

AFTER I LEFT THE show, I still listened until they moved to Sirius. After all, I wasn't going to pay to hear myself get insulted. I didn't really talk to Artie that often, but we did spend a little tim e together, both in person and on the phone. One time they had a comedy gig in LA and Artie invited me, so I took one of *The Tonight Show* producers and Budd Friedman's stepson, Ross Mark. The gig was set up at some club by Michael Sponberg, who was the promotions guy at KLSX, and at the after-party we were all hanging out laughing and drinking. I had fun with the old gang—Artie, Gary, KC. At one point I went up to take a shit, and Ralph, in his ultimate infancy, took a picture of whatever shit didn't flush down the toilet. The dude is such a nitwit. "The Reverend" Bob Levy was there and kept begging me to do an interview with him for the "Win John's Job" contest.

What was he, out of his mind?

Anyway, when we were about to leave, Sponberg approaches me. Keep in mind, here was a guy I did numerous appearances for—organizing them, booking them, and appearing at them. Well, he approaches Ross and me at the exit and goes, "Are you going to pay for that?"

I said, "What? Pay for what? It was an open bar."

Then he started calling me a cheap fuck over and over again. Even after I explained to him that I was a guest of Artie's. Finally, he called me a cheap fuck for the last time. I looked him right in the eyes and said, "Michael, if you call me that one more time, I'm going to beat the living shit out of you."

He looked really scared, shut up, and walked away. What an asshole. He was trying to show what he thought was the anti–Stuttering John line drawn by Howard.

I looked at Artie, and he was like, "John, don't worry about it, I invited you here."

When *The Tonight Show* went to Las Vegas for a week of shows, it just so happened that *The Howard Stern Show* was doing a week in Las Vegas at the Hard Rock Hotel. The same week! Go figure! It was within the first two months of my employment there. This was also the first time that Executive Producer Debbie Vickers was ecstatic with her decision to hire me. Not only did I do a really successful correspondence piece called "I'll Bet on Anything," but we did a live contest after and it killed.

We were doing a shoot for *Access Hollywood* at a blackjack table at the Paris Hotel, and right in the middle of it, resident *Tonight Show* promotional hottie Carrie Simons approached me and said, "We must leave now, Debbie has to speak to you."

I was perplexed, but okay.

As I walked down to Debbie's office, James Karidis, a cameraman for the show, was eating a bagel. He looked up at me and said, "Sorry about your friend Artie."

Carrie shushed him and we walked into Debbie's office. She sat me down across from her and said, "John, I'm sorry to be the one to say this, but your friend Artie died." She told me he was found dead in his Hard Rock Hotel room.

I started crying, I lost it. I couldn't bring myself to believe it.

I grabbed the phone, called the Hard Rock, and got a hold of Mike Gange. I was like, "Mike, get up to Artie's room!" He asked why and I told him it had just been reported that Artie was dead. "I don't know if it's true, just get up to his room now!" I said.

He finally got security and Artie was alive.

It turned out it was just a prank call made by Captain Janks.

THE BETRAYAL

I STARTED APPEARING ON Artie Lange's podcast after he launched it in 2016. It was fun, at first. We would tell some old stories from *The Howard Stern Show*, reminisce on how Howard had become everything he once mocked, and talk about our glorious days on the road. Artie would take us all out to lunch after and all was good. In fact, there was one time after a late podcast that Artie and I took a ride together to The Comedy Cellar, and it was there that I told him I was up to be Anthony Cumia's cohost. My manager was in discussions with Anthony's producer, Keith Moresca, about the job. Keith told my manager that

RAUL JULIA:
"DON'T YOU THINK JOHNNY CARSON LOOKS LIKE THE CRYPTKEEPER IN *TALES FROM THE CRYPT?*"

Anthony's first choice was his former on-air mate Jim Norton, the second was Ron Bennington, and the third was me. Every time I did Anthony's show, I did really well—in fact, Keith, Anthony, Ben, and Garret all told me that I got the best reviews from fans out of any guest. So I was telling Artie all of this, and he said to me, "Why would you want to do Anthony's show? Why not just do a show with me?"

I said sure, I would love to do that.

Then he said, "Well, it's not going to be a fifty-fifty split."

I said, "All right, but why?"

"Because I'm funnier."

Whoa. I said, "Artie, whatever split you want is fine with me."

His ego was getting bigger than his belly, but the key here is Artie asking me why I would want to be Anthony Cumia's cohost…we all know what happened shortly after that. Anyway, things on Artie's podcast gradually changed from fun to ugly. I started doing his show and Artie wouldn't even be there. I'd show up and it was just his producer, Dan "The Enabler" Falato.

I'd ask Dan where Artie was, and he would say, "Oh, he had to do something in the city but he'll be right back." Then an hour later, Artie would show up, make a beeline to his bedroom, and not come out for like twenty minutes. The other guests would be there and we would start the podcast. It would be fine at first, but then suddenly it would get dark. Artie would start trashing me and the guests, trashing Howard and Gary, and then take a break and go to the bedroom. About twenty minutes later, he would begin trashing me again—even about this book, telling me that it wasn't going to be interesting. In my head I was like, "Artie, you barely even wrote your own book." Yeah, one day Artie admitted to me that he had a writer to write his book. He would start trashing my comedy, even though he hadn't seen it in seventeen years, and then in the middle of it his nose would start bleeding. I would hand him napkins while on the podcast!

Once after the show ended, Artie went back to his bedroom, and I said, "Hey, Dan, is Artie snorting coke again?"

Dan gave an ambiguous nonanswer, saying, "I have never seen any coke here." What an asshole.

Artie's bad behavior continued; he became an angry guy, trying to do Howard's act only without the charm. I started doing my own podcast with comedian Tammy Pescatelli, and that's when all hell broke loose.

RAUL WAS COOL; UNFORTUNATELY, HE DIED A FEW YEARS LATER.

We had agreed to do a podcast for both shows simultaneously. Tammy and I showed up to Artie already mid-heroin/coke-induced stupor. We started the podcast, and before we knew it, Artie started going on a rant against Larry the Cable Guy, saying that his picture didn't deserve to be on a comedy club because he was a hack. I'm like, since when did Artie become the judge of all that is comedy. In my head I'm thinking, "Artie, you're one of the biggest hacks I know."

Put it this way: when I opened for Artie, over and over again he was doing bits about a gay *Cheers* bar called Queers. Wow, Artie, what a reach there. He would actually sing the theme song. He would do black Santa jokes, saying that it would give "ho, ho, ho," a new meaning.

That's pretty hacky stuff, and yet he's goofing on Larry!

What a fucking hypocrite.

Then I start defending Larry, saying, "Artie, he's a funny character, much like Rodney was," and Artie started asking me who I thought was funnier, Larry or Jay Leno?

I was like, they're both funny, Artie.

He demanded that I choose.

I said they're both funny.

The argument continued with Tammy, who loves Larry, and Russ Meneve— I know, I'd barely heard of him either.

The other problem was that some of these comedians were afraid to battle Artie. They were all little spineless cowards. Russ, of course, agreed with Artie, and I just repeated that I loved them both and that I thought they were both funny. Artie would start reading Larry the Cable Guy jokes to prove his point and then go back to goofing on me.

That day, while I was driving over with my friend Justin, I made a conscious decision that this would be the last straw. I thought, "If Artie starts with me one more time, I'm going to hit him below he belt. I'm going to out-bully the bully."

Which, ultimately, I did.

I had hoped that if I kicked him in the nuts enough verbally, Artie would get up and bull rush me and then I could kick the living shit out of him. You have to understand, I had an agreement with Artie that he would never goof on my stand-up, since it was how I make a living, and that he would never goof on my family. So what did Artie do? He started goofing on my stand-up and bringing up my kids.

JOHNNIE COCHRAN:

So I unleashed on him, Stuttering John style.

I said, "Hey, Artie, how did that bleach taste?"

Artie shut up. *He* started stuttering.

Then I said, "Hey, Artie, how many times did you stab yourself? Eight? Or was it nine?"

He started to pull back.

I hit him with another one. "Artie, you realize the only reason you are alive is because your mother was bringing you chicken parmigiana so that you could feed your fat ass and found you bleeding in your bed."

He didn't know what to do. Then I felt bad, started easing up. I said, "Look, Artie, stop trying to kill yourself, stop blaming yourself for your father's death. It's not your fault. You're a talented, funny guy with lots of money and fans."

After the show, I apologized and asked the Enabler to edit that whole evil rant of mine out. He grimaced. "Ah, man, you know how much work that's going to be?" So now I felt even guiltier. Finally, after leaving, I texted Dan the Enabler and told him that if he didn't want to edit it out, then don't. Which he didn't.

So now, every time Artie gets mad about it, I ask myself: If it was that damaging to his family and himself, then why didn't he get lazy-ass Dan to edit it out? Fuck, it's not my fault he's useless. Artie would go on in later shows to say that I couldn't outwit him. Which is bullshit; it's just that he's a loud, heroin-induced bully with his minions around to agree with him.

Later on, things calmed down, and Artie and I made up. He started sending me these crazy texts, saying things like, "John, I'm a better actor than you," "I'm a better comedian," "I'm a better writer," and then a few texts later, "John, I love you man, I'm sorry." I showed this twisted set of texts to Doug Goodstein just so he could see how crazy Artie had become. Doug's jaw dropped. Artie called me, apologized, and we made up. Artie even offered to put me on some of his gigs.

Artie was playing Club Nokia and asked me to open up for him. There were other comics there, and I was hanging out with Artie in his dressing room. Artie said, "Are they paying you?" and I said, "Yeah, but not very much," and Artie said, "I'll send you more." But Artie had become very good at making false promises. For instance, when I first did Artie's podcast, I asked him if I could cohost and/or write. After my first appearance, Artie promised me that if he doubled his listeners, he would give me the job. Well, after Radar Online did a story about that show, Artie called me to tell me that he had quadrupled his subscribers, but he never did give me that job.

Anyway, back at Club Nokia, we were in his dressing room, and I told him, "Look, Artie, I know that I'm going to get booed before I can even get to the mike by some disgruntled Stern fans." He was like, "No, man, people love you, don't worry."

Well, the place was sold out, and the guy before me announced my name. Ninety-nine percent of the people applauded, but eight Mexican dudes in the bleacher seats started unleashing a torrent of boos and didn't stop through my whole fifteen-minute set. It was just tons of boos mixed with a few *you sucks*. It was just like the night I lost my virginity.

I tried to be nice at first, joked that "I didn't know my family was coming." Then I went with politeness and said, "Guys, come on, people paid good money to see the show, relax." Finally, I got pissed and said, "I'll tell you what, why don't you booers up there come down on the stage and I'll beat your fucking asses in like I did Crazy Cabbie."

The place cheered, but I left the stage still pissed. I wanted to go up to the bleachers to beat the shit out of every one of them, but the Enabler said, "Don't you dare," and I didn't want to screw it up for Artie.

Around this time, I just happened to be on the phone with Artie complaining about some legal fees concerning my divorce. I was going through a re-fi on my house to lower the rates and was really upset about it. Artie said, "John, do you want me to send you two grand to pay for the lawyer?"

I said, "Really? That's really generous, Artie. You don't have to, though."

He said, "Just let me send you the money, you don't even have to pay me back, and I promise I'll never say anything about it."

I said sure. Shit, no hassles with my stocks and 401k, that's great. And I had every intention of paying him back. Then I announced my run for senator and Artie started trashing me nonstop. The truth is, initially, I did it as a goof after Trump won. I was pissed and figured heck, if a reality star can become president, then why not a stuttering senator?

The Artie onslaught continued with each guest—first with Doug Stanhope, then with Jackie, and then with Grillo, which is when that dimwit decided to goof on my kids. I couldn't believe Artie wouldn't have edited that out.

LARRY THOMAS (THE "SOUP NAZI" ACTOR FROM SEINFELD):

It continued with Jim Florentine and Gilbert Gottfried. Just nonstop abuse from what I thought was a good friend and someone I loved. Artie was relentless. Strung out, nasally, gravelly, and just plain mean. I made it a point the next time that I went to New York, I was going to go down to the Comedy Cellar and punch him in the face.

That opportunity arose when I was in Manhattan with my brother-in-law, Doug. I suggested we go to the Comedy Cellar. I knew what I was going to do if I saw Artie: I'd either punch him or hug him, all pivoting on the first words he said to me. If it were an apology, then a hug. Anything less—whack!

When I got there, I saw Jim Norton and his new Art Garfunkel–looking cohost Sam sitting with the forever-disturbed Anthony Cumia. Jim and Sam left, and I hung out with Anthony for a little while. I told Anthony what I was going to do but Artie never showed. Anthony and I went downstairs, where Ray Romano was performing. (Man, he was really good.) It was finally getting late and I was beat, so my brother-in-law and I left. Anthony did his show, and he said Artie finally showed up fifteen minutes after I had left.

He dodged a bullet. I mean, I probably wouldn't have punched him, considering that if I hit him in the nose it would probably explode and he would die. Although knowing Artie and his death wish, he might have enjoyed that.

Finally Artie called me once again to apologize after we went through a Twitter war. We had exchanged insults back and forth for days or maybe weeks. Then one day I posted a picture of my beautiful daughter Lily Belle and I on her birthday or at an award ceremony for her, and Artie saw it and decided to change his tune. He started tweeting niceties, then texted me, saying he didn't want to be the guy that Stuttering John tells his kids he hates. He finally called me and apologized for everything.

This became the typical Artie: one day he's your best friend, and the next day he's a complete asshole. His personality with heroin was like a box of chocolates; you never knew which one you were going to get. He was finally arrested in his parking garage for heroin possession.

Later on, Artie got offered the cohosting position with Anthony Cumia. What a hypocrite. They called me and had me on the air and I pretended not to care. It was sad for me, not only because I didn't get the job but because this also meant that Artie's hatred and anger would soon would soon carry over to Anthony's show, which would ultimately kill any desire for me to do that show ever again.

They asked me to do the show live, and since I had a show on Long Island to promote, I did it, and regretted every minute of it.

Artie arrived his usual half an hour late, and man, did he look bad. I shook his hand and it was covered in Vaseline. I asked him why, and he said that it was because he had dry skin—which Anthony still believes. I was like, yeah, right. The Vaseline was all over his nose, which I assumed was to prevent his nose from bleeding. Yet during the show, his nose started bleeding anyway, and I asked the staff to hand him tissues. Artie had four slits in each one of his knuckles, which I had heard was what heroin addicts do to shoot it into their knuckles. Who knows? Artie was a mess and was falling apart. A few minutes into the show, Artie, Anthony, and some unknown comedian started goofing on me. Artie was relentless, and his hateful cancer of a mood had spread to Anthony. I finally left, saying that I wanted to watch football with my brother. Which was true, plus they'd overbooked the show.

The following night, Anthony came to my show at Governors Brokerage in Bellmore, Long Island. He showed up an hour early with a girl that looked like he picked her up from a junior high playground. I did my set and did really well. My family and friends were there, and Anthony laughed his ass off. I heard him and saw him and so did my brother, who recognized his irritating cackle. The next night Anthony and Artie spent an hour trashing me and my stand-up. How uninteresting is their show if almost every one is dedicated to trashing me? Anthony said the parking lot was empty. Yeah, pock-face, that's because you showed up an hour early!

Artie started chiming in and I turned it off.

I sent a text to Keith Moresca saying that I was upset Anthony would lie and not give an honest assessment of my show. The next day they trashed me again, and another ridiculous Twitter war began, culminating in the ex-con Cumia goofing on my underage kid and posting a picture of her. I heard that Artie stood up for me and told Anthony he would leave the studio if he bashed my kid. Wow—Artie still had a little bit of a heart. My kids got abused through social media, and I even had to call a lawyer and get a cease and desist drawn up. Even a heroin-addicted Artie knows you don't mess with people's kids. Shit, even the mob knows that.

Artie continued snorting narcotics and eventually blew a hole through his nose, with pieces falling into his lungs, and underwent emergency surgery.

JOEY ADAMS (NOW DECEASED HUSBAND OF GOSSIP COLUMNIST CINDY ADAMS):
"WHEN WAS THE LAST TIME YOU SAW HALLEY'S COMET?"

A short time later, he went to the hospital again for an unknown reason. A.J. Benza, reporting for Radar Online at the time, contacted me, telling me that Artie had emergency heart surgery, so I tweeted that people should pray for him, as I thoroughly believe in the power of prayer.

Somehow, A.J. got the story wrong, and Artie started another Twitter rant bashing me. I guess he had low blood sugar or something.

He canceled another gig in Akron, Ohio, and screwed the venue promoter. This seemed to be an ongoing occurrence, as I soon learned, when Artie asked me to book a show with us together in Boston as kind of a reunion show. My agent tried, but the promoter said he would never book Artie again after he was a no-show at Foxwoods.

Say what you want about my stand-up, but at least I'm professional enough to show up.

As I'm writing this book, Artie was arrested once again for heroin possession and was flown to rehab. The photos accompanying the story all show Artie with his nose blown up ten times the size of Karl Malden's. All I can say now is that I pray for Artie and hope he has a healthy recovery.

ROBIN QUIVERS: FRIEND...UNLESS HOWARD IS INVOLVED

THE FIRST TIME I met Robin was as she limped into the studio on crutches. She'd broken her leg somehow, probably from bending down to kiss Howard's ass. I immediately got asked to park Robin's car—a thing I hated since it took me off my other, more important duties, like labeling the cassettes for the show and securing where Gary's blinders were when he needed to take a nap. In the middle of winter, I'd have to drive her Saab down three avenues to her parking garage and then run back to the studio to make sure everything was ready before the show began. But I never complained. I knew from past experience to never complain at a job, that it was a bad precedent to set. Plus, I was working on my favorite radio show of all time!

I started to joke around with Robin and we became fast friends. We would go out to lunch together, go to the movies, goof on Jackie and Gary. It was kismet. When the Channel 9 show began, Robin would drive me to the studio

I REALLY DIDN'T WANT TO DO THIS, BECAUSE JOEY WAS SO OLD IT LOOKED LIKE HE WAS GOING TO CROAK IN TEN MINUTES. I WAS EGGED ON BY KEVIN, SO I DID IT, BUT I FELT BAD AFTERWARD.

in Secaucus. We would talk and talk, so much so that the producer Dan Forman was convinced Robin and I were having an affair. We do have a disagreement on one thing, however: When Robin dropped me off at the subway station, we kissed goodbye. It was on the lips, but I still maintain that Robin slipped me a little bit of her tongue. I brought it up on the air, but she emphatically denied it. But I don't know, I'm pretty sure I felt her tongue enter my mouth. Later on, after I left, she started schtupping Jim Florentine, so maybe she secretly had a thing for longhaired, funny white guys.

I would do odd favors for Robin, one of which was cat-sitting her cats at her apartment in Queens. I'd go there once a day and be nervous as hell that I'd screw something up, like let the cat out or something. I even gave the bastards Poland Spring bottled water for fear that Robin would kill me if I gave them tap water.

I would tease Robin periodically on the air, goofing on her many diets, cleanses, and hobbies. When she was on the Atkins one, I would order her hamburgers and she would only eat the meat, and I would tell Howard on the air that Robin's wolfing down a bunch of burgers. It was all in good fun, and God knows she teased me. She also took singing lessons with my vocal instructor, Katie Agresta, and she sang on my album. Scott Einziger iso'd her vocals, and Fred would play it on the air constantly. It was embarrassing, and of course she hated me for it. Our on-air battles culminated with her saying that she wanted to take a crap in my face!

She was mad at me because I turned down a Heineken trip to Amsterdam because my wife didn't want to fly. The Heineken people had met with me and Baba Booey, Tom Chiusano, and a few salesmen from K-Rock. They wanted us to go to Amsterdam, which seemed cool at the time. I was already a little irritated with them because when I told them that I did all of the Heineken commercials on the air with Howard, they had no idea. I was like, *shit, man, I'm your Howard fucking Stern spokesperson and you have no idea?!*

Fuck those guys, and the truth is, I barely drank Heineken—I was an Amstel Light guy.

Anyway, I finally turned the trip down because my wife was pregnant and I think it was right after 9/11. Gary went to tell them the bad news, and they looked at Gary and said, "Fuck John." Gary reveled in telling me they said this, and I have not had a Heineken since. Fuck those corporate assholes. So, because

MARIO CUOMO (FORMER GOVERNOR OF NEW YORK):

I wasn't going to go, they asked Robin and she went and hated every minute of it. She did a tirade on me on the air. I was like, "Shit, I didn't force you to go," but sometimes, reasoning with a menopausal woman like Robin is a futile task. So I just laughed it off.

Robin and I maintained our friendship until my last week on the show. She saved her best betrayal of me for last. She told Howard that more and more people would soon leave if he kept paying them shit. She said, "Howard, you better look over your shoulder, because people are going to leave." She even confided in me on a phone call that she might leave and do her own thing. Then she about-faced it on the air. About four years after I left, she came to LA and called me, we had dinner, and I confronted her about it. She said she'd been between a rock and a hard place and that she was friends with both of us, but the show was where her bread was buttered. I understood, somewhat, but I could have used her support at that time.

About eight years after that, she called me. I guess she had become a part of this hallmark group where you have to apologize for any wrong that you had done to someone, so she called me to apologize. She had called Jackie, Grillo, and KC as well, but I said there was nothing I was upset about. I felt no animosity, and we still exchange occasional texts to this day.

BACK ON *THE STERN SHOW*

Every Thursday we would have a creative meeting, and this was when I'd started to notice some non–Howard-like stuff going on. Gary had hired his new protégé, KC Armstrong, to help him produce the show. KC had a radio show in college that Gary liked and he was Gary's butt boy. He was an ex-football jock with a whole host of his own problems and he would pitch these segments in the creative meeting, and I slowly realized what was going on: KC was pitching these phony bits that would illicit angry calls.

The whole cool thing about Howard's show was that everything was real. Why would he start doing phony shit? He would have fake doctors on as guests, who would say they're performing plastic surgery on kids just to get the audience angry. It was sensationalism at its worst. It was like something a hack morning zoo would do. I then had to field the calls from these people, and the whole thing was just a bit boring to me.

It was like Howard was believing what KC thought was cool. Then again, Howard believed what Ralph suggested, so there's that. I mean, really, Ralph got hired as a makeup/wardrobe guy after sending in a fan letter. The guys from E! and I would laugh in the control room at Howard's dumb outfits. One day Ralph had him in a Charlie Brown shirt. We were on the floor laughing. The best was Howard's picture in *Private Parts*, where a fifty-year-old Howard was dressed like Kurt Cobain. At that same shoot, Ralph was goofing on me because I had a blue suit on with brown shoes. He said they didn't match.

What a dummy. Half the news guys in New York were wearing that. Howard finally had the wherewithal to take Ralph off of hair and makeup and hire a professional.

Anyway, this new bunch of phony bits from KC brought the show's integrity down a notch. Howard had hired a monologue writer to write him monologue jokes, so around seven o'clock each morning, Howard would read this page of jokes and try and make it seem like he was just speaking off the cuff. It was so completely embarrassing. Artie and I would sit there uncomfortably, and even Robin had a hard time laughing through the embarrassment.

I'M A CELEBRITY...GET ME OUT OF HERE! LITERALLY!

A TALENT BOOKER FOR a new show called *I'm a Celebrity...Get Me Out of Here!* faxed my agent an offer to have me be a contestant on the show. What an opportunity. Over $100,000 for two weeks in a rainforest in Australia. How could I turn it down? It was more than I was making at *Stern* for a whole year. I called Howard to ask him for permission. He asked me to wait because he thought it might be a show that he and Adam Corolla were doing and he wanted to make sure they weren't stealing his idea. I waited nervously, thinking he would say no. Finally, after about a week, he gave me the okay. I told Gary it would be over in two weeks, maybe sooner if I got voted off, but it might be more than that if I actually lasted, and I told my program director, Steven Kingston, the same thing.

Remember that—it'll become important later on.

DAVID DINKINS:

I flew to California and met my agent, Jason Burns, at the airport. We had a few drinks before I departed first-class to Australia. I saw Melissa Rivers, another show contestant, on the plane, although I didn't speak to her since Deena Katz, the show's producer, told me not to speak to the other contestants before the show.

I had a photo op with all of the other contestants when I arrived in Australia. It was me, Bruce Jenner, Melissa Rivers, Alana Stewart, Nikki Ziering, Maria Conchita Alonso Escuela Bonita and other random Spanish words I can think of. The chick had like ten names. There was also Chris Judd, Tyson Beckford, Robin Leach, and Downtown Julie Brown. I was having a severe panic attack, as you can tell by the pictures. I looked extremely ill.

We started the show. I started helping everyone, was nice to the other contestants, and the producers were shocked. They wanted that asshole from *The Howard Stern Show*. They didn't know I was really just a nice guy—a wiseass, sure, but ultimately a nice guy.

I did ask the pertinent questions, but not in a confrontational way. I asked Melissa Rivers if it was tough for her to live in her mom's shadow, and more importantly, if her breasts were real. She said yes and offered to show them to me if I brought back food by winning a challenge.

I said, "No, thank you." Hey, I'm a gentleman!

She said it was hard for her to live in Joan's shadow.

I asked Bruce Jenner why he got that bad nose job, and he said he never liked his long nose. Little did I know that Bruce always secretly identified as a woman. I'm telling you, the Caitlyn news was shocking to me. We both lived in Calabasas, and we hung out after the show. This guy was the most staunch, "Shoot 'em up, ask questions later" kind of conservative Republican.

They had a shrink shack in the jungle with a licensed psychologist; Alana Stewart went there like five times a day!

I never complained even though it rained on us every day. The only dry thing I had left was my underwear. (Okay, partially dry. I do have hemorrhoids, you know.) The other celebs would bitch and moan, but not me. Hey, I went camping all my life—what are a few raindrops for a hundred grand? On the other hand, Tyson would be screaming at the camera, "Get me my fucking agent!" and at one point Melissa Rivers stood up on her cot and screamed, "Where is my fucking migraine medication!"

I thought for sure after that tirade she would lose, but somehow, they never aired that. I wonder why. The power of Joan, maybe? I guess that shadow doesn't always suck.

I know that when Bruce and I were given some wine, he made a racist comment about Tyson Beckford after Tyson whined about taking out the garbage or something. Bruce was like, "Well, you know how those people are." Kris Jenner was home watching the live feed, and she was like, "Holy shit, Bruce, shut the fuck up, we're going to lose half of our friends!" So she called and they didn't air it.

Bruce was so oblivious to things. For instance, Chris Judd was on there crying about his break-up with Jennifer Lopez after she left him for Ben Affleck, and the next day Bruce was telling all of us how handsome his son Brody was and that he looked just like Ben Affleck! Julie, Melissa, and Chris were stunned.

I was playing for my friend Kevin Kalinowski's charity: The Spinal Cord Society. My friend Kevin had become a quadriplegic after a pole-vaulting accident at Plainedge High School. The other celebrities had huge charities, like Make-A-Wish, getting votes by phone to keep them on the show. I would pray while lying on the cot that Jay Leno would be goofing on the show and that one day, I could be a guest on his show. That was my dream. I've always felt that if you got to be a guest on *The Tonight Show*, you made it somehow.

Well, despite the small charity I was playing for and the fact that Joan Rivers was on every show asking people to vote for her daughter, I made it to the very end. When I walked off, my wife greeted me and told me she had a surprise for me—I was booked on *The Tonight Show* the next day.

Holy fuck! I got chills down my spine.

My excitement didn't last too long, though, because when I got to my room at the hotel, I called *The Howard Stern Show* and got lambasted on air by Howard for not letting them know I'd be gone that long. I did tell Gary, but in his ass-covering way, he said I never told him. Steve Kingston acknowledged that I did tell him it would be over two weeks if they kept voting me through, but whatever, it was just another example of Gary covering his ass. As the great Joey Ramone once said, "Welcome to my nightmare."

Personally, I think Howard was madder that I came across as a nice guy, and that somewhere deep down he wished people would see him in that way. He tried to do that eventually with *America's Got Talent*.

KIRK DOUGLAS:
"WHEN YOU WORKED WITH FARRAH FAWCETT, DID YOU SEE HER NAKED?"

Fuck it. I tried calling him twice to get permission to do *The Tonight Show* so as to not piss him off, but he never called me back. I flew to LA, wrote the jokes in the town car on the way there, and had a great segment with Jay. So much so that, immediately after the show, the executive producer, Debbie Vickers, and the head writer, Joe Medeiros, offered me a correspondent job.

Everything just worked perfectly. I was at the right place, at the right time, doing the right thing. This was a dream come true.

I remember when I asked Don Fuckwald to book me on *Letterman* and he asked me what I was going to do. What am I going to do, Don? Kill it, that's what I'm going to do, you bald motherfucker.

I would have loved to see his stupid face when I became the announcer on *The Tonight Show*.

I was so proud of myself, and I suddenly didn't give a fuck what Howard was going to say to me when I got back. I knew he was just jealous of how well I did on the reality show. But what was I going to do? Was it my fault that Da Da Dummy couldn't remember what I told him? Steve Kingston clearly could.

After the taping of *The Tonight Show,* we all went back to my hotel to watch it. Gary happened to be in LA at the time, so he came. I asked him if I could be a correspondent for the show, and he said Howard would never let me do it.

So Suzanna, Downtown Julie Brown, her husband, Gary, and I were in the hotel that NBC put me up in to watch *The Tonight Show*—and the hotel didn't get NBC! We ended up driving all over town to find a place and landed at a bar where I got the bartender to tune the television to NBC and we watched the show there, but we could only read the subtitles because they couldn't put the volume on!

Anyway, I had to give *The Tonight Show* an answer, and after much deliberation and after what Gary had said, I was forced to turn it down. A few months later, they asked me again. (Little did I know that the segment producer, Dave Berg, wanted me to be the next Ed McMahon.)

So I went to Robin Quivers to ask her for advice. She told me that I wasn't a kid anymore and to set up a meeting with Howard's assistant, Laura, like an adult. So I did. A few days later, on the air, Howard said that he knew I was trying to meet with him but that he didn't want to meet with me, that he couldn't care less about my career or me.

ALL HE KEPT SAYING TO ME WAS, "WHAT ARE YOU SAYING?" THIS ALSO BECAME A SOUND BITE FOR FRED.

I went back to Robin, and she said I should try again. I did. I called Laura, and a few days later Howard said the same thing on the air, something like, "John, I know you're trying to meet with me, but I don't give a shit about you or your career, do whatever you want, I don't care."

I went back to Robin. She said, "Well, John, now you're on your own. Do what you got to do."

I turned it down yet again. I couldn't believe I was turning down a TV gig on *The Tonight Show* for a guy that called me a loser on a regular basis.

Back at home, Suzanna agreed to give me one more kid. After all, I'm Puerto Rican, I wanted ten. Suzanna was Jewish, and she said she would have three at the most. So we went to this spinning-the-sperm place to help the odds of having another boy. I guess they spin the sperm to ensure that the male sperm is more than the female sperm. It cost me like $3,000. I would go home when Suzanna was ovulating, put my arm around her, and jerk off into a lab cup. It was so romantic. Then the doctor would use a turkey baster thing to insert my sperm into her vagina. It didn't work the first time, so I shelled out more money, and the second time it took.

A few days later, we found out we were having yet another girl.

I took Suzanna to the Astro Diner, and we commiserated. Well, she was fine with it, but I was disappointed. For like two days, I thought that my dream of having a son named Oscar had been washed away. Finally, though, I embraced it.

What did it matter? Right?

So we picked the name Sadie, which I loved, and the middle name Rita, after my Danish aunt who had passed away due to colon cancer, and we were set. We started preparing the room for her arrival. I was very happy again to be having another kid.

A few weeks later, I was working on some editing and I got a call from Suzanna telling me that Sadie wasn't moving, that she thought she'd lost the baby. I hurried out of the studio and planned to meet Suzanna at NYU to make sure she was right, or hopefully wasn't. It was rush hour so I couldn't find a cab, so I got on a bus. I remember sitting in the front of the bus and bawling my eyes out uncontrollably.

I felt guilty over my disappointment when I first heard that I was having another girl, and then a cliché entered my mind. When people ask you if you want a girl or a boy, the thing to say is that you just want a healthy baby.

MAGIC JOHNSON:

Well, now I had experienced it firsthand. When I got to NYU with tears in my eyes, we checked with the doctor, and as he did the sonogram, we saw the dead, lifeless baby in her womb. An image that haunted me for years. Then we had to go to another uptown hospital to have Sadie removed. I hugged a crying Suzanna and consoled her. I have never cried so hard in my life.

•••

A FEW MONTHS LATER, my family and I were in LA because I was meeting with agents and managers. Debbie Vickers's assistant, Suzy, called me and asked me to come by Debbie's office.

Little did I know that Debbie was about to make me an offer I couldn't refuse.

I met with her in her office and we hit it off immediately. She told me that the one time that she listened to *Stern* she heard me saying that I cried over a scene in Jennifer Lopez's *Maid in Manhattan*. She said she cried over that scene too, and immediately we were kindred spirits. What a beautiful and amazing woman. I immediately had a secret crush on her. She said they really loved my personality on *I'm a Celebrity...Get Me Out of Here!*, and how would I like to be the new announcer on *The Tonight Show*?

I was flabbergasted, to say the least. It was like a message from God. I called my wife, and she was so happy because she knew how much I wanted to leave *Stern*.

They said they would soon set up a correspondent audition and a time for me to go into their announcer's booth to prove I wouldn't stutter when I announced.

I went home thrilled that I might have found my ticket out.

Could I possibly be free?

Wait, John, not so fast.

I still had to prove myself worthy as a correspondent. I called in sick one day and flew to LA for the audition. They took me to Hollywood Boulevard and Joe Medeiros, the head writer at the time, said, "Do what you can." I was so nervous that I wouldn't do well, but it turned out I did.

Then I got the news that Rick Ludwin, one of the NBC executives, was an avid Howard Stern fan and he was dead set against the idea of me being the announcer. My friend and agent, Jason Burns, told me, "John, be proactive. Record some announcing demos," and so I went into Scott the Engineer's studio. I told him I was up for some big truck-racing announcer gig and asked him if he could please record some announcements from both *The Tonight Show* and *Letterman* for me. It was so fucking hard, considering that I was recording just down the hall from Howard. I did like ten different versions, always checking the door, with all different celebrities—hence the "Niggarless Cage" and "Jennifa Aniston," which would later become popular thanks to Scott the Engineer. Yes, he betrayed me. I asked him to erase the tapes, but he didn't. He put them in the computer's trash bin but then retrieved them when I left.

He wasn't as stupid as I thought.

I can't say I blame him, considering all the practical jokes I played on him in the past. But in all honesty, I did help him make money. It was me that came up with his push-up contest where he made like $20,000, but whatever. We edited the best tapes and I sent them along to *The Tonight Show*.

They loved it!

I figured I was in. After all, I was their number-one choice to replace Edd Hall. But wait, there's more! It wasn't going to be so easy...

The Tonight Show still had some concerns that I would stutter while announcing. My agent told Debbie that much like Carly Simon and Mel Tillis, who don't stutter when they sing, I would not stutter while announcing, that it was virtually impossible as my vocal cords were moving in rhythm, and my lips just wouldn't lock up. I was out there another time doing a weekend at the Irvine Improv, and Debbie asked me to come in to prove that I could announce in their booth without stuttering. She, Joe Medeiros, and the show's audio engineer Patrick Smith were there, and they gave me a bunch of crap to announce.

I did all of them effectively, no stutter.

A few weeks later, they flew me in to meet with Jay. After all, he had to okay the deal, and he had to see if he could get along with me. I met him at *The Tonight Show* in their private screening room to watch *Kill Bill 2* with Joe Medeiros and his wife, Justine. We watched the movie and then had dinner at Dan Tana's, a famous LA Italian joint. I was nervous as shit to make a good impression, but we had a blast. We went out for ice cream after dinner and then

DAVID LETTERMAN:

"WHEN YOU KISS A GIRL, DOES HER TONGUE EVER GET CAUGHT IN THAT BIG SPACE?"

"IS YOUR MOTHER ON PROZAC OR IS SHE ALWAYS SMILING LIKE THAT?"

went back to his house to watch TV. We watched *The Iron Chef*. We goofed and joked about it while Jay smoked a pipe.

Shit, I didn't know he smoked. I was like, "Well, if he's smoking, can I light up a cig?" I asked Joe, and he said no.

The night was perfect. Jay and I hit it off, and I thought I was in. Little did I know that there was a bigger obstacle that had to be overcome before this could happen. Rick Ludwin was still making a lot of noise behind the scenes. He was continuing to argue that I would discredit the franchise, and I heard from Joe Medeiros that he was killing the deal.

I was devastated, but what could I do?

My dream was slipping away.

Again, I decided to be proactive. I edited together a reel of my best moments from *I'm a Celebrity...Get Me Out of Here!* and sent them in. Weeks went by. Every once in a while I'd call Joe, and he said it didn't look good but that it wasn't a completely dead deal. Eventually, Joe told me they had one last try. Jay was going to call Rick and say this is the guy he wanted. I waited in nervous anticipation. I remember somebody got me a massage as a gift for my birthday or something, so I decided to use it to ease my tensions. It was a gloomy, rainy day in Manhattan. I got the massage, obsessing over the thought that my chances were dead, but I convinced myself to not give up hope. After I left, I felt numb.

I took to the streets of the Village in my Birkenstocks, looking for a church. I wanted to pray. Heck, God had listened to me on numerous occasions in the past—why not now? It was dusk and beginning to get dark, and I couldn't find an open church. I walked all around the Village, desperate. I wanted this job so bad. After all, this was my ticket out. I knocked on church doors but got no answer.

I finally remembered the glorious church where I met my wife in *Tony n' Tina's Wedding*. The gate was locked, but I literally stuck my head through the rungs and prayed, "Dear God, please give me this break. Please, if there's anything You can do, please hear me now."

I went home, hugged my wife, and went to bed, knowing that I had to get up at five o'clock to start my workday.

Miraculously, I got a call from Joe the next day. Apparently, Jay called Rick and Rick acquiesced.

"DO YOU WEAR WHITE SOCKS EVEN WITH A TUXEDO?"

"DO YOU KNOW THAT YOUR HAIR LOOKS LIKE A MAP OF ITALY?"

I was in!

Thank you, God! Thank you, Jay! Thank you, Debbie! Thank you, Joe! Thank you, Dave Berg! Thank you, Deena Katz! Thank you, Suzanna! Thank you, Knight! Thank you, Lily Belle! Thank you, my future son Oscar! Thank you, Howard! Thank you, Mom and Dad! Thank you, Universe!

And now for the best part: to tell Tom Chiusano I was done.

But that moment would take time. There were still negotiations to tackle, and I had to be on the show for a while longer. Knowing that I had my ticket out, I endured. Keep in mind that Tom was a guy who, while he had cancer and stood a very good chance of dying of it, told me, after I'd asked him for a raise after ten years on the job, "John, I'll die of cancer before I give you fifty grand a year." This was a guy that, in lieu of a raise, gave me and my family health insurance, but then a few months later the company's health insurance policy changed and he took it away from me. I pleaded with him in his office, saying that it was my part of my deal.

He said that if he did it for me, he'd have to do it for everybody.

Bullshit!

Once the deal was finally in place, I signed the contract after an appearance in Philly. I wanted to tell Howard in person the next day. We were all supposed to go to Atlantic City that weekend, though Suzanna and I passed on Howard's offer to fly in his helicopter. If, God forbid, he had a negative reaction to the news, he might not want us to even go, so why not give the ride to somebody else? I was on the way to Howard's condo, but my wife was on the phone with Beth, and I said, "Let me talk to him."

I told him, and initially he was happy for me. He was like, "Of course, let's celebrate in Atlantic City."

But within minutes of our arrival, Beth informed my wife that although Howard wasn't mad at me, he was really pissed at Jay because he thought Jay should have told him. Truth is, Jay offered to call him when I was in his office months before, but I said no. I said it should come from me. After fifteen years and having given me my start, he should hear it from me first.

We had fun in Atlantic City, but the next two weeks…

We were off the first week, so that Monday I went in to tell Tom Chiusano. I walked into his office and sat down in front of his desk. I told him I was giving my two weeks' notice.

JACK NICHOLSON:
"SINCE YOUR SISTER IS REALLY YOUR MOTHER, DO YOU SEND HER A MOTHER'S DAY CARD?"

He asked why, and I told him I was going to be the new announcer on *The Tonight Show*. He leaned over toward me in his chair and said, "No way."

I said, "Yes, Tom," and I thought to myself, *Yes way, yes fucking way— I'm leaving your miserable salary and finding a better life for myself and my family. No more gigs every weekend to make enough money to live in Manhattan and raise my family. Heck, my second child barely knows me because I'm away so much trying to make money to pay the bills.*

I recalled being in Tom's office once and asking for a raise. The program director said, "Look, John, nobody else wants you."

Well, I guess he was wrong.

That weekend I was performing at the Tempe Improv, doing stand-up. I was not looking forward to the following week of Howard bashing me, though Robin called my wife, assuring her that I was doing the right thing. She then talked to me on the phone, and I remember it like it was yesterday. I was in my Tempe hotel room and she was like, "John, you're doing the right thing, Howard doesn't pay anybody here. I always tell him to look over his shoulder because more and more people are going to leave. I've been also thinking about doing my own thing, and you're doing the right thing for you and your family."

I felt so much better.

Cut to Monday morning, when she says, "Howard, I can't believe he's leaving!"

I was shocked and betrayed, and the next week would be brutal. I took the hits on the air. Howard had hung out with Mel Karmazin that Sunday before the Monday morning show and Mel told him I was wrong for leaving after all Howard had done for me. That became Howard's mantra.

Thanks, Mel. Now go back into your billion-dollar mansion and laugh at the crappy salaries you paid us working slobs all this time.

Plain and simple, I am grateful to Howard for giving me my start, but if you do a good job, give him plenty of airtime—doesn't it at all even out? At what point does it become both of us helping each other? Adam Sandler may owe Lorne Michaels for putting him on *SNL,* but didn't he provide a good service to Lorne? Doesn't that balance out at some point? And I can see him being mad if I was making millions, but after fifteen years of loyal service, my radio salary was only $85,000.

I don't blame Howard for my pay—I really don't—and the fact of the matter is that if I wanted to leave because of my bad salary, I could've. But I decided

JACK ANGRILY RESPONDED, "NO."
TRUTH IS, I KNOW A GIRL WHO SLEPT WITH JACK, AND SHE CLAIMS HE CALLS HIS PENIS "LITTLE STEVIE."

to stay and make money in other ways. And the truth is, the papers had it dead wrong. I think my first year at *The Tonight Show* I made $250,000, but I wanted to leave *The Howard Stern Show* so badly that I would've taken half. Shit, I probably would've taken $50,000!

I got beaten up in the studio by everyone, with the exception of Artie. Fred played the announcements that Scott had given to him and Howard just beat me up. Robin took Howard's side, and Gary and Ralph all joined in. Later on, my voice coach Marice Tobias, who I got to help me with the announcing gig, told me something I will never forget. She said that when you put a bunch of crabs in a bucket, eventually one of them will try and get out. The other ones then grab the fleeing crab and pull it back in. How does that equate? Well, because they're jealous that I'm getting out and they're not, and what does it say about them? Why hadn't they created an opportunity to leave?

On my last day, the most honest person affiliated with the show was, believe it or not, Mary Dell'Abate. Gary had her on speakerphone and she said, "Congratulations, John—we are so jealous."

I love Mary. Gary couldn't say it, but Mary could.

She knew how hard it was to take the verbal abuse from Howard. Gary had lamented about it to me, so I'm sure he lamented about it to her. I also knew that there was a time when Fred couldn't take it and wanted to leave too. In fact, Alison, his wife, told me she had talked him out of it.

Robin decided to throw a going-away party for me. I refused to go. She called me and said, "Why aren't you going?" I said, "Robin, you stabbed in the fucking back!" She said, "John, get over it, there are people from the show who want to see you off." So I went, but Howard didn't show.

That night I was on my way to do *Tough Crowd*, Colin Quinn's show, before I left for LA. I called Howard to see if he was really mad at me. It was the most honest and humble Howard I had ever spoken to. He said something like, "John, I'm not mad at you, and you know what, maybe I should've had you in the studio full-time. Maybe I should have put you in the Jackie chair, and maybe things would have been different."

Truth is, they would've been. But in hindsight, I'm glad I left when I did, having heard what the show has become.

CLAUDIA SCHIFFER:

YOKO TURKO

HOWARD AND ROBIN WERE always easily falling for these health-and-betterment scams. Well, Howard read some book called *Getting Things Done* written by Marci Turk and fell for it hook, line, and sinker. He hired her immediately. She became Baba Booey's boss and ran the show, if not the entire network. I've heard that at this point, Howard walks down his own hallway. The hallway must be cleared out and free from staff or guests, and nobody is allowed to approach Howard or try to talk to him while he exits the building.

What the fuck has happened to Howard?

They fired Jackie from his "Joke Hunt" show a few weeks before Christmas and didn't even invite him to the Christmas party. The E! guys found out they were fired by Howard on the air. They knew it was coming, but Howard gave them the date on the air! How disrespectful. Then, to add insult to injury, Howard didn't even invite the E! guys or Jackie to his birthday show! The place wasn't even packed, and they handed out free tickets to people walking by the club. How freaking insulting. I am shocked what he has become.

Howard has banned Artie, Jackie, KC, Gilbert, Grillo, and me from the studio, which is just more hypocrisy. When Joan Rivers was banned from Johnny Carson for doing her own show, Howard went off on Johnny and *The Tonight Show* for not having her on, yet look at him now. He's banned more people than Johnny ever did. The ex-staffers he probably hates because we have been outspoken about the new Howard—but Gilbert? From what I hear, it's because he is too risqué for the watered-down, celebrity-kiss-ass fest the show has become. It's just one more example of how Howard has become everything he once loathed.

Howard used to goof on these older celebrities, like Seinfeld, who went out and got hot young supermodel wives. Yet look at him now. He has the same thing in Beth. I love Beth and really feel bad for her. You see, Beth always wanted a child and would tell my wife that, but Howard wanted no part of it. Maybe he was just too selfish to give her a child.

The weird thing is, now Howard is trying to make up with all of the celebrities he mistreated over the years. He made amends with Rosie O'Donnell, Jennifer Aniston, and Ellen DeGeneres. Heck, he even tried to reach out to Robin Williams the day before he died to apologize, yet apparently it never occurred to him to reach out to all of those staffers he abused on a daily basis. Put it this way: Howard sued Scott Einziger for producing the show *Are You Hot?* But Howard didn't only sue the production company or the network—he sued Scott directly. This was a guy who broke bread with us on a daily basis.

This I heard from a higher up at Sirius: One time, this person was fighting to double JD's paycheck. He was in a discussion with Howard about it and said, "Come on, Howard, it would make JD happy," and then Howard responded, "I don't care about his happiness, I only care about my own!"

To top it all off, Howard emailed his staffers his new philosophy, called "The Core," which goes something like:

6 bullet points

- Create original and innovative material that speak to a large audience

- Reinvent ourselves to be trailblazers not follow others

- Entertain the guy and girl driving in the car

- Elevate radio to a level that is cool

- Always speak freely and honestly

- Beat the competition and be the best

He concluded with this douche-chill statement: "Let's never lose our way, but if we do it might help to look at these and remember that we have the best broadcast out there. It's been that way for many years and it will stay that way if we remain true to these core values."

The Core was emailed to everybody, along with a picture of Howard barefooted and holding an apple core, while next to him sat a big apple core. Just what the fuck happened to this guy? Well, I received a "red flag list" that was emailed to all of his staffers in 2013. It was a list of things that no on-air staffer could mention. At the top it's marked "Subjects of Concern: Red Flag List" and includes in big red letters that for items marked with an asterisk, "IF HOWARD/ DON/GARY are not around to approve, DO NOT AIR!" Though the entire list

BILLY CRYSTAL:
"HOW BAD DO YOU THINK LETTERMAN WAS HOSTING THE ACADEMY AWARDS?"
"WILL THERE BE A MR. SATURDAY NIGHT 2?"

includes dozens of topics and clips, here are a few of my favorites (reproduced as they appear in the original document):

• Ex-wife Allison name mentions / calls (especially anything negative)

• Scott Eizenger (we can now leave in but stay away from negative comments)

• Jim Paratore (Former Howard producer that Howard sued. He was also the founder of TMZ who died in May 2012)

• Mike Fleiss (Former Howard producer who Howard also sued)

• No mention of Les Moonves & family (including Julie Chen—wife)

• Elliot Offen

• Cabbie – Per Tim, we can air Cabbie moments but we cannot interview him for any new special

• Chauncey Hayden – Per Time, we can air Chauncey moments but we cannot interview him for any future special.

• Linda McCartney singing "Hey Jude" (Nov 90)

• Comedian Bob Levy

• 1/18/06 Rachel Hunter moment where HS calls her a cunt.

• 11/15/95 Don Cornelius with Stuttering John

• Any past "negative" talk about Ellen Degeneres

• All negative Mariah Carey and Nick Cannon

• 4/16/11 HS Mom's phone call about AGT

• Any negative Kathie Lee content

• Negative referenes to Jennifer Aniston

• Angie Everheart

• Remove the Alec Baldwin "dirty little pig" voicemail

• Song "At 17" by Janis Ian/Jerry Seinfeld. **Never to see the light of day.**

P.S. To all of you who continue to ask me if Howard wears a wig, I have no idea. I know that the E! guys pulled a screenshot of him bent over while wrestling with Gary Busey that appeared to reveal some netting, but I really don't know. As for dyeing his hair, same answer.

"HOW MANY YEARS WERE YOU MARRIED BEFORE YOU CHEATED ON YOUR WIFE?"
BILLY GOT SO PISSED. THIS IS WHERE THE "IT'S NOT FUN" LINE CAME FROM.

THE TONIGHT SHOW

I STARTED THERE IN March but didn't debut until April. I was given my own computer in my own office, and I had my own dressing room downstairs with a shower. This was the job of a lifetime! They offered to paint both rooms any color that I chose, and Jay couldn't have been any nicer. He made me feel at home.

I had a meeting with Debbie Vickers; Joe Medeiros, the head writer; Larry Goitia, the supervising producer; and also the guy that signed our checks to discuss where I would be placed on the set.

This was the exact moment I knew I was doomed.

They were trying to find a spot that would be conducive to on-air banter with Jay, and their ultimate solution was for me to sit in the audience on a high chair. I begged them, saying that would be comedy death. I knew my talents were best suited for me to be on the couch next to Jay—which the segment producer, Dave Berg, also thought—but Jay would never let that happen.

I was fearful, and, man, it showed. Jay had his rhythm with Kevin, who, by the way, I liked very much. In fact, I started liking Jay better than Letterman when Kevin started. I loved their rapport, though Debbie was not a big fan of his— maybe it was because he went through like seventeen assistants in two years.

We mapped out the stage, and I didn't begrudge Debbie for her decision. There was nowhere on stage to sit. Either I'd be next to the band, which would be awkward, or stage right, which was where Debbie sat and the segment producers stood to hold up cue cards for Jay in case he forgot the topic he was supposed to cover for his interview. Jay was first and foremost about the monologue—that was his forte. It was something I would soon learn, and also something Jay was very honest about.

I remember him telling me that when Trista from *The Bachelorette* was on the show, he did a whole segment with her, then he went out to the parking lot to retrieve his car. She saw him and said, "Jay, take a picture

ALEC BALDWIN:
"GENITAL-WISE, WHO'S THE BIGGEST BALDWIN?"
"DID YOU EVER PLAY BUTT BONGO WITH KIM?"

with me!" Jay was like, "Sure, who are you?" She was like, "Jay! I'm Trista! I was just a guest on your show!" In Jay's defense, who the fuck wants to remember Trista?

One of my favorite instances of this—and I can't remember who told me this story exactly, though it was possibly Jay himself—was this one time at a charity event at the Comedy Store. Apparently, Jay saw George Lopez there and approached him. You see, George had been very vocal about his anger toward Jay for not having him on as often as he would have liked. So Jay goes up to him and says something like, "Hey, man, I hope you know that I have nothing to do with the booking of the guests—that's not my thing, and I just wanted you to know that." The guy looks at Jay and says, "Jay, I'm not George Lopez. I'm Paul Rodriguez!"

When I first started, Howard was constantly bashing Jay on the air. I felt so bad. I went up to him after rehearsal and said, "Hey, Jay, I'm sorry Howard is bashing you so much, I know that's because of me and I really apologize."

Jay put his hands on both of my shoulders and looked me in the eyes and said, "John, don't worry about it, I don't give a shit what Howard says."

He made me feel so much better. Jay is a great guy.

I immediately started writing bits and jokes for the show. Joe Medeiros liked them, so much so that they promised me a writing gig as soon as somebody was let go. I wrote this bit called "The Search for the Most Interesting Person." It was a bit where I would end up traveling through the United States to find the most talented person in each state. They gave that bit to Tom Green.

I wrote jokes and bits feverishly and would send them to Joe and Debbie. I used to hang in Debbie's office all of the time. We'd talk and I would tell her how happy I was to be there. She would say, "Give it time, soon you won't be so happy." I made a conscious decision not to bring that mindset *The Howard Stern Show* had instilled in me to *The Tonight Show*. I tried to be positive at all times and never complain. When the writers had a bit for me to do, I would do it—no questions asked. Heck, this was my dream job!

I was right, though, about becoming a glorified heckler. Once, in the early going, Jay was interviewing a guest and I screamed out something, and he looked around bewildered, like, *Who is this audience fuck screwing up my interview?*

"DO YOU EVER LOOK AT THE STAINS IN KIM'S UNDERWEAR?"
"ARE YOU JEALOUS OF A CERTAIN ROCK STAR WHO WEARS PURPLE?"

Billy Crystal was a guest on one of the Vegas shows. I'd had an earlier confrontation with him on *The Howard Stern Show*, so I asked Jay, "Hey, man, should I send Billy some flowers or chocolate? I don't know, something as an apology?" Jay said, in his famous Jay voice, "No, just avoid him." Which I did, until after the show. Then it was me, Robin Leach, and his girlfriend in the makeup room, and in walks Billy. And there, folks, I was face-to-face with a guy who wanted to kick the shit out of me for the interview I did with him at the *Forget Paris* premiere. Which everyone did. I was nervous but immediately sprang into action. I started with, "Hey, Billy, look, I'm sorry for that stuff at the premiere," and he was like, "Yeah, John, you know, it was my premiere and everything," and I was like, "Look, Billy, I know that and I'm really, really sorry," and then I got even more nervous and I said, "Billy, if it's any consolation, I loved your movie *51*."

He looked at me like I was fucking with him again, which I wasn't, and said, "*61*, John, the movie was *61*."

51 came to my head because it's Bernie Williams's number, one of my favorite Yankees. That's how I got *51* instead of *61**. I again apologized and that was that.

Even when I'm not trying to fuck with people, I'm fucking with them.

In the meantime, though, I continued working for the greatest show on earth! And why was it the greatest show on earth? Because there was free food everywhere! In radio, we paid for our own meals, but now NBC was picking up the tab! Besides that, there were so many great and talented people there, and Jay was the best! I got to meet famous celebrities and hang with them.

George Clooney, one of the nicest guys in the world, was on the stage and he saw me and said, "John, I'm so happy for you, congrats on the new gig!" I was so happy that he even knew my name!

Jerry Seinfeld saw me and offered his congratulations. He said, "John, it's good to see you moving up in the world."

I had an uncomfortable run-in with Burt Reynolds. You see, Burt's another guy I pissed off pretty bad in the past. I interviewed him once at the premiere of *Mystery, Alaska*. I asked him something and he grabbed my mike and shoved

REGIS PHILBIN:
"DO YOU HAVE F.U. MONEY?"
"IF KATHIE LEE SUCKS, SAY 'WHAT?'"

it down with my hand. I also was at a book signing of his at a mall and I got thrown out trying to interview him at the signing on the bottom floor, so then I went to the second floor and started screaming down questions, like, "Burt, why did you beat up Loni?"

Anyway, they threw me out of the entire mall.

Cut to Burt doing a guest spot on the show. I'm outside conducting the "Gasoline Games," which was done outside, across the street. At this point, the last thing Debbie needed to hear about was me and my interviewing past, especially after Howard had been bashing Jay on a regular basis. So I'm outside, and I have the earphones on so I can hear the show as we're packing up. Burt comes out, and he says to Jay sarcastically on the show, "It's nice to see well-spoken John out there." My heart nearly dropped out of my rib cage.

I was like, "Holy shit."

Jay asked him if he had a problem with me, and Burt told him, "Well, Jay, let's just say that John once asked me a very inappropriate question years back that I really took offense to."

Jay asked, "What was the question?"

Burt said, "I don't want to say, Jay, but let's just say it was an anti-Semitic question that I'd rather not repeat."

I was shitting in my pants. This was all I needed.

After the show, I asked the segment producer if I could go into Burt's dressing room to apologize, and he said that I could. I knocked on the door, and Burt said, "Come in." I walked in, and before I could say a thing, Burt was like, "Stuttering John, how the hell are ya?"

I'm like, "Burt, I thought you were pissed at me."

He said, "No, of course not. I was just messing around out there. Now say hello to my son."

I shook his son's hand. "But, Burt, what was the question I asked you?"

He said, "Oh, you asked me if I thought the Jews ran Hollywood." I apologized, and he said, "John, no problem. After my family and I watched you on *I'm a Celebrity...Get Me Out of Here!* we fell in love with you. So don't worry about it."

Relationship repaired.

Dennis Miller would never speak to me when he was a guest. I pissed him off once asking him ridiculous questions at an ESPN Zone press conference held when Dennis was made the new announcer of *Monday Night Football*. He would ignore me when we sat in rehearsal, and he would ignore me in the makeup room and in the hallways. Finally, one day he came up to me and said, "John, look, I haven't talked to you because I was still pissed about the press conference, but Jay says you're a good guy, so I'm ready to bury the hatchet." I shook his hand, and all was good with Dennis and me after that.

Another time, they wanted me to come on stage in a mankini. You know, the one made famous by Borat. So I wore it in rehearsal, and after, when I was in the makeup room, Debbie called down and said, "John, I have a question for you that's a little hard for me to ask."

I said, "You can ask me anything, Debbie. What is it?"

She said that my pubes were spilling out of the mankini, and would I mind shaving them?

So I asked my hair person, Margaret, if she would do it.

She said no fucking way. But she did give me an electric trimmer, and, not knowing what I was doing, I placed it to the sensitive part of my skin above the pubic area, and blood spewed out everywhere! Just then, lead guest and noted germaphobe Howie Mandel walks in, sees me naked, blood everywhere, and almost has a heart attack!

I mean, come on! Pubes? A little blood? It's not like I asked him to shake my hand.

He ended up spending the first three minutes of his appearance telling Jay all about it.

Howie and I became friends, and we would share stories about our OCD and what medications we were on. He even told me he was a fan of Howard, but he always turned the radio off when Howard would make fun of me for stuttering. It turns out that Howie's son stuttered at the time and it bothered him to hear a stutterer being made fun of.

Things were fun for me at *The Tonight Show*, but day after day I would hear about Howard and how he was bashing Jay. I just didn't understand it. Like, why? Why couldn't Howard just be happy for me? I knew his beating up on Jay was just transference of his anger toward me.

I continued to submit jokes to Debbie and Jay. I knew I had to increase my value there, and writing was a way to do that. I met Charlie Sheen in the midway, which was essentially the parking area where Jay, Debbie, Kevin, and

KATE PIERSON (B-52'S SINGER):

I parked. (All with our names on the spots!) Charlie said to me that after he and his then-wife Denise Richards saw me on *I'm a Celebrity...Get Me Out of Here!* they had become big fans.

Was I dreaming?

I had the easiest work schedule in my life. I didn't have to be at work until one, unless they were shooting a bit with me, which I welcomed. Gilbert Gottfried would always come by, and in his consummate cheapness, he would bring an extra bag and collect as many free magazines, candy, and snacks as possible. That man paid for nothing!

Back when I was on *The Howard Stern Show*, I booked a comedy gig with Artie and Gilbert at the Grove Theater in LA. Gilbert's agent told me that Gilbert didn't always work so well in LA, but I didn't care because I was such a huge fan. Well, I convinced KLSX General Manager Bob Moore to pay Gilbert $10,000 a show for two nights. When Gilbert and I flew out, we had adjacent seats in first class. Gilbert ordered the pancakes for breakfast, and they gave him one of those tiny bottles of maple syrup. So when we landed, I saw half of the bottle of the syrup left on Gilbert's chair. I grabbed my bag and looked down, and the maple syrup bottle was gone!

I said, "Gilbert, did you take that half bottle of syrup?"

He looked at me and said, "You caught me, didn't you?"

Oh, man. This guy is the cheapest fuck in the universe!

When he would do a guest spot on *The Howard Stern Show*, Gilbert, Artie, and I would go out to lunch, and Artie and I would pay. Afterward I'd ask Gilbert, "Do you want to share a cab?" since we both lived downtown.

"No, I'll walk."

I'd say, "Gilbert, I'll pay," and he'd say of course.

I love that cheap son of a bitch!

Anyway, back to the show in LA. I was the host and Gilbert went on after Artie, who had become a hero to Stern fans. Gilbert got on stage and Bombed— capital "B." The audience started throwing ice cubes and Buffalo wings. But, in a moment of true Gilbert genius, he decided to fuck with them some more. He'd say things like, "Have you heard the one about the blonde that walks into a bar? Ah, fuck that one, how about a priest and a rabbi are in a plane? Ah, fuck that..."

The crowd was booing incessantly. Bob Moore, the GM, whom I was sitting behind, turned around and said, "Is this the fucking guy we're paying twenty grand? Get him off the stage!"

I got on the stage and was motioning for him to leave, so in true Gilbert fashion, he decided to end with the most disgusting joke he could think of and launched into "The Aristocrats."

What a character.

STUTTERING AT *THE TONIGHT SHOW*

THERE WERE QUITE A few times when I would stutter doing a correspondence piece or while talking to Jay on air, but Debbie would have the editors edit them out. Otherwise, if we were live taping "Beach Games" or something, I would have to reach into my stuttering bag of tricks and get creative.

The best was when then–Angels pitcher Jared Washburn was throwing suntan-lotion-filled balloons at my back. I wrote a line for myself saying, "Don't worry, Jay, he's no Mariano Rivera." Mo was my favorite pitcher, but still. Why the fuck would I choose a pitcher with two of the hardest consonants for me to hit in a row? So when we go live, we get to the bit where Jared was going to throw the balloons at my back and I say, "Don't worry Jay, he's no M-M-M… Randy Johnson!" I had to change the name in a split second and come up with a different pitcher. Nobody noticed, thank God.

Another time we were shooting "Beach Games" at Venice Beach, and it really posed a problem. See, before we shot it at Paradise Cove. P's weren't a problem for me, but V's were a different story. I was shitting my pants because I knew there was no way I was going to be able to say Venice Beach without stuttering. So I sat for hours in my beach chair, trying to think of a solution. I finally came up with one where I put a silent "the" in front of "Venice," thus helping me get to the "Venice" unscathed. I called these starter words. I would use them all the time but never in this fashion, because now I was trying to hide the starter word. So we went live and again I was shitting in my pants, and I said to Jay, "We're here at the-Venice Beach…"

I said the "the" so quickly and low that nobody noticed.

BARBARA WALTERS:
"BARBARA, IS YOUR SPEECH IMPEDIMENT REAL?"

Being a stutterer is a task all its own, but you also have to be a walking thesaurus. Like, if you can't say, "great," say, "amazing." If you can't say, "right," say, "correct." I read somewhere that stutterers tend to have very high IQs—unfortunately, it was in the *Weekly World News*, and on the next page it had a story where they caught a man who was half-alligator.

Here is my list of tricks, for any stutterers reading this:

- Always have a replacement word ready when you know there's a word coming up that might pose a problem.

- Use "starter words" for words that will pose a problem. Mine were always "kind of," "fucking," and "like." Which came in handy when my girlfriend Karen's stepdad asked why I wanted to date Karen. I said, "Because I kind of fucking like her."

- Sing through sentences. It's impossible to stutter when you sing, so even if you have the rhythm in your head, you can subtly do this without anyone noticing. If you do it too strongly, though, they'll think you're a singing telegram. But, hey, at least you won't stutter.

- Raise your voice when you speak. It's very hard to stutter when you scream. In fact, when Paul Giamatti was a guest on the show, he told me that he was playing a stutterer in an M. Night Shyamalan movie. I asked him if he wanted me to coach him. He said he would be fine, but when I saw the movie, the motherfucker stuttered when he talked to himself and when he screamed. I call bullshit! Stutterers don't stutter when they talk to themselves.

- If you're really bad, bring a notebook and a pen, and this will allow you to communicate and alleviate the pressure of having to speak, thus making speaking easier. Hey, it worked for Conroy.

- Try speaking in a different accent. It's very hard to stutter doing that.

- Try speaking in a character. Like for me, the Italian kind of Andrew Dice Clay voice works.

- The fucking kicker is that when I saw *The King's Speech*, which is about the stuttering King Edward back in the 1920s, the motherfucker's speech therapist was already suggesting most of these tricks. So why the fuck did my speech therapist not know this?

SHE WAS NOT THRILLED. SHE AND HER HUSBAND TRIED WALKING AWAY,
BUT THEY WERE HEADED IN THE WRONG DIRECTION, SO I HAD TO TELL THEM WHERE TO GO.

CHELSEA HANDLER: "NICE" IS A FOUR LETTER WORD

THE FIRST TIME I met Chelsea, I didn't even know it. I was in coach on a plane to LA to pick out a house for my move to *The Tonight Show*. As we were on the runway, I popped a Xanax because I hate to fly. Chelsea immediately said, in her fast-paced delivery, "What was that?" I told her what it was, and she asked me if she could have one. I gave her one and that was that. It was weird because Chelsea is an attractive woman, but I didn't even notice that. The whole thing was so happenstance, who knew I'd be partially responsible for her addictions?

I thought nothing of the event until the segment producers Bob and Ross on *The Tonight Show* booked her to do stand-up and she told me about the flight. She was friendly then, but keep in mind that she was also a nobody. After her performance on *The Tonight Show*, they had her be a correspondent.

Around that time, my comedy tour was doing a weekend of shows at the Tempe Improv, so I offered her the gig. She gladly took it because it was good pay and the Tempe Improv was a big deal to an upcoming comic. It was Chelsea, Jason Gillearn, Ross "The Intern" Mathews, and me. John Kennedy and I would go to Ross's house and help him write jokes, as this was his first time doing stand-up.

I brought my wife, and we all met in Tempe. Dan Mer, the club owner, would not let Chelsea drink vodka at the club, and she was pissed. Dan let me drink beer because it was my anti-stuttering medication, but maybe this angered Chelsea. Who knows? We all did our sets and Chelsea, Suzanna, and I went out to dinner together. We all did great, and Ross killed. For his first time on stage, he was awesome.

The next time Chelsea was in to do the show, something had changed. She had become more popular now, and I guess it gave her license to show her true colors. I think she'd just started her E! show and had a best-selling book. I came into her dressing room to say hi and she started insulting me. I couldn't believe it. I said, "Good shows in Tempe," and she said something like, "I don't know what you were doing there."

DANNY DEVITO:

All right, let's give her the benefit of the doubt for now.

The next time I saw her was at Khloe Kardashian and Lamar Odom's wedding. We sat at the same table as Chelsea, and she completely ignored my wife and me. She even asked my wife who she was! What a complete bitch. She had Ross and Jason Gillearn on her show many times, but when I asked for one appearance to promote my movie or a stand-up show, she turned me down. Now, one might think that maybe it's just me, but that isn't the case. Ross Mark, the segment producer who opened the door for her career by booking her on *The Tonight Show*, went to one of Chelsea's parties with his wife, and Chelsea saw him there and turned her back on him. Then again, her show was on E! and she was dating the network's president, Ted Harbert—so I guess she didn't need Ross anymore.

The one thing she had our segment producers tell Jay was that he wasn't allowed to make fun of how old she looked. This from a woman who insults everyone on a daily basis.

Can't blame her, though. She does look old for her age. I heard Netflix canceled her show and replaced it with Letterman's because they wanted a younger-looking host.

KEEPING UP WITH KRIS JENNER

SOON AFTER WE MOVED to Calabasas, California, to do *The Tonight Show*, my wife came home and told me that she ran into Bruce Jenner in town. Bruce invited my family to come over on Sunday for a BBQ, so we did. It was so much fun. Bruce showed me his Olympic room, which was loaded with pictures and awards and ribbons. Heck, he had even framed the pair of shorts he wore when he won the decathlon at the Olympics. (No way Ashton Kutcher could have worn those.) This always seemed funny to me, because one time when I asked Bruce to see his gold medal, Bruce told me he had to go get it because "after all, you can't live in the past," and yet he had an entire room dedicated to the 1976 Olympics! His license plate said 10EVENTS, and he and Kris's phone number ended in 1976. Dude, your whole life—at that time—was dedicated to the past! He even gave me a signed Wheaties box with him on the cover.

My wife and I would go over to their place pretty regularly, and Kim, Kourtney, and Khloe would be lying by the pool in their bikinis. I couldn't stop staring at Kourtney; she was my favorite of the Kardashians. She had such a great body. Such perfect boobs, a great face, a great butt...

Wait, wait...

All right. I'm finished.

Anyway, one day my wife said, "Hey, Kris, why don't you do a reality show with the family like this, just hanging around the house, having friends over?"

Kris immediately loved the idea.

Sorry, America.

You have to understand, Kris had always wanted to be famous—that's part of the reason she hobnobbed with celebrities. She just yearned for that lifestyle. Anyway, my wife would go over to Kris's house to write the treatment for this reality show she had the idea for.

Well, Deena Katz, the casting producer for *I'm a Celebrity*... used to hang out with us at my parties or at the Kardashians'. We would go to Deena's house and hang with her husband, Jerry, and their kid. We became friends, and Deena heard about the show my wife was writing with Kris. Deena got a call from Ryan Seacrest asking if she knew of any shows he could produce. She told him about the Kardashian reality show and he liked it.

Here's the sick thing about it: Kris did the show and never included my wife! She didn't even give my wife a credit! I was so pissed off.

I would tell Suzanna to sue, but she would say that the universe would take care of it. And, yeah, it certainly did. The Kardashians are billionaires and I'm performing at Hey Guys Comedy Club in Iowa.

We remained friends, though. My wife and I were actually in their pilot episode. I remember Khloe coming up to me with the cameras on and asking if I thought Kris was hot and if I wanted to fuck her mom.

I thought she was trying too hard.

My wife and I were invited to the premiere, and we thought the show was contrived and God-awful! Man, did we have it wrong. It became a big hit with spinoffs. Kris would give us used furniture she didn't need, I think as a subconscious way of alleviating her guilt for not including my wife. I remember mentioning to Jerry, Deena's husband, when we were at my house how I was shocked that Kris didn't feel any guilt, and he agreed.

TOM BROKAW:

"CAN YOU SAY 'RED LEATHER, YELLOW LEATHER'?"

What are you going to do? That's Hollywood.

We were always invited to Kris's Christmas Eve party, where we would rub elbows with the likes of Sugar Ray Leonard, Jillian Barberie, and Kathy Lee Gifford. I made amends with Kathy for all of the horrible things Howard had said about her. I had actually defended her once on the air against Howard, and I damn well told her that!

At one of these parties, Kris showed us the stripper pole in her bedroom, and like eight- and nine-year-old Kylie and Kendall were swinging off of it. Then, later that night, Kylie and Kendall performed a burlesque show with seductive dancing on top of a piano! Jillian and I looked at each other like, *Whoa, is this really happening?* Meanwhile Kris had this proud smile on her face. I don't know if it was because she approved of the dance or because she saw dollar signs in her newest nutty flock of freakazoids.

Suzanna and I had decided to try for another kid, this time no spinning. We decided to do it the natural way, although I did read the book on how to have a boy. Apparently the guy should have a little caffeine right before the day of ovulation. The book also stipulated no jerking off and only wearing boxers. It said the woman should avoid caffeine, and that when the time came, we should have sex doggie style, making sure that she came first. (Which for me—ahem—isn't a problem. I put the stud in Stuttering John!) Anyway, afterward, she's supposed to stay in doggie-style position for four minutes, helping the male sperm to swim faster to the egg.

Hey, man, that's what the book said. Albeit, that book was *Playboy*.

Suzanna, like the trooper that she was, stayed in that position and, miraculously, a few months later we found out we were having a boy! I was so excited. I thought this was God's way of teaching me the lesson of Sadie. I paid my penance, and this was his gift to me. Oscar David Melendez was the first baby born in the San Fernando Valley on New Year's morning. As a result, a newspaper came to take a picture and do a story.

The night before, New Year's Eve, we had a party, so we had people over and we had just gotten done with dinner. Heck, even Bruce and Kris Jenner were there. Kris actually told Suzanna that she would have the baby that night. Well, anyway, we were done with dinner and my wife was washing dishes. Suddenly, she ran into the bathroom. I followed her and was like, "Honey, what's wrong?" She told me that her water just broke. I was like, "Well, that

"ARE THERE NEWS GROUPIES?"

"HAS ANYONE EVER ASKED YOU IF YOU'RE GAY?"

doesn't mean you have to stop washing the dishes. We have people over, and I'm ready for dessert!" So I took her to the hospital, and she complained the whole time. I mean, most women would love to be on the back of a Harley. Then she's on the delivery room table, I'm massaging her head, and she's in pain, so I'm happy.

I'm only kidding, ladies. I wasn't massaging her head.

The doctor said to me, "Look, I can rush this and save you money on the yearly taxes."

I was like, "Um, no, Doc, it's my kid. I'd rather you take your time."

It was also because I had an OCD thing where I already got my mind set for January 1 before I left my house.

My OCD gets real bad when it comes to my kids.

Eventually, the doctor told me it was time. He said, "It's time to see your baby being born—come on over here."

I said no.

He asked why and told me to get over there, and again I said no.

He said, "Why?"

I said, "Every one of my friends tells me that if you see the baby being born, you'll never want to have sex with your wife again."

He said that was ridiculous and to come on over, and so finally I did. And it looked like a CSI crime scene. There was blood everywhere, my wife was stretched out like two feet—it looked like a manhole with a mustache! Then the baby's head got stuck, and the doctor pulled out these huge pliers called forceps. So he's got the forceps in there, the baby's heads in there, the doctor's hands are in there, I'm like, "Honey, the next time we go on vacation, we can pack everything in there! Laptop? No problem!"

But then the baby comes out and he's so cute. Unfortunately what happens is this huge purple sack of blood and puss comes spilling out of my wife—the doctor calls it the placenta, and I affectionately call it the gag bag—and then the doctor's like, "Do you have any questions?"

Uh, yeah. Are you going to have sex with her, because I'm fucking traumatized!

Then the doctor asks me to cut the umbilical cord. I say no and we argue again and he wins again, so I put down my beer, cut the cord, and we bring the baby home. He's sleeping in his little crib next to my wife and he starts

PETER JENNINGS:

crying, and my wife gets up! Rips her shirt off! Rips her bra off! And then she jams her nipple straight in the kid's mouth! I'm thinking I'd be lucky to get that on Christmas.

But all jokes aside, I was so proud and grateful to get my second son, Oscar. I still thank God each day. My favorite number has always been three, and now I have my three lovely kids.

THE CONAN CONSPIRACY

A FEW MONTHS INTO my tenure at *The Tonight Show*, we all got called down into the conference room so Jay could make a big announcement. The room was packed wall-to-wall with employees nervously awaiting what Jay was about to tell us.

Jay lied, and I guess he had to, but he did. He said, "Hey, guys, I just want to say that I've decided to retire from doing this show after my new five-year contract is up. I thank you all for being here and working hard to make this show number one, but I think it's time that I focus on other things. I wish Conan O'Brien the best, as he will be the next host of *The Tonight Show*."

"What the fuck!" I screamed out. "Jay, I haven't even unpacked yet!"

Everybody laughed nervously, but it was a sad day in *Tonight Show* history. Traci Fiss, a segment producer, sat across from me crying, and it seemed everyone was going through the numbers in their heads as to whether they could save enough in the next five years to retire on. We all shuffled out and contemplated our futures.

Now, this was all bullshit. Jay Leno was forced out by Conan O'Brien.

Conan had had enough of hosting *The Late Night Show*, and he wanted to be the next *Tonight Show* host. But rather than graciously wait for Jay to retire on his own, Conan forced his hand. And so the cowardly asses at NBC, rather than make a stand against Conan, chose to make a stand against Jay. They thought Conan had the youth demographic, but they didn't realize that Conan's big ratings were mostly because of the great lead-in that Jay gave him. They would rather remove Jay, who was number one in late night, for Conan, an elitist, Harvard-graduate snob.

Jay couldn't believe that a network he was loyal to for so many years would treat him like this. I know he felt this way, because I would hang with him after each show in his bunker as he got changed. It was the two of us and Jack Coen, who was the monologue coordinator, and NBC patsy Rick Ludwin. Jay didn't trust Rick, but he knew how to play the game. Jay would sometimes make comments like, "Hey, fire the guy who's on top—you NBC guys are geniuses!" But he put on a good face for the media. He would lie and say it was time for him to move on, but every one of us at NBC knew this was all bullshit. This was the job that Jay loved.

As the five-year end was nearing, we all thought we were going to get picked up by ABC. The rumor was that Jimmy Kimmel would go on later and Jay would go on before him. This was exciting news, we thought, because that would've undoubtedly meant more money, but then NBC started to get cold feet. What if Conan failed? They suddenly realized their huge blunder and wanted to have their cake and eat it too.

And so they came up with this plan to give Jay a ten-o'clock show, which would allow them to keep him at the network. Jay initially balked. He told the NBC execs that the show would fail and that he didn't want to do it. They begged, and because Jay is a loyal guy, he finally accepted. The problem was, we would be out of work for three months while the new show was being prepped. That's three months with no salary. The move to *The Jay Leno Show*, which aired at ten, was bittersweet for me because I finally got the staff writing job I was offered when initially I signed my *Tonight Show* contract, but I would no longer be the announcer. Jay had said in interviews that he had Kevin and that he always felt awkward having to play to not one but two people, and I must say I felt awkward too. By sitting with the audience, I felt like a glorified heckler. Jay would goof on me because I always looked surprised when he would go to me, but that was because it happened so infrequently! The only way it would have worked is the way segment producer Dave Berg initially saw it when he booked me the first time: on the couch like Ed McMahon. But Jay would never have it. The good news, however, was that I got the coveted staff writer job. Another one of my dreams had come true, and I was now a unionized television writer with a pension!

As we were doing *The Jay Leno Show*, Conan was bombing as host of *The Tonight Show*. The NBC execs were beginning to question what they'd done, and they decided to offer Jay the 11:30 slot with the idea of moving Conan and *The Tonight Show* back to 12:05. Conan balked, however, but the network went ahead and offered Jay his old job back anyway. Again, Jay never wanted to leave in the first place and he was nothing if not loyal, so he gladly accepted the offer to return—infuriating Conan even further.

And while we thought we were once more in the clear, things would only get more complicated. In the middle of Jay's new five-year deal for *The Tonight Show*, NBC decided that they wanted Jimmy Fallon to come in and host the show once the deal was up, as they felt he could appeal to a younger demographic. The only problem was that the network wanted to give the job over to Fallon in February of 2014 so that they could promote him during the Olympics—even though Jay's contract wasn't up until September. Jay agreed to leave, but only on one condition: that each of his 150 staff members were paid through September.

True to word, every employee on the show got paid—in one lump sum, no less—thanks to Jay's loyalty. For me alone, that meant a six-figure payout, never mind what the rest of the staff was making. This kind of behavior is widely known and exactly who Jay is. To this day, it's what inspires loyalty to Jay from all of his former employees, even though Jay himself has been known to remark, "Hey, I was number one—and *I* still got fired."

JAY LENO-CD

JAY HAD IT BAD, like I did. When he would walk around the halls, he had to run his hands around each side of the walls and tap them. During one hiatus, they removed the busted wall next to Jay's desk. See, apparently, Jay would accidentally bang his humongous head against the wall and it caused a hole. Well, when Jay got back from hiatus and they'd replaced the broken wall with a new one, Jay demanded that they find the old wall with the hole and put it back. I don't know why I should be surprised at this—after all, this was a guy whose dressing room had a shitload of junk everywhere. There was shit that he saved from the eighties. We actually found a sandwich in a box that was dated 1998!

"ARE WOMEN EASIER TO DEAL WITH AFTER MENOPAUSE?'
PHIL ANGRILY RESPONDED, "THAT'S NOT FUNNY."

The guy was a hoarder and incredibly ritualistic. For instance, when the show started and the announcement was playing, Jay had to touch this certain doorknob that led to the stage. It was a ritual he had to complete before every monologue. So one day my good friend and fellow writer, Anthony Caleca, thought it would be funny to stand right in front of the doorknob while this was going on. Jay did not know what to do! He started small talk with Anthony as he tried to find the least embarrassing solution to the problem at hand. Finally, he quickly just reached around Anthony's back, his head touching Anthony's, and he grabbed for the doorknob, touched it, and ran up the stairs to the stage. It was funny, but as a fellow OCD sufferer, I let Anthony know how cruel it was.

Why should I be surprised? Again, this was a guy who had like fifty denim shirts and pants and would wear them every day. His excuse was that it made it easier to pick out clothes. I didn't buy that for a second. I mean, here was a guy that had never touched his *Tonight Show* money ever; he just lived off of his stand-up money. I think he has that old-school mentality of "It could all go away," and he had to hoard money like a squirrel hoarding nuts. I wish I had that problem.

> When Jay was a kid growing up in Massachusetts, his teacher decided to surprise the kids with a field trip to Fenway Park. When they pulled up to the park, a defiant Jay refused to get out of the bus. The teacher said, "Leno, get out of the bus, we're going to go watch the Red Sox." Jay said, "No." The teacher was getting pretty angry. "Why not?" he asked. Jay said, "Because I don't like baseball. I didn't ask to do this, so I'm not going." And so the pissed-off teacher had to sit in that damn bus the whole time the game was being played, while the other two teachers took the kids to the game!

When I was hired as a staff writer, I began coming up with drop-ins, which were essentially a video joke or prop during the monologue riffing off a news story or topic from that day or the day before. They served to break up the monologue and provided a cut point in case some of the opening jokes bombed. I had become quite successful at writing them and had accounted for seven of my own segments, some of which were recurring. I would also write monologue jokes. The other writing assignments were props and jokes for bits, cold opens, and drop-ins. I started submitting these, and Rob Young, a seasoned

MARÍA CONCHITA ALONSO:
"ARE YOU ROSIE PEREZ?"
"DO YOU HAVE A GREEN CARD?"

writer, came to my office and said, "John, you're getting a ton of drop-ins on. Why not pitch them and produce them yourself?"

I said sure. Little did I know that I was about to embark on the hardest, most cumbersome writing job in the building. Rob meant well, but man, this was work. See, I was happy churning out segments and bits from the confines of my own office. I was doing really well, in fact—our head writer, Jack Coen, told one of our editors, Teo Konuralp, that he wished he had ten of me on his writing staff. I just kept churning out good, original material, and Jack was pleased. He once jokingly told me on a motorcycle ride to Big Bear that he would love to fire me, but I was doing too well. Jay was happy too. On several occasions he would come up to me and say, "John, you know we bust your balls, but you are really doing a good job. Keep it up."

I was happy. I was writing for a TV show and was excelling at it! Then I attended my first drop-in meeting. Heck, I'd give it a shot. It took place in Jay's office, which was tiny, because again, Jay had that working-man mentality, hence the denim, and he never demanded a big office. In fact, when we shot bits that allegedly took place in Jay's office, they were always shot in Jack's office, which was much nicer.

> Rob was one of the funniest writers on the show and one of my best friends there. He knew I was a staunch Giants fan. The morning after the Saints won the Super Bowl, I stuck my head in his office to congratulate him.
>
> He said, "John, have the Giants ever lost a Super Bowl?"
>
> I said, "Yes, once."
>
> He deadpanned, "What's that like?"
>
> I laughed my ass off. The motherfucker.

So there I was in my first drop-in meeting. It was me, two other drop-in writers—Troy Thomas and Rob Young—the head graphic guy, the head of the research department, Jay, Jack, Jack's assistant Adam, and the cameraman/segment director. We were all crammed into Jay's office. I pitched like seven drop-ins from the TV shows I'd watched with my wife and kids the night before. Rob and Troy pitched stuff from the research department the day before. Jack was livid. He said something to Rob and Troy like, "Why is the new guy the only one who's pitching me new stuff from the top shows from the night before?" He was pissed, and when we walked back into Rob's office, Rob lost it! He was like, "What the fuck does he want from me? We are given the shows by the research department!"

I felt bad, but I knew that now I was going to have to pitch every morning and this was a lot of work. At four every day, Troy, Rob, and I received about two and a half hours of footage from all of the TV shows from the day and night before and brought it home to watch. Then we came up with our five pitches for the next morning. We would edit our jokes on Final Cut Pro, which we all had on our computers. We'd get up super early and drive in and meet in Rob's office around eight to make sure that we didn't have any overlapping drop-ins. Rob was the senior guy, so he would pitch first; Troy and I would alternate being in second and third position. At 9:30 a.m., we would get a call from Adam, Jack's assistant, to come down to Jay's office to pitch. As our turn began, we would plug our computers into Jay's TV and begin our pitches. If we got stuff approved, we went into a production meeting at 10:30 a.m. and told all of the departments—research, props, casting, graphic, clearances, and such—what we needed. Then we started to write our scripts for what Jay and our actors would say. At noon, I would go into the briefings with Jay, Debbie, and the segment producers who had a guest on that day. We would eat lunch from a five-star restaurant and the segment producers would brief Jay on the segments. I would come up with jokes, bits, and cold opens for those celebrities.

> When Jay was doing poorly in school, his parents had to meet with Jay and his elementary school guidance counselor. After a brief discussion, the guidance counselor said, "You know, Mr. and Mrs. Leno, college isn't for everybody…maybe Jay should consider a career in the fast-food industry."

After that, we'd shoot the drop-ins, edit them with our three editors, record the voiceover, and deal with graphics to make sure that our special effects were completed to the best of our ability. If we got it done by 2:30 p.m. it would be played at the rehearsal. If not, at 3:45 p.m., Jay, Jack, the stage manager, the other drop-in guys, and the writer's assistant would watch the drop-in. If it got approved, it was sent to the director's booth to air.

MATTHEW BRODERICK:
"HOW DO YOU SUCCEED IN BUSINESS WITHOUT TRYING?"
"DID YOU DRIVE HERE?"

EASY FOR YOU TO SAY

Then the whole cycle would begin again.

We received the most abuse as far as the writers were concerned, but to have your drop-in played and for it to get laughs somehow made it all worth it. The great thing about writing a cold open was that I got to direct huge celebrities. I remember when my cold-open writing partner John Kennedy and I wrote one for Quentin Tarantino. After I got it accepted, I got to go downstairs and wait for Quentin to be ready to shoot. While shooting the first take with Quentin, he went off script and the improv pushed it too long. I had to say to him, "Look, Quentin, a cold open is at most only thirty seconds, so is it cool if you just try and stay with the script?" He said, sure, John. And as I walked out of the room, I thought, *Wow, how crazy is this? Stuttering John is directing Quentin Tarantino!*

I directed Charlie Sheen on one of the cold opens, and after the shoot, he started to tell me that he too was a stutterer. He said that he stuttered on R's, and it was hard growing up because his sister and his brother had names that began with R. Afterward, he invited me to his Super Bowl party, and I ended up going. Charlie had this elaborate setup in the backyard of his mansion. He had ice sculptures of both teams' logos. He brought in chefs from the top cooking shows, too.

The only thing missing from the party? Charlie.

He never left his bedroom. He didn't even attend his own party!

Don Rickles was a guest while I was doing the show, and I was excited to see him. I was a big fan and loved him in *Kelly's Heroes*. When Don arrived, he walked down the hallway to makeup. He saw our Asian page and started bending up and down and making fake Chinese words. Next he saw our six-foot-five senior segment producer, Stephanie Ross, and went, "Hey, Stretch, get your uniform on, coach needs you in the game."

I laughed my ass off.

He sat in the makeup chair, and I came over and said hi.

He said to me, "Look, I watch you on the show all the time—you got to talk more. You're funny, don't let Jay talk over you. He just wants to keep you down, he doesn't want anyone to be funnier than him. Kevin is not

HOW THE HECK WAS I TO KNOW THAT MATTHEW KILLED SOMEONE WHILE DRIVING?
I DON'T THINK HE WAS HAPPY WITH THE QUESTION.

funny—you are. You got to talk more, I watch every night, I watch every night...You know what I'm saying, Rob?"

I'm like, "Um, I'm John."

"Whatever," he said. "Just talk more."

As for pitching things, I only pissed Jay off a couple of times. Once, there was this news reporter doing a piece on how this new technology can put you in any movie. The reporter put herself in *Casablanca* right next to Humphrey Bogart, and so I pitched Jay on taking the news reporter out and replacing her with him, except we'd do it with *Deliverance*. He was like, "I'm not going to get fucked in the ass! Why not have me suck a few cocks too!"

The only other time I pitched something to Jay that I feared would piss him off was after Rob complimented me on my series of drop-ins called "Would His Hair Look Better as a Beard?" which I'm pretty sure I wrote when I was stoned. Rob said, though, that he had a slight problem with another one of my recurring drop-ins called "Is His Head Bigger Than Mine?" in which we'd have a picture of a celebrity's head in space and then, to the *2001: A Space Odyssey* theme, a picture of Jay's head would come in and eclipse the celebrity's. Rob's problem with it was that he that the pictures could be manipulated to be as small or as large as I wanted. He thought a better, more realistic bit would be "What Weighs More than Jay's Head?"

I said, "You mean like, what weighs more—Jay's head or a standard-sized pumpkin?"

He said yes, and we decided on pitching it.

I said, "Rob, we both have to pitch this to Jay, because I don't want to pitch it alone."

He said fine, but when we walked into Jay's office, he hung out in the back and I did all the talking. Jay was like, "All right, if you think that's funny."

So then I brought in a bathroom scale and had Jay lie down on his office floor and we weighed his gargantuan head! The only problem was that Jay wouldn't really put his full weight on the scale. I think he was really insecure about his head and didn't want the bit to work. His head kept weighing in at four pounds!

Now, come on, even the average head is eight pounds!

PAUL SORVINO:

"HAS WOODY ALLEN LOST HIS MIND?"

"WHAT ARE THE ODDS THAT JOHN TRAVOLTA WILL EVER STAR IN ANOTHER DECENT MOVIE?"

And though the image of Jay lying down with his head on a bathroom scale was a priceless one I will always cherish, the bit never aired, nor was it ever mentioned again.

> My favorite moments on *The Tonight Show* were in rehearsal. That's where we would show Jay the comedy piece and our drop-ins. One of Jay's favorite stories that he loves to tell about me was when the first lady, Michelle Obama, was a guest. We were in rehearsal and they'd just played one of my drop-ins. Jay was like, "I don't know, is that funny?" I said, "Yeah, Jay, come on, it's fucking funny!" and Jay was like, "Shhhhh, John, keep it down, the first lady is here." I responded, "Oh Jay, like the first lady never heard the word fuck before?"

Once a month, the show would order from Pink's Hot Dogs. Jay would ask the writing assistant to go down and get him two hot dogs before the afternoon briefing. He would then hide them in his top desk drawer and take occasional bites on the sly.

See, he feared Debbie Vickers, because she wanted Jay to watch his weight. Those two were like an old married couple. Or better yet, Debbie was like Jay's mother. After Jay wolfed down the dogs, he went into the briefing and ate another high-scale lunch. Debbie would make sure Jay worked out with a trainer once a day, although we all knew what Jay's workout session was: he'd walk for twenty minutes on the treadmill, do two sets of bench presses with like fifty pounds, and then take a shower. The guy never lost any weight, but at least he appeased Debbie.

One time when Jay was on the floor in rehearsal, they played a bit, and Debbie, who was watching from her office, didn't like it. Debbie called down to Jay and told him angrily not to air the bit. While Debbie was scolding him on the phone, Jay starting making faces and hand gestures, goofing on Debbie. Then Debbie reminded him, "Jay, I can see what you're doing!"

I was in a 7-Eleven once and saw they had hot-dog-flavored potato chips. I immediately picked up a bag for Jay, because he loved doing the "How fat are we in America?" bit. Anyway, when Jay brought it out in rehearsal, Debbie told him to eat one and then give the bag to the prop guy because she didn't want him eating potato chips during the monologue. Jay didn't listen. The whole

"SHOULD ANAL SEX BE LEGALIZED EVERYWHERE?"

PAUL SORVINO SCARED THE SHIT OUT OF ME, IMPLYING HE HAD MOB CONNECTIONS AND THAT I SHOULD BACK OFF. PAULEY FROM ROCKY WAS THE ONLY OTHER ACTOR TO SCARE ME OFF WITH THAT IMPLICATION.

monologue, Jay ate the entire bag of chips, doing jokes while spitting potato chips everywhere!

> When Jay was a kid, his father set up one of those freestanding basketball hoops on the driveway. Jay hated playing basketball, and his father knew that. Well, since Jay wasn't the best student, his parents had gotten him a tutor. One day the tutor was backing his car into Jay's driveway. Jay was directing him where to turn, and at this point Jay saw an opportunity and backed the tutor's car right into the basketball hoop, knocking it down and breaking it. When Jay's father got home, he asked the tutor what had happened. The tutor was like, "I'm so sorry, Mr. Leno, I was being so careful. I even had Jay direct me when I was backing in." Jay's father knew immediately. "Jay backed you in? Jay, get over here!"

For the briefings, one writer besides Jay had to attend the meeting to come up with funny stuff for the guests. When we were doing *The Jay Leno Show* at 10:00 p.m., I started coming up with segment ideas with the producers. We all got along so well that when the show went back to 11:30 p.m., I told Debbie I would probably be good in the briefings. She agreed, so every day at noon I attended the briefings. It took an hour away from producing my drop-ins, but it allowed me to write and pitch cold opens and come up with ideas for guests for the show, which I'd done for Howard as well. So we would sit down in this big conference room and order in from five-star restaurants. The segment producers would brief Jay on what they were going to talk about, and occasionally I would supply them with either a drop-in bit for the guest or a prop bit or even questions for the guest.

When Barack Obama was on, I got two of my questions in and it worked well with him. My partner in crime, Ross Mark—one of the segment producers—and I would text each other back and forth when Ross's old partner, Bob Read, would pitch. Bob was a segment producer and I loved him, but this guy had a gift for gab. He would take like five minutes just to go over the guest's credits and tell Jay what a big fan of his the guest was. He would brief a five-minute segment for like forty-five minutes. Ross and I would text back and forth, "Yawn," "Z-Z-Z," or the occasional, "Is this guy ever going to shut the fuck up?" text. Debbie would look at us laughing and

DAN RATHER:

sometimes get annoyed. I'm not sure if she knew what we were up to, but it was funny.

Jay would sit there, listen, and eat his second lunch of the day. And he would always tell us stories of when he was a kid. Here are some of the best ones. How do I remember them? Because he would tell them over and over again, and never remember that he already told you the same story a half-dozen times.

> Jay would tell us this joke in the briefing, but also would tell the guests in their dressing rooms: One day a husband and wife are in the gynecologist's office, and the doctor informs them that the wife is suffering from uterine cancer. The couple is so sad and dismayed, so the husband pleads with the doctor, asking if there's anything, anything that he can do. The doctor says, "Well, there is one small chance," and he explains that one time another wife was suffering from the same thing, and her husband went down on her every day and every night, and then after six months, miraculously, the wife went into remission.
>
> So, the husband had his task at hand. Every day and every night for six months, he went down on his wife. When his wife went to the doctor, he found out that yet another miracle had happened: his wife had gone into remission. She called her husband to tell him the good news and then drove home with a bottle of champagne to celebrate
>
> When she got home, she found her husband on the living room couch, crying his eyes out. She said, "Honey, what's wrong? I'm cured," and the husband looked up, and in between cries he said, "Yeah, but I could have saved Mom."

THE WRITERS' STRIKE

POOR JAY GOT SCREWED again. When the writers' guild went on strike, Letterman managed to get some waiver that allowed him to keep his staff. Jay, on the other hand, did not. Jay was never the favorite. I mean, in the twenty-odd years that he hosted The Tonight Show, his writers never received an Emmy, which is total bullshit because his material was just as good if not better than Letterman's and all of the other shows that had won. It just was never going to happen, as the staff would tell me, because some considered Jay a sellout. He went down the middle, making fun of both political parties. He appealed to the mainstream, and some said he'd lost his edge. In my mind, the motherfucker was smart and knew it was better to not polarize half the audience. Plus, if you really watched the show, as I did for ten years, Jay did do edgy stuff, but the critics never noticed it.

The strike was a tough time for the producers, the writers, the guys in the middle (like myself), and especially Jay. He was on his own, with the exception of a few nonwriters who submitted jokes. I would never submit a joke during the strike because I perceived it as unethical, although some did, and the wall between the writers and producers was never thicker. Debbie was so irritated by Anthony Caleca, my friend and another writer, who would protest loudly with a megaphone outside her window. Man, the producers hated the writers around this time, but I stayed neutral. I was Switzerland during all of this.

Well, the one thing I did do, because it wasn't writing, was stay in rehearsal with Jay and give him my critique on the jokes, bits, and drop-ins he had. On various occasions I'd be eating lunch across the way from the show and Jay would summon me to come to rehearsal. He would actually tell staffers to go find me. It was amazing to me that Jay Leno respected and valued my opinion. It made sense, because I would always be brutally honest about everything. Sometimes, before and after the strike, it irritated some of the writers that Jay valued my opinion over theirs. Look, I did the same thing for Howard, and I think that's why we became friends, because he knew I had a good sense of comedy and that I would speak my mind, no matter whose feelings got hurt. Jay would request old monologues from his monologue coordinator, Lisa Nelson, and revamp the jokes into current events. Jay is no sham of a writer, and he would write his own jokes. Somehow, he survived the strike. Truth be told, Jay is a quick, witty motherfucker, and one of the funniest people that I have ever met. In fact, he still remained number one over Letterman. But this did seem to convince the producers that they didn't need the writers, and there were a lot of hard feelings between the departments thereafter.

ANTHONY QUINN:

"WHICH WOULD YOU PREFER, SOMEONE TO PICK YOUR NOSE OR SOMEONE TO SUCK YOUR EAR WAX OUT WITH A STRAW?"

NATIONAL LAMPOON PRESENTS ONE, TWO, MANY

I GOT A CALL from my friend Marco telling me he had an investor looking to put money into a movie. Marco was the guy who was trying to get me investors years ago, when I had written that script for my wife and me, yet he never found funding. I polished up the script and headed out to New Jersey to meet with the investor. He liked what I told him, and he liked the script, so he put up more than $500,000 for me to make the movie. As you probably know, that is an incredibly low budget, but I knew if I could pull a few favors with equipment and songs and such, I'd be able to make it.

First, we had to cast the film, and this was the last straw in what would finally lead to my divorce with Suzanna. I argued with both Marco and the investor to have Suzanna star in the part that I wrote for her, but they both balked. The investor demanded that I get a name and somebody with more experience. I broke the news to my wife, and she was really upset. There was nothing I could do. As I figured it, I would put Suzanna in a smaller role, and if the movie was a success, I would write another one and get her in a bigger part. She was not having any of it. She was really pissed, and I can't say I blame her—but I had no choice.

We cast Bellamy Young as the female lead. She had a lot of film and television credits and was beautiful and talented. We cast comedian Jeff Ross as my best friend, and Jm J. Bullock as my psychologist. We shot the film at some low-budget building that seconded as a place where swingers had orgies. There were used condoms all over the place, but it was cheap.

I loved when I saw Jeff Ross reading his script before the audition. I was walking down the stairs and he looked up at me and said, "Hey, man, this is really funny. Did you write this?"

That was a pretty cool experience, since Jeff is a great comic that I respect.

I told him that I did, and he said good job. We shot some stuff outdoors in Manhattan and some stuff at Griffith Park. The outdoor shots looked great.

ANTHONY CALMLY RESPONDED, "BOTH VERY UNPLEASANT."

I was able to get a great digital camera from the Camera House for cheap because the guy was a fan. My favorite parts were the kissing scenes with Bellamy. Heck, she would give me full tongue, and since I was acting, I wasn't cheating! Man, did I get aroused during these scenes. I was harder than a fence pole! We'd make out for like two minutes straight! You can see some of it in the movie. Bellamy was awesome, and she soon became a big star on the show *Scandal*.

HOWARD GOES BALLISTIC ON ME!

I WAS MADE AN offer by some time-share company to call into radio shows and plug their Vegas business. One of the call-ins was to Adam Carolla's show. It was early in the morning, and I had just gotten done with like twenty calls in a row. I was on the phone with Adam, and he started asking me about Howard. He asked me if I wished I had been paid more, and of course I said yes. Who the fuck wouldn't want to get paid more? Shit, look how much the pelican took from Sirius. This motherfucker always wanted to get paid more. I said that it was hard because Howard would get pissed when anyone on the show did outside appearances, but he wouldn't fight for us to get nice raises. Hence his Larry "Bud" Melman comparison.

I thought nothing of the interview, but when I was driving to National Lampoon to promote my movie, I started getting calls that Howard was going batshit crazy on me. He would say his usual shit—that I was a no-talent, ungrateful loser—and the same bullshit he would say on the air to me. I didn't understand what I said that was so bad, so I called Gary and asked him and said I meant nothing bad by it. The story was covered in the *Post*, and I waited for things to simmer down. They finally did, and Suzanna and Beth set up a dinner with us at Howard's Southampton Mansion.

It was a beautiful, sprawling place on the beach. We knocked on the door and Howard and Beth answered. Howard and I hugged, and all was good. Howard gave us a tour of the place, which took like two hours. He had medieval fireplaces flown in from England and Italy. He had two kitchens—one for him, if he wanted to cook, and the other for his personal chef. He had a beautiful

MARSHA MASON:

spacious living room overlooking his patio, his infinity pool, and the beach. He took us down on his elevator into the entertainment room, where he had a bowling alley and a pool table. We went upstairs to see Beth's wing of the house and then Howard's. There were like forty rooms in this place!

Anyway, we had a few drinks and Howard and I started talking. He told me he bought the house with the Sirius stock he sold. He then was real honest and told me how good I was at doing the interviews. It was a really great conversation. He scolded me for smoking and then told me how he was pissed at Jay for not paying us while we waited for the ten o'clock show to begin. I thought that was kind of hypocritical, since Howard never gave a fuck about how little I was paid during the K-Rock days—but, hey, he was truly caring about me.

It was a fun night. Howard asked me if I was pissed about not being the show's announcer anymore, and I told him I wasn't. I was more proud of being a staff writer, which was true, although both would have been nice. We sat down for dinner and the chef served fish, which I don't eat, and Howard felt so bad. I told him not to worry and ate bread. Heck, I was more concerned with drinking and smoking anyway.

We said our goodbyes. That would be the last time I would ever see them both.

JIMMY KIMMEL—LOVE ME, HOWARD

JIMMY HAD ALWAYS HAD this bizarre fascination with Howard Stern. When Jay had *The Jay Leno Show*, which aired at ten o'clock after the whole Conan debacle, my friend Ross Mark produced a segment called "Ten Questions" or something like that. It was a segment where a guest was given the softball questions in advance and the guest had time to give a funny retort. Well, one time we had Jimmy Kimmel on the segment. Jimmy was going to do it via satellite from his studio. Keep in mind, Jay had been very nice to Jimmy, even when their shows ran head to head, Jay would still have him on to plug it. Jay is also great friends with Adam Carolla, who is Jimmy Kimmel's buddy.

They were getting ready to do the segment, and all of us at *The Tonight Show* could hear the feed. As I was listening to Jay make small talk with Jimmy, I could tell that Jimmy was being cold and standoffish, and I wanted to run down to tell Debbie that Jimmy was going to sabotage him, but how did I know for sure? Instead, I waited and watched, and I was right. Jimmy pounded Jay for taking the ten o'clock job, saying things like, "Don't you know when it's time to retire?" and "Don't you have enough cars?"

Jay was blindsided by this pile of puss, and I was pissed, as was Debbie. Ross felt betrayed that this scumbag would do that to Jay. But you have to realize that Jimmy was in bed with Howard Stern. I think Jimmy has this "love me, Daddy" thing going on with Howard, and since Howard didn't like Jay, I guess Jimmy felt he had to follow suit.

He even had to make a Howard reference at the end of the 2016 Academy Awards, saying, "Hit him with the Hein." He's such a Howard sycophant. I remember going to a bar one night in Studio City, and I happened to sit next to a Kimmel writer. We argued for an hour over this incident. His argument was that it was the same thing I did for Howard, asking celebrities questions. I disagreed because Jay was already friends with Jimmy. There's a big difference. Whatever the case may be, Jimmy Kimmel is not a nice guy.

Later on, Jay did an article for the *Los Angeles Daily News* saying that he liked Colbert and Fallon but he thought that Kimmel had a mean streak in him. Jay said that he was a comic, and as such, if you insulted someone, you would do it to their face—as opposed to Jimmy, a radio guy, who insulted people from afar.

The whole irony to Jimmy's relationship with Howard was that Howard always accused Jay of stealing his bits, but the truth is, it was Jimmy who stole from Howard on a regular basis, and he stole from us too! I'll give you one example of how Jimmy Kimmel virtually lifted a bit of ours from *The Tonight Show* and called it his own. Granted he could argue he'd gotten the idea independent of us, but we had run the bit umpteen times.

Rob Young, my fellow drop-in writer, had a bit that he called "How Long Will It Take?" Rob's bit was funny as hell. I'll never forget the first one. He found a video of the world's smallest man standing underneath the world's tallest woman while she wore a skirt. Well, Rob's bit had the title come up, "How Long Will It Take?" And then a timer was set. The little guy took about ten seconds to look up the tall woman's skirt.

Genius.

Well, Jimmy lifted the bit pretty much verbatim and made his an entire segment!

GEORGE FOREMAN:

What a creep.

Shit, Jimmy copied Howard by having his family on the show. Jimmy is a thief. Not Jay. Trust me. Any real Stern fan knows that Jimmy steals from Howard's show all of the time and there's no way Howard doesn't know it, but he says nothing because he'd rather be at war with Jay.

> When I was at *The Howard Stern Show*, all I ever heard was that Jay Leno stole Jaywalking from The Homeless Game. Heck, even I believed it. So when I got to *The Tonight Show*, I confronted Joe Medeiros, the head writer at the time, about it. Now, keep in mind I did the first Homeless Game, and it actually was at the Yankee parade after they had won in 1996. It was KC's idea, actually. When I asked Joe, he said that they'd been doing Jaywalking since 1988 and officially did it every week in 1992, and he could pull video to prove this. I was shocked!

KATHY GRIFFIN: SENSITIVE ARE WE?

> One time I was hanging with Kathy in her dressing room before she went on, and I was in my traditional collared button-down shirt and suit jacket that they dressed me in, and we were shooting the shit. Well, after the show, I changed into my jeans, T-shirt, and leather jacket, went outside to my parking spot, put on my New York Giants motorcycle helmet, jumped on my Harley, and took off. I ended up pulling up alongside Kathy's limo at a traffic light. I told her to roll down the window. She did and said, "Who are you?" I was like, "Kathy, it's me, John. I changed." Without missing a beat, she said, "Into who? Dennis Hopper?"

I LOVE KATHY GRIFFIN. As far as I'm concerned, she is one of the funniest female comics I've ever seen. She's very quick-witted, like Joan Rivers was. I was on her show *My Life On The D-List* once when we were backstage at *Last Comic Standing*. We had a great time. I was cracking jokes, she was laughing, and I thought to myself, *If she's on the D-list, then I'm on the Y-list. Like, why the fuck am I here?*

There was one instance, though, when Kathy got completely sensitive and started crying after being a guest on *The Tonight Show*. I remember it vividly. She was on the couch and she held up two pictures: one of her, and one of her former costar Brooke Shields. And Jay, being the funny shoot-from-the-hip kind of guy, said, "Is that the before-and-after picture?"

Now, I thought it was funny, but Kathy apparently didn't. She was crying in her dressing room and her cameras were there shooting her reality show, and poor Jay had to go into her dressing room and apologize. This continued in the parking lot, with Kathy crying. Now look, I get that some might think it was insensitive, but Kathy is a comedian! She should be able to handle a joke. That being said, all in all, I like Kathy.

HOWARD GOES OFF ON ME AGAIN

WHEN WE WERE DOING *The Jay Leno Show* at ten o'clock, we had to churn out more comedy bits because we needed two instead of *The Tonight Show*'s one per hour. We had about twenty writers including myself, and I was excelling. Jay and Jack, the head writer, would compliment me on my work.

Anyway, one of our writers came up with this bit of who can make a better Super Bowl pick, Terry Bradshaw or a chicken? I heard about it but thought nothing of it. Apparently, after the bit, Howard started saying that Jay stole the idea from him, and this couldn't be further from the truth. Heck, shows have been doing that bit since the fifties. One day, I was on Facebook, and the guys were all accusing me of stealing bits from *The Howard Stern Show*, and there were even people saying Howard was accusing me of stealing his bits. So I just wrote back that I'm not stealing any bits and not to drink the Kool-Aid. Now, look, I didn't even equate the term with Jim Jones. I was just repeating what our executive producer would say sometimes in the briefings.

I guess the guy took my line, cut and pasted it out of context, and sent it to the show. Howard got it and went ballistic on me yet again. This would be the last time I would ever be in his good graces. I couldn't believe that little comment threw him out of whack, but that's Howard, a guy who ripped into people on a regular basis but couldn't take it himself. I mean, if you consider all

STEVE MARTIN:
"DOES GOLDIE HAWN'S ASS LOOK THAT GREAT IN PERSON?"

the crap he gave me, all of the insults, all of the put-downs—this is what sets him off?

He should change his name to the Drama Queen of All Media.

In 2017, I decided to reach out to him. I messaged Beth on Facebook and asked her to forward it to Howard. It read, "Hey, Howard, I know we have said some pretty shitty shit to each other but I just want to say that I apologize if I hurt you. I will always consider you a friend. Best, John."

Believe it or not, Howard wrote back to me saying, "John, thanks for saying that, it's all good, Howard."

Well, that was it. We made up, but Howard would never have me on the show again. I am now *persona non grata*. It's fine, though. The show and Howard have both become something I'm not sure I would even recognize anymore.

> I was at a housewarming party for Bob Read, who was one of our segment producers, and the comedian Ant was there. I noticed he was wearing a belt buckle with writing on it, and I asked him what it said, as I thought it said "Jail Bait." He was livid, and he walked outside into the hallway all pissed off. I didn't know what I said to offend him, so I went out in the hallway and grabbed his head and tried to hug him, saying something like, "Hey, man, what's up? We're friends. What got you so pissed?"
>
> He looked at me with complete anger in his eyes and screamed, "Get the fuck away from me!" He scrambled quickly out of there. I didn't understand what I had done until Bob informed me that when I grabbed his head, I moved his wig all the way to the side. His hair hat was on the side of his face!

ME AND THE MOB

AROUND THIS TIME, MY friend Marc, who got the financing for my movie, had just acquired the rights to the John Gotti Jr. story. I was ecstatic, since I had a three-percent ownership in the company. The first time we met, John took us to his restaurant in Oyster Bay, where he went into the kitchen and cooked. He made like a shrimp marinara dish. He asked me if I was hungry and I said yes, but

I was allergic to shellfish. He was annoyed by this. "Who's allergic to shellfish? Just eat the damn thing."

I did.

I wasn't going to piss off this famous mobster in his own kitchen. I thought, "So I break out in painful hives all over my body—big deal!"

One time we went to a restaurant in New Jersey to have lunch with John. I was given the seat next to the former Don of the Gambino crime family, and they brought out a big tray of chicken cutlet parmigiano. I picked up a giant piece and the chicken slipped, fell hard on my plate, and splattered sauce all over John Gotti Jr.'s jacket!

He looked calmly at me and said, "You know you just spilled sauce all over my jacket."

I was shitting in my pants. I was like, "I'm sorry, Mr. Gotti! I'm sorry, Mr. Gotti!

He wiped the sauce off and said, "You know, in the old days, if something like that happened, we'd all be in on it and make the guy who did it think he was getting whacked."

So I dodged a bullet there. Literally. Thank God it wasn't the old days. I mean, I've woken up next to some cows before, but never a horse!

Another time, we were having dinner with John Travolta, his wife, and Joe Pesci. We were having a good time, and I said to Joe, "You know, Joe, it's because of you that every day on social media I get called a stuttering prick!" He laughed out loud. Joe also told me that the whole "Do I amuse you" scene was witnessed by him at one of my favorite Jersey restaurants, the Belmont Tavern. He saw a head mob guy do that exact same thing to an underling, and Joe brought it to Scorsese, who loved it.

AMERICA'S GOT HOWARD?

I HAVE ALWAYS MAINTAINED the reason Howard got so mad at me for doing *I'm a Celebrity...Get Me Out of Here!* had nothing to do with my saying it would take two or three weeks, but because it meant I had been or was getting accepted by the mainstream—and that was what Howard had always craved. In my opinion,

LARRY KING:
"WHY COULDN'T YOU GET IT UP FOR MARILYN CHAMBERS?"
"ISN'T IT TIME FOR YOU TO PROPOSE?"

he couldn't stand to see and hear all of the positive reviews I was getting. Shit, how dare I get that acceptance? Followed by me getting to be a guest on *The Tonight Show* and killing it on there—that was his worst nightmare. One of "his" guys did well without him—not as his flunkie, not as a wise guy asking goofy questions, but as a nice, funny man who the other celebrities on the show adored and embraced. Gary even told me, "Hey, John, I want that guy on my show." I knew that was the real issue. Why do you think he beat me up so bad?

Later, he decided to appear on *America's Got Talent*. And people thought *I* sold out going to *The Tonight Show.*

Howard had always yearned for the approval of others, much like he had always wanted the approval from his father. He would have rather been hobnobbing with his favorite celebrities than bashing them, but how was he to do that? He tried once with that dreadful E! interview show that lasted one season. It became quite apparent that Howard was just not as funny without the gang.

When Howard was on *America's Got Talent*, they had a stuttering comic on. After his set, Howard gushed about him, telling him he was an inspiration! I watched this and nearly kicked my foot through my computer screen. *This* guy was the inspiration? How about the stutterer you tormented for years, yet who still managed to shrug it off and eventually become the announcer on *The Tonight Show*? How about that guy?

My oldest kid called me to tell me that he saw it and what a hypocrite Howard was. Artie called me too, with the same lament. I was stunned. God bless Howie Mandel, who must have struggled to hold in what he really thought.

JUST WHEN I THOUGHT I WAS OUT, THEY PULLED ME BACK IN: MY PHONY PHONE CALL TO DONALD TRUMP

AFTER *THE TONIGHT SHOW* ended, I thought my life in the spotlight was basically over. I wrote for other shows, was the executive producer for a radio show, and started doing my podcast. As I had done before, I embarked on reinventing myself—and that started with me announcing my run for the US Senate. I love politics and thought that might be the next step. As I starting doing my podcast

"WHEN YOU HAVE A PROBLEM ON THE AIR, LIKE YOU HAVE TO BURP OR FART, DO YOU USE THE 'COUGH' BUTTON?"
LARRY WASN'T HAPPY.

from my news studio, my producer (and former campaign manager) Royce D'Orazio suggested I should call the White House. After all, I was friends with Donald Trump, so maybe he would take the call. It seemed interesting, but we had a bigger guest that week in Jackie "The Jokeman" Martling.

The next week I tried to book KC, who was too busy, so I said to Royce, "Sure, let's call the White House." We Googled the number for the White House and called the switchboard. When I called as "Stuttering" John Melendez, they didn't put me through and just hung up.

No big deal, really. The same thing happens when I call DirecTV.

Royce suggested that I say I was New Jersey Senator Bob Menendez, since it's only one letter off. It's like the *My Cousin Vinny* bit where Pesci says, "Not Gallo, Callo." I put on a fake awful English accent and said I was Sean Moore.

They said, "Who?"

I said Sean as in Connery and Moore as in Roger, and that I was a big James Bond fan, which should have been an immediate indication that I was faking. After all, I didn't name myself.

Then they said President Trump was in Fargo, North Dakota, and I was like, "Holy shit, they just gave the location of the president to a stuttering idiot. Why not give me his latitude and longitude?" They said that would see what they could do and then we hung up. A few minutes later, I get a call back on my cell phone, and the screener on the other line from the White House said they just had one question: Why am I calling from an 818 area code?

I said we were on holiday and they bought it. Hook, line, and stutter, as if my cell phone area code changes when I travel.

They said they'd have someone representing the president call me back! How unbelievable is that? Almost as unbelievable as KC being too busy to call in to my show.

We ended the podcast. I went home, took a shower, and drove to a date in Beverly Hills—which explains the shower. As I was driving, I got a call from Jared Kushner, Trump's son-in-law, from aboard Air Force One! I answered the phone in my Long Island–accented voice, but then switched to Sean Moore. How does this guy not know that? Jared asked what the senator wanted to speak about, and I pulled something out of my ass about how the senator had a long conversation with the president a few weeks ago and that he just wanted some closure on it. Jared said Trump was in a meeting but that he would pull him

CHEVY CHASE:
"ARE YOU STILL WEARING YOUR TOUPEE?"
"HOW LONG DO YOU THINK IT WILL BE BEFORE DAN AYKROYD EXPLODES?"

out if I wanted him to. I said no, just have him call me back—because I knew I had to figure out how to record it. I could have asked the NSA for it later, but I thought it might be easier just to record it myself.

I called my fellow prankster friend Justin in, and he said to patch him in if/when the president called and that he would record it. Twenty minutes later, Air Force One called me and said they had the president on the phone. Again, I answered in my Long Island accent but then changed to my English one. I scrambled to get Justin on the line while driving, and then, after a few bumbling attempts, I finally got it.

I said, "Are you there, Bob?" and Justin said yes—which was my cue that everything was rolling. I took over from there.

After about thirty seconds of dead air, Donald picked up the phone and said, "Hi, Bob."

I then proceeded to have a four-minute conversation about immigration reform, saying that we had to get the kids at the border back with their families, and then grilled him on who his next Supreme Court Justice pick would be.

He answered everything and even gave me a timeline for when he would announce his pick. At the end of the conversation, we said our goodbyes and then I slipped in and a "baba booey" to you all. I was in total shock.

We attached the call to my podcast the next day, and we released it, and then…nothing. We called Rachel Maddow, and her producer was not interested. Royce and I started to think that maybe this wasn't as big of a deal as we'd thought. I mean, we'd just infiltrated the White House and exposed them and their screening process, as well as Jared Kushner's ineptitude, and…nothing?

I called my friend at the *Daily Mail* who does many Stern stories, Adam Levy. He ran the story, but they called it a hoax. I called the *Huffington Post*, and they said they couldn't run it because they couldn't verify that it was real. Two friends at the pub I hang out with didn't even believe me. Like it's common for people in pubs to exaggerate, or something. Come on!

But then everything turned. *Politico* reported that a Washington insider said the White House was scrambling to find out how this had happened. Before I knew it, I was on CNN, MSNBC, *Inside Edition*, NBC, CBS, *TMZ*, and in the *Daily News*, *New York Post*, and *The New York Times*! I was getting discussed in every country from Denmark to Japan! I tripled my Twitter followers. It was unbelievable!

"WERE YOU HIGH WHEN YOU SAID YOU'D BEAT DAVID LETTERMAN?"
"DID YOU EVER THINK YOU'D SEE THE DAY THAT GARRETT MORRIS IS MORE HAPPENING THAN YOU?"

After a Friday night celebration, I came home only to have two neighborhood kids tell me there were two guys in suit jackets knocking on my door. They said they were from the Secret Service, showed their badges, and said they were looking for me.

Shit, what I had done? It was just a prank! I didn't think I'd broken any laws.

I did a few more media outlets, but then my agent said that the Secret Service had contacted her (This was unbelievable! My agent actually called me!) because they were looking to talk to me. We called Stormy Daniels's attorney, Michael Avenatti, and he agreed to represent me. I called the Secret Service, and they confirmed that they wanted to meet me, and I asked them if they were going to arrest me, or was this just to ask me questions?

They said they couldn't tell me.

I was shitting, literally. (I'd called them from the bowl at Pickwick's Pub—that's my throne away from home.) I asked if I should bring a lawyer and they said it was up to me. Fuck, I was going to go to jail for this shit. (I mean, was Pickwick going to press charges? It was pretty nasty.)

I checked the law, and it says that you can get in trouble for impersonating a public official, but only if you were doing it for monetary gain. I made an appointment to meet the Secret Service the next day, which was a Monday, and I got off the bowl and called Avenatti. He told me he would handle it. He called them and told me he needed time to brief me, and finally, a few days later, he called me and said he asked them if they were going to arrest me, and they said no—but when he asked them to sign papers saying as much, they wouldn't. So Avenatti instructed me to lie low on Twitter and not to appear on any more TV shows for a little while. He said I shouldn't poke the bear, and we canceled an upcoming CNN interview.

Kathy Griffin called me and said that these people don't fuck around, that they had her on the no-fly list after her picture with a decapitated Trump head. And wouldn't you know it, as I'm sitting here writing this chapter just a few mere weeks after my chat with the president, I'm looking at two fresh letters from the IRS informing me that I owe $15,000 in back taxes.

On the other hand, I'm getting offers to do new and exciting things. I've since sicned a production deal with The Idea Factory, Daryl Silver's company, for a show called *Poking the Bear*.

All in all, I have to admit, I really am blessed.

"DO YOU TELL YOUR KIDS THAT YOU'RE AN ACCOUNTANT, OR DO YOU TELL THEM THE UGLY TRUTH?"
"DOES IT BOTHER YOU THAT NOT ONLY DID YOU FAIL, BUT THAT NOBODY KNOWS OR CARES THAT YOU FAILED?"

MY CHARMED LIFE

WELL, THAT IS MY story. I've always felt like the poor man's Forrest Gump. I've gotten to do everything I've always wanted to do—but I was too stupid to invest in Apple stock. When Dee Snider was a guest on *The Howard Stern Show* and Howard asked me to go out on the street and find a person to ask questions about Mayor Dinkins or something—I went out and brought back a dude who didn't even know what planet he was on, and it turned out to be great radio. Dee looked at me and said, "John, you lead a charmed life." And that's just it. I have led a charmed life. I have been one of the luckiest, most blessed, most fortunate motherfuckers on the planet. I am grateful to Howard Stern for giving me my start. I don't hate the man. In fact, quite the contrary. I love him. I just think, like all of us, he is flawed.

I am grateful for all of the people in this world, like Wayne Rice, Steven Weber, Amy Yasbeth, Crystal Bernard, the *Wings* producer, Al Martin, Ted Nugent, and Ozzy Osbourne, as well as all of the bands that let me open for them. I thank people like Sam Kinison and Willie Barcena for the kind words, and I thank God for hearing my prayers. I thank Jay Leno, Joe Medeiros, and Debbie Vickers for picking me above the rest. (Heck, there were four staff members who asked Debbie for the job, but she said no. One of them was the future head writer!)

Thanks to Rob Young for his friendship and support over the years. He changed my life when he suggested that I pitch and produce my own video drop-ins at *The Tonight Show*. And I swear I'll get back it him if it's the last thing that I do.

Thanks also to Ross Mark, Helga Pollock, Dax and Beth Mark, Jamie Park, Mike Schiff, Walter Lewis, Tom Patino, Anthony Caleca, Kevin Castro, and Larry Goitia.

I thank National Lampoon for putting out my movie and Steven Kingston for giving me my radio show. I thank my good friends Craig Kallman and John Titta for signing me to my record and publishing deals. I thank Randy Cantor

CHEVY ASKED ME, "HOW DOES IT FEEL WORKING FOR A BULLY?" HE ELABORATED ON HOW BIG OF A BULLY HOWARD WAS. I DIDN'T AGREE WITH HIM IN THE MOMENT—BUT ALL THESE YEARS LATER, CHEVY DID HAVE A POINT.

for producing both of my records and Wayne and Craig at Razor and Tie for signing me. I thank Sting, Gene Simmons, Nuno Bettencourt, Barry Williams, Grandpa Al Lewis, and Gilbert Gottfried for appearing in my video. I thank Nigel Dick for directing it. I thank Bellamy Young, Jeff Ross, Jm J. Bullock, and Sandra Taylor for being in my movie. I thank Michael DeLorenzo for directing it and my good friend Marco Fiore for getting it funded. Mike Froch and Len Sclofani. I thank Modi, Jim Florentine, Otto and George, Nick Di Paolo, Craig Gass, Artie Lange, "The Reverend" Bob Levy, Greg Giraldo, Mike Bocchetti, Greg Fitzsimmons, Jason Gillearn, Ross Mathews, Russ Meneve, Jim Norton, and, yes, even Melrose Larry Green for going on the road with me.

Thanks to Richie Wilson, Scott Depace, and Doug Goodstein. And thanks to Jackie and Fred for writing all those great questions.

I thank my friends—Mike Novara, Danny and Dawn Godfrey, Douglas Keller, Justin Schwartz, Alex Anguiano, Bruce and Lynne Valero, Bob LaValley, Paul "Jiggs" Dwyer, Pat Carley, Jerry and Kim Aschettino, Joe Carroll, Eric Moller, Felix and Lisa Hannenman, Roger Paul, Derek Panza, Joel Gold, Steven Weinberger, John Kmiotek, Royce D'Orazio, Merdad Sogand and Ashkon Saiiti, Tommy Cassel, Sterling Youngman, Neil Politz, Darren Anderson, Josh Richmond, Tony Nassaney, Chris "Haha", Eric Bohlander, Peter Hayes, Craig and Denise Phelps, John Passant, Tamara Boedecker, Allan Shields, Paul Smurthwaite, Chris Flood, Phil Nickelson, Dermot, Mick, John Hill, Camille Caiozzo, Peter, Bella, Marjan, Greg, Michael Flood, Ralph, Kim, Chris, and Craig Holman. As well as Claire Caruso, Joanne Brett, KC, Stacie, Kayla, Jen, Sal, and everyone at Pickwick's Pub. I thank the universe.

Thanks to Father Martin, for making church bearable, and Miss Wyland, Miss Casement, Dr. Manley, Mr. Dunne, and Dr. Marcropolis for making school fun.

Thanks to Karen Harris and Dan Forman. Thanks also to Jason Burns, the Jerry Maguire of agents.

Thanks to Gretchen Bonaduce, and thanks to my friends Tyson, Guy, Julia, Hailie, and everyone at Rare Bird Books. And thank you to Rainn Wilson, Dan Whitney, Kathy Griffin, Richard Lewis, AJ Benza, Tabitha Stevens, Steve Guttenberg, and Jillian Barberie.

And a big thank you to all of the people I may have accidentally forgotten.

O.J. SIMPSON:

"WOULD YOU SIGN MY KNIFE?"

I thank my siblings, Roy, Susan, and Joyce, and my sister-in-law Liz and also Margaret. I thank all of my nieces: Jennifer, Lisa, and Lacie; my nephews: Chris, Sean, Joey, and Nick; and my cousins, including Carolynn and Artie, Annamay and Jimmy, Gailee and Bob, and Mary. (I'm Puerto Rican, if I included all of their names we'd need a whole other chapter.)

Thanks to Mom and Dad for all of their love and support. Most of all, I thank my ex-wife Suzanna for not only loving and supporting me, but also for giving me my three great kids, and I thank my kids—Knight, Lily, and Oscar— for being so amazing.

Follow your dreams, believe in yourself, don't feed into the word "can't," and God bless you all.